ERNST CASSIRER was born in Breslau on July 28, 1874. Upon graduation from the University of Berlin, he continued his studies in philosophy at the University of Marburg. He taught at the Universities of Berlin and Hamburg until his departure from Germany in 1932 to accept an appointment at Oxford. In 1941, Cassirer came to America to teach at Yale where he remained until 1944. The last year of his life was spent as a visiting professor at Columbia University. He died in New York on April 13, 1945.

Cassirer's first works were in the field of epistemology. By 1904, he had completed the first two volumes of his monumental four-volume history of epistemology, *The Problem of Knowledge*, the final volume of which was in the process of translation at the time of his death. His first great systematic work, *Substance and Function*, was published in 1910.

After the First World War, Cassirer began working out the theory of symbolic forms, his major contribution to twentieth-century philosophy, which has earned him a place with Bergson, Croce, Dewey, Santayana, and Whitehead. The three volumes of *The Philosophy of Symbolic Forms* were brought out between 1923 and 1929, and the first of these to appear in America has recently been published by the Yale University Press.

The last twelve years of Cassirer's life were devoted to an application of the philosophy of symbolic forms to the various realms of human culture—to art and the social sciences. AN ESSAY ON MAN, completed in 1944, is the major work of this period.

To Charles W. Hendel
in friendship and gratitude

AN ESSAY ON MAN

An Introduction

to a Philosophy of Human Culture

BY ERNST CASSIRER

DOUBLEDAY

ANCHOR

BOOKS

DOUBLEDAY & COMPANY, INC., GARDEN CITY, NEW YORK

BOOKS BY ERNST CASSIRER
PUBLISHED BY YALE UNIVERSITY PRESS

An Essay on Man

The Myth of the State

The Problem of Knowledge

The Philosophy of Symbolic Forms, Volume I

Preface

PART I WHAT IS MAN?

PART II MAN AND CULTURE

Preface

The first impulse for the writing of this book came from my English and American friends who repeatedly and urgently asked me to publish an English translation of my *Philosophy of Symbolic Forms*.[1] Although I should have liked very much to comply with their request, after the first tentative steps I found it impracticable and, under the present circumstances, unjustifiable to reproduce the former book in its entirety. As for the reader, it would have taxed his attention to the utmost to read a three-volume study dealing with a difficult and abstract subject. But even from the point of view of the author it was scarcely possible or advisable to publish a work planned and written more than twenty-five years ago. Since that time the author has continued his study on the subject. He has learned many new facts and he has been confronted with new problems. Even the old problems are seen by him from a different angle and appear in a new light. For all these reasons I decided to make a fresh start and to write an entirely new book. This book had to be much shorter than the first one. "A big book," said Lessing, "is a big evil." When writing my *Philosophy of Symbolic Forms* I was so engrossed in the subject itself that I forgot or neglected this stylistic maxim. Now I feel much more inclined to subscribe to Lessing's words. Instead of giving a detailed account of facts and a lengthy discussion of theories I have tried in this present book to concentrate upon a few points that seemed to me to be of special philosophical importance and to express my thoughts as briefly and succinctly as possible.

Still the book has had to deal with subjects that, at first sight, may seem to be widely divergent. A book concerned with psychological, ontological, epistemological questions and containing chapters on Myth and Religion, Language and Art, on Science and History, is open to the objection that it is a *mixtum compositum* of the most disparate and heterogeneous things. I hope that the reader after having read these pages will find this objection to be unfounded. It was one of my principal aims to convince him that all the subjects dealt with in this book are, after all, only *one* subject. They are different

1. 3 vols., Berlin, Bruno Cassirer, 1923–29.

roads leading to a common center—and, to my mind, it is for a philosophy of culture to find out and to determine this center.

As to the style of the book it has been, of course, a serious drawback that I have had to write it in a language that is not my native tongue. I should hardly have overcome this obstacle without the help of my friend James Pettegrove, of New Jersey State Teachers College. He has revised the whole manuscript and given me his kind advice on all linguistic and stylistic questions. But I am also very much indebted to him for many valuable and pertinent remarks regarding the subject matter of the book.

I did not mean to write a "popular" book on a subject that, in many respects, is resistant to any popularization. On the other hand this book is not destined for scholars or philosophers alone. The fundamental problems of human culture have a general human interest, and they should be made accessible to the general public. I have tried, therefore, to avoid all technicalities and to express my thoughts as clearly and simply as possible. My critics should, however, be warned that what I could give here is more an explanation and illustration than a demonstration of my theory. For a closer discussion and analysis of the problems involved I must ask them to go back to the detailed description in my *Philosophy of Symbolic Forms*.

It is my serious wish not to impose a ready-made theory, expressed in a dogmatic style, upon the minds of my readers. I have been anxious to place them in a position to judge for themselves. Of course it has not been possible to lay before their eyes the whole bulk of empirical evidence upon which my principal thesis rests. But I have tried at least to give ample and detailed quotations from the standard works on the various subjects. What the reader will find is not at all a complete bibliography—even the titles of such a bibliography would have far exceeded the space that has been allowed me. I have had to content myself with citing those authors to whom I myself feel most indebted and with selecting those examples that seemed to me to be of typical significance and of paramount philosophical interest.

By the dedication to Charles W. Hendel I wish to express my feeling of deep gratitude to the man who, with indefatigable zeal, helped me to prepare this book. He was the first to whom I spoke about its general plan. Without his keen interest in the subject matter of the book and his friendly personal interest in its author I should hardly have found the courage to publish it. He has read the manuscript several times, and I have always been able to accept his critical suggestions. They have proved to be very helpful and valuable.

The dedication has, however, not only a personal but also a "symbolic" meaning. By dedicating this book to the Chairman of the Department of Philosophy and to the Director of Graduate Studies at Yale University I wish to express to the Department itself my cordial thanks. When, three years ago, I came to Yale University it was an agreeable surprise to find a close coöperation that extended to a wide field. It was a special pleasure and a great privilege to work together with my younger colleagues in conjoint seminars on various subjects. This was, indeed, a new experience in my long academic life —and a very interesting and stimulating one. I shall always keep in grateful memory these conjoint seminars—one in the philosophy of history, another in the philosophy of science, a third in the theory of knowledge, held by Charles Hendel and Hajo Holborn, F. S. C. Northrop and Henry Margenau, Monroe Beardsley, Frederic Fitch, and Charles Stevenson.

I have to regard this book, to a large extent, as an outcome of my work at the Graduate School of Yale University and I avail myself of this opportunity to express my thanks to the Dean of the Graduate School, Edgar S. Furniss, for the hospitality offered to me these last three years. A word of cordial thanks is also due to my students. I have discussed with them almost all the problems contained in this book and I trust that they will find many traces of our common work in the following pages.

I am grateful to the Fluid Research Fund of Yale University for a research grant that helped me to prepare this book.

Ernst Cassirer

Yale University

I   WHAT IS MAN?

1   The Crisis in Man's Knowledge of Himself

1   That self-knowledge is the highest aim of philosophical inquiry appears to be generally acknowledged. In all the conflicts between the different philosophical schools this objective remained invariable and unshaken: it proved to be the Archimedean point, the fixed and immovable center, of all thought. Nor did the most sceptical thinkers deny the possibility and necessity of self-knowledge. They distrusted all general principles concerning the nature of things, but this distrust was only meant to open a new and more reliable mode of investigation. In the history of philosophy scepticism has very often been simply the counterpart of a resolute *humanism*. By the denial and destruction of the objective certainty of the external world the sceptic hopes to throw all the thoughts of man back upon his own being. Self-knowledge—he declares—is the first prerequisite of self-realization. We must try to break the chain connecting us with the outer world in order to enjoy our true freedom. "La plus grande chose du monde c'est de scavoir être à soy," writes Montaigne.

Yet even this approach to the problem—the method of introspection—is not secure against sceptical doubts. Modern philosophy began with the principle that the evidence of our own being is impregnable and unassailable. But the advance of psychological knowledge has hardly confirmed this Cartesian principle. The general tendency of thought is nowadays again directed toward the opposite pole. Few modern psychologists would admit or recommend a mere method of introspection. In general they tell us that such a method is very precarious. They are convinced that a strictly objective behavioristic attitude is the only possible approach to a scientific psychology. But a consistent and radical behaviorism fails to attain its end. It can warn us against possible methodological errors, but it cannot solve all the problems of human psychology. We may criticize or suspect the purely introspective view, but we cannot suppress or eliminate it. Without introspection, without an immediate awareness of feelings, emotions, perceptions, thoughts, we could not even define the field of human psychology. Yet it must be admitted that by following this way alone we can never arrive at a comprehensive view of human nature. Introspection reveals to us only that small sector of human life which is accessible to our individual experience. It can never cover the whole field of human phenomena. Even if we should succeed in collecting and combining all the data, we should still have a very meager and fragmentary picture—a mere torso—of human nature.

Aristotle declares that all human knowledge originates from a basic tendency of human nature manifesting itself in man's most elementary actions and reactions. The whole extent of the life of the senses is determined by and impregnated with this tendency.

"All men by nature desire to know. An indication of this is the delight we take in our senses; for even apart from their usefulness they are loved for themselves; and above all others the sense of sight. For not only with a view to action, but even when we are not going to do anything we prefer seeing to everything else. The reason is that this, most of all senses, makes us know and brings to light many differences between things."[1] This passage is highly characteristic of Aristotle's conception of knowledge as distinguished from Plato's. Such a philosophical eulogy of man's sensuous life would be impossible in the work of Plato. He could never compare the desire for knowledge with the delight we take in our senses. In Plato the life of the senses is separated from the life of the intellect by a broad and insurmountable gulf. Knowledge and

1. Aristotle, Metaphysics, Book A. 1 980ᵃ 21. English trans. by W. D. Ross, The Works of Aristotle (Oxford, Clarendon Press, 1924), Vol. VIII.

truth belong to a transcendental order—to the realm of pure and eternal ideas. Even Aristotle is convinced that scientific knowledge is not possible through the act of perception alone. But he speaks as a biologist when he denies this Platonic severance between the ideal and the empirical world. He attempts to explain the ideal world, the world of knowledge, in terms of life. In both realms, according to Aristotle, we find the same unbroken continuity. In nature as well as in human knowledge the higher forms develop from the lower forms. Sense perception, memory, experience, imagination, and reason are all linked together by a common bond; they are merely different stages and different expressions of one and the same fundamental activity, which attains its highest perfection in man, but which in a way is shared by the animals and all the forms of organic life.

If we were to adopt this biological view we should expect that the first stages of human knowledge would deal exclusively with the external world. For all his immediate needs and practical interests man is dependent on his physical environment. He cannot live without constantly adapting himself to the conditions of the surrounding world. The initial steps toward man's intellectual and cultural life may be described as acts which involve a sort of mental adjustment to the immediate environment. But as human culture progresses we very soon meet with an opposite tendency of human life. From the earliest glimmering of human consciousness we find an introvert view of life accompanying and complementing this extrovert view. The farther we trace the development of human culture from these beginnings the more this introvert view seems to come to the fore. Man's natural curiosity begins slowly to change its direction. We can study this growth in almost all the forms of the cultural life of man. In the first mythological explanations of the universe we always find a primitive *anthropology* side by side with a primitive *cosmology*. The question of the origin of the world is inextricably interwoven with the question of the origin of man. Religion does not destroy these first mythological explanations. On the contrary, it preserves the mythological cosmology and anthropology by giving them new shape and new depth. Henceforth self-knowledge is not conceived as a merely theoretical interest. It is not simply a subject of curiosity or speculation; it is declared to be the fundamental obligation of man. The great religious thinkers were the first to inculcate this moral requirement. In all the higher forms of religious life the maxim "Know thyself" is regarded as a categorical imperative, as an ultimate moral and religious law. In this imperative we feel, as it were, a sudden reversal of the first natural instinct to know—we perceive a transvaluation of all values. In the histories of all the religions of the world—in Judaism, Buddhism, Confucianism, and Christianity—we can observe the individual steps of this development.

The same principle holds good in the general evolution of philosophical thought. In its earliest stages Greek philosophy seems exclusively concerned with the physical universe. Cosmology clearly predominates over all the other branches of philosophical investigation. It is, however, characteristic of the depth and comprehensiveness of the Greek mind that almost every individual thinker represents at the same time a new general *type* of thought. Beyond the physical philosophy of the Milesian School the Pythagoreans discover a mathematical philosophy, while the Eleatic thinkers are the first to conceive the ideal of a logical philosophy. Heraclitus stands on the border line between cosmological and anthropological thought. Although he still speaks as a natural philosopher, and he belongs to the "ancient physiologists," yet he is convinced that it is impossible to penetrate into the secret of nature without having studied the secret of man. We must fulfil the demand of self-reflection if we wish to keep hold of reality and to understand its meaning. Hence it was possible for Heraclitus to characterize the whole of his philosophy by the two words *edizêsamên emauton* ("I have sought for myself").[2] But this new tendency of thought, although in a sense inherent in early Greek philosophy, did not come to its full maturity until the time of Socrates. Thus it is in the problem of man that we find the landmark separating Socratic from pre-Socratic thought. Socrates never attacks or criticizes the

2. Fragment 101, in Diels, *Die Fragmente der Vorsokratiker*, ed. by W. Krantz (5th ed. Berlin, 1934), I, 173.

theories of his predecessors. He does not intend to introduce a new philosophical doctrine. Yet in him all the former problems are seen in a new light because they are referred to a new intellectual center. The problems of Greek natural philosophy and of Greek metaphysics are suddenly eclipsed by a new question which seems henceforth to absorb man's whole theoretical interest. In Socrates we no longer have an independent theory of nature or an independent logical theory. We do not even have a coherent and systematic ethical theory —in that sense in which it was developed in the later ethical systems. Only one question remains: What is man? Socrates always maintains and defends the ideal of an objective, absolute, universal truth. But the only universe he knows, and to which all his inquiries refer, is the universe of man. His philosophy—if he possesses a philosophy—is strictly anthropological. In one of the Platonic dialogues Socrates is described as being engaged in a conversation with his pupil Phaedrus. They are walking, and after a short time they come to a place outside the gates of Athens. Socrates bursts into admiration for the beauty of the spot. He is delighted with the landscape, which he praises highly. But Phaedrus interrupts. He is surprised that Socrates behaves like a stranger who is being shown about by a guide. "Do you ever cross the border?" he asks. Socrates puts symbolic meaning into his reply. "Very true, my good friend," he replies, "and I hope that you will excuse me when you hear the reason, which is, that I am a lover of knowledge, and the men who dwell in the city are my teachers, and not the trees, or the country." [3]

Yet when we study Plato's Socratic dialogues nowhere do we find a direct solution of the new problem. Socrates gives us a detailed and meticulous analysis of individual human qualities and virtues. He seeks to determine the nature of these qualities and to define them: goodness, justice, temperance, courage, and so on. But he never ventures a definition of man. How is this seeming deficiency to be accounted for? Did Socrates deliberately adopt a roundabout approach—one that allowed him only to scratch the surface of his problem

3. Plato, Phaedrus 230A (Jowett trans.).

without ever penetrating into its depth and its real core? But here, more than anywhere else, we should suspect Socratic irony. It is precisely the negative answer of Socrates which throws new and unexpected light on the question, and which gives us the positive insight into the Socratic conception of man. We cannot discover the nature of man in the same way that we can detect the nature of physical things. Physical things may be described in terms of their objective properties, but man may be described and defined only in terms of his consciousness. This fact poses an entirely new problem which cannot be solved by our usual modes of investigation. Empirical observation and logical analysis, in the sense in which these terms were used in pre-Socratic philosophy, here proved inefficient and inadequate. For it is only in our immediate intercourse with human beings that we have insight into the character of man. We must actually confront man, we must meet him squarely face to face, in order to understand him. Hence it is not a new objective content, but a new activity and function of thought which is the distinctive feature of the philosophy of Socrates. Philosophy, which had hitherto been conceived as an intellectual monologue, is transformed into a dialogue. Only by way of dialogical or dialectic thought can we approach the knowledge of human nature. Previously truth might have been conceived to be a sort of ready-made thing which could be grasped by an effort of the individual thinker, and readily transferred and communicated to others. But Socrates could no longer subscribe to this view. It is as impossible—says Plato in the *Republic*—to implant truth in the soul of a man as it is to give the power of seeing to a man born blind. Truth is by nature the offspring of dialectic thought. It cannot be gained, therefore, except through a constant coöperation of the subjects in mutual interrogation and reply. It is not therefore like an empirical object; it must be understood as the outgrowth of a social act. Here we have the new, indirect answer to the question "What is man?" Man is declared to be that creature who is constantly in search of himself—a creature who in every moment of his existence must examine and scrutinize the conditions of his existence. In this scrutiny, in this critical attitude toward human life, consists the real value of human life. "A life which is unexamined," says Socrates in his *Apology*, "is not worth living." [4] We may epitomize the thought of Socrates by saying that man is defined by him as that being who, when asked a rational question, can give a rational answer. Both his knowledge and his morality are comprehended in this circle. It is by this fundamental faculty, by this faculty of giving a response to himself and to others, that man becomes a "responsible" being, a moral subject.

2   This first answer has, in a sense, always remained the classical answer. The Socratic problem and the Socratic method can never be forgotten or obliterated. Through the medium of Platonic thought it has left its mark[5] on the whole future development of human civilization. There is perhaps no surer or shorter way of convincing ourselves of the deep unity and perfect continuity of ancient philosophic thought than by comparing these first stages in Greek philosophy with one of the latest and noblest products of Graeco-Roman culture, the book *To Himself* written by the Emperor Marcus Aurelius Antoninus. At first sight such a comparison may appear arbitrary; for Marcus Aurelius was not an original thinker, nor did he follow a strictly logical method. He himself

4. Plato, *Apology* 37E (Jowett trans.).

5. In the following pages I shall not attempt to give a survey of the historical development of anthropological philosophy. I shall merely select a few typical stages in order to illustrate the general line of thought. The history of the philosophy of man is still a desideratum. Whereas the history of metaphysics, of natural philosophy, of ethical and scientific thought has been studied in all detail, we are here still at the beginning. During the last century the importance of this problem has been felt more and more vividly. Wilhelm Dilthey has concentrated all his efforts upon its solution. But Dilthey's work, however rich and suggestive, remained incomplete. One of the pupils of Dilthey, Bernhard Groethuysen, has given an excellent description of the general development of anthropological philosophy. But unfortunately even this description stops short of the last and decisive step—that of our moden era. See Bernhard Groethuysen, "Philosophische Anthropologie," *Handbuch der Philosophie* (Munich and Berlin, 1931), III, 1-207. See also Groethuysen's article, "Towards an Anthropological Philosophy," *Philosophy and History, Essays Presented to Ernst Cassirer* (Oxford, Clarendon Press, 1936), pp. 77-89.

thanks the gods that when he had set his heart on philosophy he did not become a writer of philosophy or a solver of syllogisms.[6] But Socrates and Marcus Aurelius have in common the conviction that in order to find the true nature or essence of man we must first of all remove from his being all external and incidental traits.

"Call none of those things a man's that do not fall to him as a man. They cannot be claimed of a man; the man's nature does not guarantee them; they are no consummations of that nature. Consequently neither is the end for which man lives placed in these things, nor yet that which is perfective of the end, namely the Good. Moreover, if any of these things did fall to a man, it would not fall to him to contemn them and set his face against them, . . . but as it is, the more a man can cut himself free, . . . from these and other such things with equanimity, by so much the more is he good." [7] All that which befalls man from without is null and void. His essence does not depend on external circumstances; it depends exclusively on the value he gives to himself. Riches, rank, social distinction, even health or intellectual gifts—all this becomes indifferent (*adiaphoron*). What matters alone is the tendency, the inner attitude of the soul; and this inner principle cannot be disturbed. "That which does not make a man himself worse than before cannot make his life worse either, nor injure it whether from without or within." [8]

The requirement of self-questioning appears, therefore, in Stoicism, as in the conception of Socrates, as man's privilege and his fundamental duty.[9] But this duty is now understood in a broader sense; it has not only a moral but also a universal and metaphysical background. "Never fail to ask thyself this question and to cross-examine thyself thus: What relation

6. Marcus Aurelius Antoninus, *Ad se ipsum* (*eis heauton*), Bk. I, par. 8. In most of the following passages I quote the English version of C. R. Haines, *The Communings with Himself of Marcus Aurelius Antoninus* (Cambridge, Mass., Harvard University Press, 1916), Loeb Classical Library.

7. Marcus Aurelius, *op. cit.*, Bk. V, par. 15.

8. *Idem*, Bk. IV, par. 8.

9. *Idem*, Bk. III, par. 6.

have I to this part of me which they call the ruling Reason
(to hêgemonikon)?" [10] He who lives in harmony with his own
self, his demon, lives in harmony with the universe; for both
the universal order and the personal order are nothing but
different expressions and manifestations of a common underlying principle. Man proves his inherent power of criticism, of
judgment and discernment, by conceiving that in this corre-
lation the Self, not the Universe, has the leading part. Once
the Self has won its inner form, this form remains unalterable
and imperturbable. "A sphere once formed continues round
and true." [11] That is, so to speak, the last word of Greek
philosophy—a word that once more contains and explains the
spirit in which it was originally conceived. This spirit was a
spirit of judgment, of critical discernment between Being and
Non-Being, between truth and illusion, between good and evil.
Life in itself is changing and fluctuating, but the true value
of life is to be sought in an eternal order that admits of no
change. It is not in the world of our senses, it is only by the
power of our judgment that we can grasp this order. Judgment
is the central power in man, the common source of truth and
morality. For it is the only thing in which man entirely depends on himself; it is free, autonomous, self-sufficing.[12]
"Distract not thyself," says Marcus Aurelius, "be not too
eager, but be thine own master, and look upon life as a man,
as a human being, as a citizen, as a mortal creature. . . .
Things do not touch the soul, for they are external and remain
immovable, but our disturbance comes only of that judgment
that we form in ourselves. All these things, which thou seest,
change immediately, and will no longer be; and constantly
bear in mind how many of these changes thou hast already
witnessed. The Universe—mutation, Life—affirmation." [13]

10. *Idem*, Bk. V, par. 11.
11. *Idem*, Bk. VIII, par. 41.
12. Cf. *idem*, Bk. V, par. 14. *Ho logos kai hê logikê technê dynameis
eisin heautais arkoumenai kai tois kath' heautas ergois.*
13. *Ho kosmos alloiôsis • ho bios hypolêpsis* Bk. IV, par. 3. The term
"affirmation" or "judgment" seems to me a much more adequate
expression of the thought of Marcus Aurelius than "opinion," which
I find in all the English versions I have consulted. "Opinion" (the

The greatest merit of this Stoic conception of man lies in the fact that this conception gives to man both a deep feeling of his harmony with nature and of his moral independence of nature. In the mind of the Stoic philosopher these assertions do not conflict; they are correlated with one another. Man finds himself in perfect equipoise with the universe, and he knows that this equipoise must not be disturbed by any external force. Such is the dual character of Stoic "imperturbability" (*ataraxia*). This Stoic theory proved to be one of the strongest formative powers of ancient culture. But it found itself suddenly in the presence of a new, and hitherto unknown, force. The conflict with this new force shook the classical ideal of man to its very foundations. The Stoic and the Christian theories of man are not necessarily hostile to one another. In the history of ideas they work in conjunction, and we often find them in close connection in one and the same individual thinker. Nevertheless, there always remains one point on which the antagonism between the Christian and the Stoic ideals proves irreconcilable. The asserted absolute independence of man, which in the Stoic theory was regarded as man's fundamental virtue, is turned in the Christian theory into his fundamental vice and error. As long as man perseveres in this error there is no possible road to salvation. The struggle between these two conflicting views has lasted for many centuries, and at the beginning of the modern era—at the time of the Renaissance and in the seventeenth century—we still feel its full strenth.[14]

Here we can grasp one of the most characteristic features of anthropological philosophy. This philosophy is not, like other branches of philosophical investigation, a slow and continuous development of general ideas. Even in the history of logic, metaphysics, and natural philosophy we find the sharpest oppositions. This history may be described in Hegelian terms

Platonic *doxa*) contains an element of change and uncertainty which is not intended by Marcus Aurelius. As equivalent terms for *hypolépsis* we find in Marcus Aurelius *krisis, krima, diakrisis*. Cf. Bk. III, par. 2; VI, par. 52; VIII, pars. 28, 47.

14. For a detailed account see Cassirer, *Descartes* (Stockholm, 1939), pp. 215 ff.

as a dialectic process in which each thesis is followed by its antithesis. Nevertheless there is an inner consistency, a clear logical order, connecting the different stages of this dialectic process. Anthropological philosophy, on the other hand, exhibits a quite different character. If we wish to grasp its real meaning and import, we must choose not the epic manner of description but the dramatic. For we are confronted, not with a peaceful development of concepts or theories, but with a clash between conflicting spiritual powers. The history of anthropological philosophy is fraught with the deepest human passions and emotions. It is not concerned with a single theoretical problem, however general its scope; here the whole destiny of man is at stake and clamoring for an ultimate decision.

This character of the problem has found its clearest expression in the work of Augustine. Augustine stands at the frontier of two ages. Living in the fourth century of the Christian era, he has grown up in the tradition of Greek philosophy, and it is especially the system of Neo-Platonism which has left its mark on his whole philosophy. But, on the other hand, he is the pioneer of medieval thought; he is the founder of medieval philosophy and of Christian dogmatics. In his *Confessions* we can follow every step of his way from Greek philosophy to Christian revelation. According to Augustine all philosophy prior to the appearance of Christ was liable to one fundamental error, and was infected with one and the same heresy. The power of reason was extolled as the highest power of man. But what man could never know until he was enlightened with a special divine revelation is that reason itself is one of the most questionable and ambiguous things in the world. Reason cannot show us the way to clarity, to truth and wisdom. For it is itself obscure in its meaning, and its origin is wrapped in mystery—in a mystery soluble only by Christian revelation. Reason for Augustine does not have a simple and unique but rather a double and divided nature. Man was created in the image of God; and in his original state, in which he went out from the hands of God, he was equal to his archetype. But all this has been lost through the fall of Adam. From that time on all the original power of reason has been obscured. And reason alone, when left to itself and its own faculties, never can find the way back. It cannot reconstruct itself; it cannot, by its own efforts, return to its former pure essence. If such a reformation is ever possible, it is only by supernatural aid, by the power of divine grace. Such is the new anthropology, as it is understood by Augustine, and maintained in all the great systems of medieval thought. Even Thomas Aquinas, the disciple of Aristotle, who goes back to the sources of Greek philosophy, does not venture to deviate from this fundamental dogma. He concedes to human reason a much higher power than Augustine did; but he is convinced that reason cannot make the right use of these powers unless it is guided and illuminated by the grace of God. Here we have come to a complete reversal of all the values upheld by Greek philosophy. What once seemed to be the highest privilege of man proves to be his peril and his temptation; what appeared as his pride becomes his deepest humiliation. The Stoic precept that man has to obey and revere his inner principle, the "demon" within himself, is now regarded as dangerous idolatry.

It is not practicable here to describe further the character of this new anthropology, to analyze its fundamental motives and to follow up its development. But in order to understand its purport we may choose a different and shorter way. At the beginning of modern times there appeared a thinker who gave to this anthropology a new vigor and a new splendor. In the work of Pascal it found its last and perhaps most impressive expression. Pascal was prepared for this task as no other writer had been. He possessed an incomparable gift for elucidating the most obscure questions and condensing and concentrating complex and scattered systems of thought. Nothing seems to be impermeable to the keenness of his thought and the lucidity of his style. In him are united all the advantages of modern literature and modern philosophy. But he uses them as weapons against the modern spirit, the spirit of Descartes and his philosophy. At first sight Pascal seems to accept all the presuppositions of Cartesianism and of modern science. There is nothing in nature that can resist the effort of scientific reason; for there is nothing that can resist geometry. It is a curious event in the history of ideas that it was one of the greatest and profoundest geometers who became the belated champion of the philosophical anthropology of the Middle Ages. When sixteen years old, Pascal wrote the treatise on conic sections that opened a new and a very rich and fertile field of geometrical thought. But he was not only a great geometer, he was a philosopher; and as a philosopher he was not merely absorbed in geometrical problems but he wished to understand the true use, the extent, and the limits of geometry. He was thus led to make that fundamental distinction between the "geometrical spirit" and the "acute or subtle spirit." The geometrical spirit excels in all these subjects that are capable of a perfect analysis—that may be divided into their first elements.[15] It starts with certain axioms and from them it draws inferences the truth of which can be demonstrated by universal logical rules. The advantage of this spirit consists in the clarity of its principles and in the necessity of its deductions. But not all objects are capable of such treatment. There are things which because of their subtlety and their infinite variety defy every attempt at logical analysis. And if there is anything in the world that we have to treat in this second way, it is the mind of man. What characterizes man is the richness and subtlety, the variety and versatility of his nature. Hence mathematics can never become the instrument of a true doctrine of man, of a philosophical anthropology. It is ridiculous to speak of man as if he were a geometrical proposition. A moral philosophy in terms of a system of geometry—an *Ethica more geometrico demonstrata*—is to the mind of Pascal an absurdity, a philosophical dream. Traditional logic and metaphysics are themselves in no better position to understand and solve the riddle of man. Their first and supreme law is the law of contradiction. Rational thought, logical and metaphysical thought can comprehend only those objects which are free from contradiction, and which have a consistent nature and truth. It is,

15. For the distinction between *l'esprit géométrique* and *l'esprit de finesse* compare Pascal's treatise "De l'esprit géométrique" and Pascal's *Pensées*, ed. by Charles Louandre (Paris, 1858), chap. ix, p. 231. In the passages which follow I quote the English translation of O. W. Wight (New York, 1861).

however, just this homogeneity which we never find in man. The philosopher is not permitted to construct an artificial man; he must describe a real one. All the so-called definitions of man are nothing but airy speculation so long as they are not based upon and confirmed by our experience of man. There is no other way to know man than to understand his life and conduct. But what we find here defies every attempt at inclusion within a single and simple formula. Contradiction is the very element of human existence. Man has no "nature" —no simple or homogeneous being. He is a strange mixture of being and nonbeing. His place is between these two opposite poles.

There is, therefore, only one approach to the secret of human nature: that of religion. Religion shows us that there is a double man—the man before and after the fall. Man was destined for the highest goal, but he forfeited his position. By the fall he lost his power, and his reason and will were perverted. The classical maxim, "Know thyself," when understood in its philosophic sense, in the sense of Socrates, Epictetus, or Marcus Aurelius, is therefore not only ineffectual, it is misleading and erroneous. Man cannot confide in himself and listen to himself. He has to silence himself in order to hear a higher and truer voice. "What shall become of you, then, O man! you who search out what is your true condition by your natural reason? . . . Know, then, haughty man, what a paradox you are to yourself. Humble yourself, impotent reason; be silent, imbecile nature; learn that man infinitely surpasses man, and hear from your master your true condition, which you are ignorant of. Listen to God." [16]

What is given here is not meant to be a theoretical solution of the problem of man. Religion cannot offer such a solution. By its adversaries religion has always been accused of darkness and incomprehensibility. But this blame becomes the highest praise as soon as we consider its true aim. Religion cannot be clear and rational. What it relates is an obscure and somber story: the story of the sin and the fall of man. It reveals a fact of which no rational explanation is possible. We cannot account for the sin of man; for it is not produced or necessitated

16. *Pensées*, chap. x, sec. 1.

by any natural cause. Nor can we account for man's salvation; for this salvation depends on an inscrutable act of divine grace. It is freely given and freely denied; there is no human action and no human merit that can deserve it. Religion, therefore, never pretends to clarify the mystery of man. It confirms and deepens this mystery. The God of whom it speaks is a *Deus absconditus*, a hidden God. Hence even his image, man, cannot be other than mysterious. Man also remains a *homo absconditus*. Religion is no "theory" of God and man and of their mutual relation. The only answer that we receive from religion is that it is the will of God to conceal himself. "Thus, God being concealed, every religion that does not say that God is concealed is not true; and every religion which does not render a reason for this, is not instructive. Ours does all this: *Vere tu es Deus absconditus.*[17] . . . For nature is such, that it everywhere indicates a God lost, both in man and out of man."[18] Religion is, therefore, so to speak, a logic of absurdity; for only thus can it grasp the absurdity, the inner contradiction, the chimerical being of man. "Certainly, nothing strikes us more rudely than this doctrine; and yet, without this mystery, the most incomprehensible of all, we are incomprehensible to ourselves. The knot of our condition takes its twists and turns in this abyss; so that man is more inconceivable without this mystery, than this mystery is inconceivable to man."[19]

3   What we learn from Pascal's example is that at the beginning of modern times the old problem was still felt in its full strength. Even after the appearance of Descartes' *Discours de la méthode* the modern mind was still wrestling with the same difficulties. It was divided between two entirely incompatible solutions. But at the same time there begins a slow intellectual development by which the question What is man? is transformed and, so to speak, raised to a higher level. The important thing here is not so much the discovery of new

17. *Idem,* chap. xii, sec. 5.
18. *Idem,* chap. xiii, sec. 3.
19. *Idem,* chap. x, sec. 1.

facts as the discovery of a new instrument of thought. Now for the first time the scientific spirit, in the modern sense of the word, enters the lists. The quest now is for a general theory of man based on empirical observations and on general logical principles. The first postulate of this new and scientific spirit was the removal of all the artificial barriers that had hitherto separated the human world from the rest of nature. In order to understand the order of human things we must begin with a study of the cosmic order. And this cosmic order now appears in a wholly new light. The new cosmology, the heliocentric system introduced in the work of Copernicus, is the only sound and scientific basis for a new *anthropology*.

Neither classical metaphysics nor medieval religion and theology were prepared for this task. Both of these bodies of doctrine, however different in their methods and aims, are grounded in a common principle. They both conceive the universe as a hierarchic order in which man occupies the highest place. In Stoic philosophy and in Christian theology man was described as the end of the universe. Both doctrines are convinced that there is a general providence ruling over the world and the destiny of man. This concept is one of the basic presuppositions of Stoic and Christian thought.[20] All this is suddenly called into question by the new cosmology. Man's claim to being the center of the universe has lost its foundation. Man is placed in an infinite space in which his being seems to be a single and vanishing point. He is surrounded by a mute universe, by a world that is silent to his religious feelings and to his deepest moral demands.

It is understandable, and it was indeed necessary, that the first reaction to this new conception of the world could only be a negative one—a reaction of doubt and fear. Even the greatest thinkers could not free themselves from this feeling. "Le silence éternel de ces espaces infinis m'effraye," says Pascal.[21] The Copernican system became one of the strongest instruments of that philosophical agnosticism and scepticism which developed in the sixteenth century. In his criticism of

20. For the Stoic concept of providence (*pronoia*) see, for instance, Marcus Aurelius, *op. cit.*, Bk. II, par. 3.

21. Pascal, *op. cit.*, chap. xxv, sec. 18.

human reason Montaigne uses all the well-known traditional arguments of the systems of Greek scepticism. But he adds a new weapon which in his hands proves to be of the greatest strength and of paramount importance. Nothing is more apt to humiliate us and to break the pride of human reason than an unprejudiced view of the physical universe. Let man, he says in a famous passage of his *Apologie de Raimond Sebond*, "make me understand by the force of his reason, upon what foundations he has built those great advantages he thinks he has over other creatures. Who has made him believe that this admirable motion of the celestial arch, the eternal light of those luminaries that roll so high over his head, the wondrous and fearful motions of that infinite ocean, should be established and continue so many ages for his service and convenience? Can anything be imagined so ridiculous, that this miserable and wretched creature, who is not so much as master of himself, but subject to the injuries of all things, should call himself master and emperor of the world, of which he has not power to know the least part, much less to command the whole?" [22] Man is always inclined to regard the small circle in which he lives as the center of the world and to make his particular, private life the standard of the universe. But he must give up this vain pretense, this petty provincial way of thinking and judging. "When the vines of our village are nipped with the frost, the parish-priest presently concludes that the indignation of God is gone out against all the human race . . . Who is it that, seeing these civil wars of ours, does not cry out, That the machine of the whole world is upsetting, and that the day of judgment is at hand! . . . But whoever shall represent to his fancy, as in a picture, the great image of our mother nature, pourtrayed in her full majesty and lustre; whoever in her face shall read so general and so constant a variety, whoever shall observe himself in that figure, and not himself but a whole kingdom, no bigger than the least touch of a pencil, in comparison of the whole, that man alone is

22. Montaigne, *Essais*, II, chap. xii. English trans. by William Hazlitt, *The Works of Michael de Montaigne* (2d ed. London, 1845), p. 205.

able to value things according to their true estimate and grandeur." [23]

Montaigne's words give us the clue to the whole subsequent development of the modern theory of man. Modern philosophy and modern science had to accept the challenge contained in these words. They had to prove that the new cosmology, far from enfeebling or obstructing the power of human reason, establishes and confirms this power. Such was the task of the combined efforts of the metaphysical systems of the sixteenth and seventeenth centuries. These systems go different ways, but they are all directed toward one and the same end. They strive, so to speak, to turn the apparent curse of the new cosmology into a blessing. Giordano Bruno was the first thinker to enter upon this path, which in a sense became the path of all modern metaphysics. What is characteristic of the philosophy of Giordano Bruno is that here the term "infinity" changes its meaning. In Greek classical thought infinity is a negative concept. The infinite is the boundless or indeterminate. It has no limit and no form, and it is, therefore, inaccessible to human reason, which lives in the realm of form and can understand nothing but forms. In this sense the finite and infinite, *peras* and *hapeiron*, are declared by Plato in the *Philebus* to be the two fundamental principles which are necessarily opposed to one another. In Bruno's doctrine infinity no longer means a mere negation or limitation. On the contrary, it means the immeasurable and inexhaustible abundance of reality and the unrestricted power of the human intellect. It is in this sense that Bruno understands and interprets the Copernican doctrine. This doctrine, according to Bruno, was the first and decisive step toward man's self-liberation. Man no longer lives in the world as a prisoner enclosed within the narrow walls of a finite physical universe. He can traverse the air and break through all the imaginary boundaries of the celestial spheres which have been erected by a false metaphysics and cosmology.[24] The infinite universe sets no limits to human reason; on the contrary, it is the great in-

23. *Idem*, I, chap. xxv. English trans., pp. 65 f.
24. For further details see Cassirer, *Individuum und Kosmos in der Philosophie der Renaissance* (Leipzig, 1927), pp. 197 ff.

centive of human reason. The human intellect becomes aware of its own infinity through measuring its powers by the infinite universe.

All this is expressed in the work of Bruno in a poetical, not in a scientific language. The new world of modern science, the mathematical theory of nature, was still unknown to Bruno. He could not, therefore, pursue his way to its logical conclusion. It took the combined efforts of all the metaphysicians and scientists of the seventeenth century to overcome the intellectual crisis brought about by the discovery of the Copernican system. Every great thinker—Galileo, Descartes, Leibniz, Spinoza—has his special share in the solution of this problem. Galileo asserts that in the field of mathematics man reaches the climax of all possible knowledge—a knowledge which is not inferior to that of the divine intellect. Of course the divine intellect knows and conceives an infinitely greater number of mathematical truths than we do, but with regard to objective certainty the few verities known by the human mind are known as perfectly by man as they are by God.[25] Descartes begins with his universal doubt which seems to enclose man within the limits of his own consciousness. There seems to be no way out of this magic circle—no approach to reality. But even here the idea of the infinite turns out to be the only instrument for the overthrow of universal doubt. By means of this concept alone we can demonstrate the reality of God and, in an indirect way, the reality of the material world. Leibniz combines this metaphysical proof with a new scientific proof. He discovers a new instrument of mathematical thought—the infinitesimal calculus. By the rules of this calculus the physical universe becomes intelligible; the laws of nature are seen to be nothing but special cases of the general laws of reason. It is Spinoza who ventures to make the last and decisive step in this mathematical theory of the world and of the human mind. Spinoza constructs a new ethics, a theory of the passions and affections, a mathematical theory of the moral world. By this theory alone, he is convinced, can we attain our end: the goal of a "philosophy of man," of an anthropological philoso-

25. Galileo, *Dialogo dei due massimi sistemi del mondo*, I (Edizione nazionale), VII, 129.

phy, which is free from the errors and prejudices of a merely anthropocentric system. This is the topic, the general theme, which in its various forms permeates all the great metaphysical systems of the seventeenth century. It is the rationalistic solution of the problem of man. Mathematical reason is the bond between man and the universe; it permits us to pass freely from the one to the other. Mathematical reason is the key to a true understanding of the cosmic and the moral order.

4   In 1754 Denis Diderot published a series of aphorisms entitled *Pensées sur l'interprétation de la nature*. In this essay he declared that the superiority of mathematics in the realm of science is no longer uncontested. Mathematics, he asserted, has reached such a high degree of perfection that no further progress is possible; henceforth mathematics will remain stationary. "Nous touchons au moment d'une grande révolution dans les sciences. Au penchant que les esprits me paroissent avoir à la morale, aux belles lettres, à l'histoire de la nature et à la physique expérimentale j'oserois presque assurer qu'avant qu'il soit cent ans on ne comptera pas trois grands géomètres en Europe. Cette science s'arrêtera tout court où l'auront laissé les Bernoulli, les Euler, les Maupertuis et les d'Alembert. Ils auront posés les colonnes d'Hercule, on n'ira point au delà." [26]

Diderot is one of the great representatives of the philosophy of the Enlightenment. As the editor of the *Encyclopédie* he stands at the very center of all the great intellectual movements of his time. No one had a clearer perspective of the general development of scientific thought; no one had a keener feeling for all the tendencies of the eighteenth century. It is all the more characteristic and remarkable of Diderot that, representing all the ideals of the Enlightenment, he began to doubt the absolute right of these ideals. He expects the rise of a new form of science—a science of a more concrete character, based rather on the observation of facts than on the assumption of general principles. According to Diderot, we have highly overrated our logical and rational methods. We know how to

26. Diderot, *Pensées sur l'interprétation de la nature*, sec. 4; cf. secs. 17, 21.

compare, to organize, and systematize the known facts; but we have not cultivated those methods by which alone it would be possible to discover new facts. We are under the delusion that the man who does not know how to count his fortune is in no better position than the man who has no fortune at all. But the time is near when we shall overcome this prejudice, and then we shall have reached a new and culminating point in the history of natural science.

Has Diderot's prophecy been fulfilled? Did the development of scientific ideas in the nineteenth century confirm his view? On one point, to be sure, his error is obvious. His expectation that mathematical thought would come to a standstill, that the great mathematicians of the eighteenth century had reached the Pillars of Hercules, proved to be entirely untrue. To that eighteenth-century galaxy we must now add the names of Gauss, of Riemann, of Weierstrass, of Poincaré. Everywhere in the science of the nineteenth century we meet with the triumphal march of new mathematical ideas and concepts. Nevertheless, Diderot's prediction contained an element of truth. For the innovation of the intellectual structure of the nineteenth century lies in the place that mathematical thought occupies in the scientific hierarchy. A new force begins to appear. Biological thought takes precedence over mathematical thought. In the first half of the nineteenth century there are still some metaphysicians, such as Herbart, or some psychologists, such as G. Th. Fechner, who cherish the hope of founding a mathematical psychology. But these projects rapidly disappear after the publication of Darwin's work *On the Origin of Species*. Henceforth the true character of anthropological philosophy appears to be fixed once and for all. After innumerable fruitless attempts the philosophy of man stands at last on firm ground. We no longer need indulge in airy speculations, for we are not in search of a general definition of the nature or essence of man. Our problem is simply to collect the empirical evidence which the general theory of evolution has put at our disposal in a rich and abundant measure.

Such was the conviction shared by the scientists and philosophers of the nineteenth century. But what became more important for the general history of ideas and for the development of philosophical thought was not the empirical facts of evolution but the theoretical *interpretation* of these facts. This interpretation was not determined, in an unambiguous sense, by the empirical evidence itself, but rather by certain fundamental principles which had a definite metaphysical character. Though rarely acknowledged, this metaphysical cast of evolutionary thinking was a latent motivating force. The theory of evolution in a general philosophical sense was by no means a recent achievement. It had received its classical expression in Aristotle's psychology and in his general view of organic life. The characteristic and fundamental distinction between the Aristotelean and the modern version of evolution consisted in the fact that Aristotle gave a formal interpretation whereas the moderns attempted a material interpretation. Aristotle was convinced that in order to understand the general plan of nature, the origins of life, the lower forms must be interpreted in the light of the higher forms. In his metaphysics, in his definition of the soul as "the first actualization of a natural body potentially having life," organic life is conceived and interpreted in terms of human life. The teleological character of human life is projected upon the whole realm of natural phenomena. In modern theory this order is reversed. Aristotle's final causes are characterized as a mere *"asylum ignorantiae."* One of the principal aims of Darwin's work was to free modern thought from this illusion of final causes. We must seek to understand the structure of organic nature by material causes alone, or we cannot understand it at all. But material causes are in Aristotle's terminology "accidental" causes. Aristotle had emphatically asserted the impossibility of understanding the phenomenon of life by such accidental causes. Modern theory takes up this challenge. Modern thinkers have held that, after the innumerable fruitless attempts of former times, they have definitely succeeded in accounting for organic life as a mere product of chance. The accidental changes that take place in the life of every organism are sufficient to explain the gradual transformation that leads us from the simplest forms of life in a protozoon to the highest and most complicated forms. We find one of the most striking expressions of this view in Darwin himself, who is usually so very reticent with regard to his philosophical conceptions. "Not only the various domestic races," observes Darwin at the end of his book, *The Variation of Animals and Plants under Domestication*, "but the most distinct genera and orders within the same great class—for instance, mammals, birds, reptiles, and fishes—are all the descendants of one common progenitor, and we must admit that the whole vast amount of difference between these forms has primarily arisen from simple variability. To consider the subject under this point of view is enough to strike one dumb with amazement. But our amazement ought to be lessened when we reflect that beings almost infinite in number, during an almost infinite lapse of time, have often had their whole organization rendered in some degree plastic, and that each slight modification of structure which was in any way beneficial under excessively complex conditions of life has been preserved, whilst each which was in any way injurious has been rigorously destroyed. And the long-continued accumulation of beneficial variations will infallibly have led to structures as diversified, as beautifully adapted for various purposes and as excellently co-ordinated as we see in the plants and animals around us. Hence I have spoken of selection as the paramount power, whether applied by man to the formation of domestic breeds, or by nature to the production of species . . . If an architect were to rear a noble and commodious edifice, without the use of cut stone, by selecting from the fragments at the base of a precipice wedge-formed stones for his arches, elongated stones for his lintels, and flat stones for his roof, we should admire his skill and regard him as the paramount power. Now, the fragments of stone, thought indispensable to the architect, bear to the edifice built by him the same relation which the fluctuating variations of organic beings bear to the varied and admirable structures ultimately acquired by their modified descendents." [27]

But still another, and perhaps the most important, step had to be taken before a real anthropological philosophy could

27. Darwin, *The Variation of Animals and Plants under Domestication* (New York, D. Appleton & Co., 1897), II, chap. xxviii, 425 f.

develop. The theory of evolution had destroyed the arbitrary limits between the different forms of organic life. There are no separate species; there is just one continuous and uninterrupted stream of life. But can we apply the same principle to human life and human *culture?* Is the cultural world, like the organic world, made up of accidental changes?—Does it not possess a definite and undeniable teleological structure? Herewith a new problem presented itself to all philosophers whose starting point was the general theory of evolution. They had to prove that the cultural world, the world of human civilization, is reducible to a few general causes which are the same for the physical as for the so-called spiritual phenomena. Such was the new type of philosophy of culture introduced by Hippolyte Taine in his *Philosophy of Art* and in his *History of English Literature.* "Here as elsewhere," said Taine, "we have but a mechanical problem; the total effect is a result, depending entirely on magnitude and direction of the producing causes . . . Though the means of notation are not the same in the moral and physical sciences, yet as in both the matter is the same, equally made up of forces, magnitudes, and directions, we may say that in both the final result is produced after the same method." [28] It is the same iron ring of necessity that encloses both our physical and our cultural life. In his feelings, his inclinations, his ideas, his thoughts, and in his production of works of art, man never breaks out of this magic circle. We may consider man as an animal of superior species which produces philosophies and poems in the same way as silkworms produce their cocoons or bees build their cells. In the preface to his great work, *Les origines de la France contemporaine,* Taine states that he is going to study the transformation of France as a result of the French Revolution as he would the "metamorphosis of an insect."

But here another question arises. Can we be content with counting up in a merely empirical manner the different impulses that we find in human nature? For a really scientific insight these impulses would have to be classified and systematized. Obviously, not all of them are on the same level.

28. Taine, *Histoire de la littérature anglaise,* Intro. English trans. by H. van Laun (New York, Holt & Co., 1872), I, 12 ff.

We must suppose them to have a definite structure—and one of the first and most important tasks of our psychology and theory of culture is to discover this structure. In the complicated wheelwork of human life we must find the hidden driving force which sets the whole mechanism of our thought and will in motion. The principal aim of all these theories was to prove the unity and homogeneity of human nature. But if we examine the explanations which these theories were designed to give, the unity of human nature appears extremely doubtful. Every philosopher believes he has found the mainspring and master-faculty—*l'idée maîtresse*, as it was called by Taine. But as to the character of this master-faculty all the explanations differ widely from, and contradict, one another. Each individual thinker gives us his own picture of human nature. All these philosophers are determined empiricists: they would show us the facts and nothing but the facts. But their interpretation of the empirical evidence contains from the very outset an arbitrary assumption—and this arbitrariness becomes more and more obvious as the theory proceeds and takes on a more elaborate and sophisticated aspect. Nietzsche proclaims the will to power, Freud signalizes the sexual instinct, Marx enthrones the economic instinct. Each theory becomes a Procrustean bed on which the empirical facts are stretched to fit a preconceived pattern.

Owing to this development our modern theory of man lost its intellectual center. We acquired instead a complete anarchy of thought. Even in the former times to be sure there was a great discrepancy of opinions and theories relating to this problem. But there remained at least a general orientation, a frame of reference, to which all individual differences might be referred. Metaphysics, theology, mathematics, and biology successively assumed the guidance for thought on the problem of man and determined the line of investigation. The real crisis of this problem manifested itself when such a central power capable of directing all individual efforts ceased to exist. The paramount importance of the problem was still felt in all the different branches of knowledge and inquiry. But an established authority to which one might appeal no longer existed. Theologians, scientists, politicians, sociologists, biologists, psychologists, ethnologists, economists all approached the problem from their own viewpoints. To combine or unify all these particular aspects and perspectives was impossible. And even within the special fields there was no generally accepted scientific principle. The personal factor became more and more prevalent, and the temperament of the individual writer tended to play a decisive role. *Trahit sua quemque voluptas:* every author seems in the last count to be led by his own conception and evaluation of human life.

That this antagonism of ideas is not merely a grave theoretical problem but an imminent threat to the whole extent of our ethical and cultural life admits of no doubt. In recent philosophical thought Max Scheler was one of the first to become aware of and to signalize this danger. "In no other period of human knowledge," declares Scheler, "has man ever become more problematic to himself than in our own days. We have a scientific, a philosophical, and a theological anthropology that know nothing of each other. Therefore we no longer possess any clear and consistent idea of man. The ever-growing multiplicity of the particular sciences that are engaged in the study of men has much more confused and obscured than elucidated our concept of man." [29]

Such is the strange situation in which modern philosophy finds itself. No former age was ever in such a favorable position with regard to the sources of our knowledge of human nature. Psychology, ethnology, anthropology, and history have amassed an astoundingly rich and constantly increasing body of facts. Our technical instruments for observation and experimentation have been immensely improved, and our analyses have become sharper and more penetrating. We appear, nevertheless, not yet to have found a method for the mastery and organization of this material. When compared with our own abundance the past may seem very poor. But our wealth of facts is not necessarily a wealth of thoughts. Unless we succeed in finding a clue of Ariadne to lead us out of this labyrinth, we can have no real insight into the general character of human culture; we shall remain lost in a mass of dis-

29. Max Scheler, *Die Stellung des Menschen im Kosmos* (Darmstadt, Reichl, 1928), pp. 13 f.

connected and disintegrated data which seem to lack all conceptual unity.

2   A Clue to the Nature of Man: the Symbol

The biologist Johannes von Uexküll has written a book in which he undertakes a critical revision of the principles of biology. Biology, according to Uexküll, is a natural science which has to be developed by the usual empirical methods—the methods of observation and experimentation. Biological thought, on the other hand, does not belong to the same type as physical or chemical thought. Uexküll is a resolute champion of vitalism; he is a defender of the principle of the autonomy of life. Life is an ultimate and self-dependent reality. It cannot be described or explained in terms of physics or chemistry. From this point of view Uexküll evolves a new general scheme of biological research. As a philosopher he is an idealist or phenomenalist. But his phenomenalism is not based upon metaphysical or epistemological considerations; it is founded rather on empirical principles. As he points out, it would be a very naïve sort of dogmatism to assume that there exists an absolute reality of things which is the same for all living beings. Reality is not a unique and homogeneous thing; it is immensely diversified, having as many different schemes and patterns as there are different organisms. Every organism is, so to speak, a monadic being. It has a world of its own because it has an experience of its own. The phenomena that we find in the life of a certain biological species are not transferable to any other species. The experiences—and therefore the realities—of two different organisms are incommensurable with one another. In the world of a fly, says Uexküll, we find only "fly things"; in the world of a sea urchin we find only "sea urchin things."

From this general presupposition Uexküll develops a very ingenious and original scheme of the biological world. Wishing to avoid all psychological interpretations, he follows an entirely objective or behavioristic method. The only clue to animal life, he maintains, is given us in the facts of comparative anatomy. If we know the anatomical structure of an animal species, we possess all the necessary data for reconstructing its special mode of experience. A careful study of the structure of the animal body, of the number, the quality, and the distribution of the various sense organs, and the conditions of the nervous system, gives us a perfect image of the inner and outer world of the organism. Uexküll began his investigations with a study of the lowest organisms; he extended them gradually to all the forms of organic life. In a certain sense he refuses to speak of lower or higher forms of life. Life is perfect everywhere; it is the same in the smallest as in the largest circle. Every organism, even the lowest, is not only in a vague sense adapted to (*angepasst*) but entirely fitted into (*eingepasst*) its environment. According to its anatomical structure it possesses a certain *Merknetz* and a certain *Wirknetz*—a receptor system and an effector system. Without the coöperation and equilibrium of these two systems the organism could not survive. The receptor system by which a biological species receives outward stimuli and the effector system by which it reacts to them are in all cases closely interwoven. They are links in one and the same chain which is described by Uexküll as the *functional circle (Funktionskreis)* of the animal.[1]

I cannot enter here upon a discussion of Uexküll's biological principles. I have merely referred to his concepts and terminology in order to pose a general question. Is it possible to make use of the scheme proposed by Uexküll for a description and characterization of the *human world?* Obviously this world forms no exception to those biological rules which govern the life of all the other organisms. Yet in the human world we find a new characteristic which appears to be the distinctive mark of human life. The functional circle of man is not only quantitively enlarged; it has also undergone a qualitative change. Man has, as it were, discovered a new method of adapting himself to his environment. Between the receptor system and the effector system, which are to be found in all

1. See Johannes von Uexküll, *Theoretische Biologie* (2d ed. Berlin, 1938); *Umwelt und Innenwelt der Tiere* (1909; 2d ed. Berlin, 1921).

animal species, we find in man a third link which we may describe as the *symbolic system*. This new acquisition transforms the whole of human life. As compared with the other animals man lives not merely in a broader reality; he lives, so to speak, in a new *dimension* of reality. There is an unmistakable difference between organic reactions and human responses. In the first case a direct and immediate answer is given to an outward stimulus; in the second case the answer is delayed. It is interrupted and retarded by a slow and complicated process of thought. At first sight such a delay may appear to be a very questionable gain. Many philosophers have warned man against this pretended progress. "L'homme qui médite," says Rousseau, "est un animal dépravé": it is not an improvement but a deterioration of human nature to exceed the boundaries of organic life.

Yet there is no remedy against this reversal of the natural order. Man cannot escape from his own achievement. He cannot but adopt the conditions of his own life. No longer in a merely physical universe, man lives in a symbolic universe. Language, myth, art, and religion are parts of this universe. They are the varied threads which weave the symbolic net, the tangled web of human experience. All human progress in thought and experience refines upon and strengthens this net. No longer can man confront reality immediately; he cannot see it, as it were, face to face. Physical reality seems to recede in proportion as man's symbolic activity advances. Instead of dealing with the things themselves man is in a sense constantly conversing with himself. He has so enveloped himself in linguistic forms, in artistic images, in mythical symbols or religious rites that he cannot see or know anything except by the interposition of this artificial medium. His situation is the same in the theoretical as in the practical sphere. Even here man does not live in a world of hard facts, or according to his immediate needs and desires. He lives rather in the midst of imaginary emotions, in hopes and fears, in illusions and disillusions, in his fantasies and dreams. "What disturbs and alarms man," said Epictetus, "are not the things, but his opinions and fancies about the things."

From the point of view at which we have just arrived we

may correct and enlarge the classical definition of man. In spite of all the efforts of modern irrationalism this definition of man as an *animal rationale* has not lost its force. Rationality is indeed an inherent feature of all human activities. Mythology itself is not simply a crude mass of superstitions or gross delusions. It is not merely chaotic, for it possesses a systematic or conceptual form.[2] But, on the other hand, it would be impossible to characterize the structure of myth as rational. Language has often been identified with reason, or with the very source of reason. But it is easy to see that this definition fails to cover the whole field. It is a *pars pro toto*; it offers us a part for the whole. For side by side with conceptual language there is an emotional language; side by side with logical or scientific language there is a language of poetic imagination. Primarily language does not express thoughts or ideas, but feelings and affections. And even a religion "within the limits of pure reason" as conceived and worked out by Kant is no more than a mere abstraction. It conveys only the ideal shape, only the shadow, of what a genuine and concrete religious life is. The great thinkers who have defined man as an *animal rationale* were not empiricists, nor did they ever intend to give an empirical account of human nature. By this definition they were expressing rather a fundamental moral imperative. Reason is a very inadequate term with which to comprehend the forms of man's cultural life in all their richness and variety. But all these forms are symbolic forms. Hence, instead of defining man as an *animal rationale*, we should define him as an *animal symbolicum*. By so doing we can designate his specific difference, and we can understand the new way open to man—the way to civilization.

3   From Animal Reactions to Human Responses

By our definition of man as an *animal symbolicum* we have arrived at our first point of departure for further investigations. But it now becomes imperative that we develop

2. See Cassirer, *Die Begriffsform im mythischen Denken* (Leipzig, 1921).

this definition somewhat in order to give it greater precision. That symbolic thought and symbolic behavior are among the most characteristic features of human life, and that the whole progress of human culture is based on these conditions, is undeniable. But are we entitled to consider them as the special endowment of man to the exclusion of all other organic beings? Is not symbolism a principle which we may trace back to a much deeper source, and which has a much broader range of applicability? If we answer this question in the negative we must, as it seems, confess our ignorance concerning many fundamental questions which have perennially occupied the center of attention in the philosophy of human culture. The question of the *origin* of language, of art, of religion becomes unanswerable, and we are left with human culture as a given fact which remains in a sense isolated and, therefore, unintelligible.

It is understandable that scientists have always refused to accept such a solution. They have made great efforts to connect the fact of symbolism with other well-known and more elementary facts. The problem has been felt to be of paramount importance, but unfortunately it has very rarely been approached with an entirely open mind. From the first it has been obscured and confused by other questions which belong to a quite different realm of discourse. Instead of giving us an unbiased description and analysis of the phenomena themselves the discussion of this problem has been converted into a metaphysical dispute. It has become the bone of contention between the different metaphysical systems: between idealism and materialism, spiritualism and naturalism. For all these systems the question of symbolism has become a crucial problem, on which the future shape of science and metaphysics has seemed to hinge.

With this aspect of the problem we are not concerned here, having set for ourselves a much more modest and concrete task. We shall attempt to describe the symbolic attitude of man in a more accurate manner in order to be able to contradistinguish it from other modes of symbolic behavior found throughout the animal kingdom. That animals do not always react to stimuli in a direct way, that they are capable of an indirect reaction, is evidently beyond question. The well-known experiments of Pavlov provide us with a rich body of empirical evidence concerning the so-called representative stimuli. In the case of the anthropoid apes a very interesting experimental study by Wolfe has shown the effectiveness of "token rewards." The animals learned to respond to tokens as substitute for food rewards in the same way in which they responded to food itself.[1] According to Wolfe the results of varied and protracted training experiments have demonstrated that symbolic processes occur in the behavior of anthropoid apes. Robert M. Yerkes, who describes these experiments in his latest book, draws from them an important general conclusion.

"That they [symbolic processes] are relatively rare and difficult to observe is evident. One may fairly continue to question their existence, but I suspect that they presently will be identified as antecedents of human symbolic processes. Thus we leave this subject at a most exciting stage of development, when discoveries of moment seem imminent."[2]

It would be premature to make any predictions with regard to the future development of this problem. The field must be left open for future investigations. The interpretation of the experimental facts, on the other hand, always depends on certain fundamental concepts which have to be clarified before the empirical material can bear its fruit. Modern psychology and psychobiology take this fact into account. It seems to me highly significant that nowadays it is not the philosophers but the empirical observers and investigators who appear to be taking the leading roles in solving this problem. The latter tell us that after all the problem is not merely an empirical one but to a great degree a logical one. Georg Révész has recently published a series of articles in which he starts off with the proposition that the warmly debated question of so-called *animal language* cannot be solved on the basis of mere facts of animal psychology. Everyone who examines the differ-

1. J. B. Wolfe, "Effectiveness of Token-rewards for Chimpanzees," Comparative Psychology Monographs, 12, No. 5.
2. Robert M. Yerkes, *Chimpanzees. A Laboratory Colony* (New Haven, Yale University Press, 1943), p. 189.

ent psychological theses and theories with an unbiased and critical mind must come at last to the conclusion that the problem cannot be cleared up by simply referring to forms of animal communication and to certain animal accomplishments which are gained by drill and training. All such accomplishments admit of the most contradictory interpretations. Hence it is necessary, first of all, to find a correct logical starting point, one which can lead us to a natural and sound interpretation of the empirical facts. This starting point is the *definition of speech* (*die Begriffsbestimmung der Sprache*).[3] But instead of giving a ready-made definition of speech, it would be better perhaps to proceed along tentative lines. Speech is not a simple and uniform phenomenon. It consists of different elements which, both biologically and systematically, are not on the same level. We must try to find the order and interrelationships of the constituent elements; we must, as it were, distinguish the various geological strata of speech. The first and most fundamental stratum is evidently the language of the emotions. A great portion of all human utterance still belongs to this stratum. But there is a form of speech that shows us quite a different type. Here the word is by no means a mere interjection; it is not an involuntary expression of feeling, but a part of a sentence which has a definite syntactical and logical structure.[4] It is true that even in highly developed, in theoretical language the connection with the first element is not entirely broken off. Scarcely a sentence can be found—except perhaps the pure formal sentences of mathematics—without a certain affective or emotional tinge.[5] Analogies and parallels to emotional language may be found in abundance in the animal world. As regards chimpanzees

3. G. Révész, "Die menschlichen Kommunikationsformen und die sogenannte Tiersprache," *Proceedings of the Netherlands Akademie van Wetenschappen*, XLIII (1940), Nos. 9, 10; XLIV (1941), No. 1.

4. For the distinction between mere emotive utterances and "the normal type of communication of ideas that is speech," see the introductory remarks of Edward Sapir, *Language* (New York, Harcourt, Brace, 1921).

5. For further details see Charles Bally, *Le langage et la vie* (Paris, 1936).

Wolfgang Koehler states that they achieve a considerable degree of expression by means of gesture. Rage, terror, despair, grief, pleading, desire, playfulness, and pleasure are readily expressed in this manner. Nevertheless one element, which is characteristic of and indispensable to all human language, is missing: we find no signs which have an objective reference or meaning. "It may be taken as positively proved," says Koehler, "that their gamut of *phonetics* is entirely 'subjective,' and can only express emotions, never designate or describe objects. But they have so many phonetic elements which are also common to human languages, that their lack of articulate speech cannot be ascribed to *secondary* (glosso-labial) limitations. Their gestures too, of face and body like their expression in sound, never designate or 'describe' objects (Bühler)." [6]

Here we touch upon the crucial point in our whole problem. The difference between *propositional language* and *emotional language* is the real landmark between the human and the animal world. All the theories and observations concerning animal language are wide of the mark if they fail to recognize this fundamental difference.[7] In all the literature of the subject there does not seem to be a single conclusive proof of the fact that any animal ever made the decisive step from subjective to objective, from affective to propositional language. Koehler insists emphatically that speech is definitely beyond the powers of anthropoid apes. He maintains that the lack of this invaluable technical aid and the great limitation of those

6. Wolfgang Koehler, "Zur Psychologie des Schimpansen," *Psychologische Forschung*, I (1921), 27. Cf. the English ed., *The Mentality of Apes* (New York, Harcourt, Brace, 1925), App., p. 317.

7. An early attempt to make a sharp distinction between propositional and emotional language was made in the field of the psychopathology of language. The English neurologist Jackson introduced the term "propositional language" in order to account for some very interesting pathological phenomena. He found that many patients suffering from aphasia had by no means lost the use of speech but that they could not employ their words in an objective, propositional sense. Jackson's distinction proved to be very fruitful. It has played an important part in the further development of the psychopathology of language. For details see Cassirer, *Philosophie der symbolischen Formen*, III, chap. vi, 237–323.

very important components of thought, the so-called images, constitute the causes which prevent animals from ever achieving even the least beginnings of cultural development.[8] The same conclusion has been reached by Révész. Speech, he asserts, is an anthropological concept which accordingly should be entirely discarded from the study of animal psychology. If we proceed from a clear and precise definition of speech, all the other forms of utterances, which we also find in animals, are automatically eliminated.[9] Yerkes, who has studied the problem with special interest, speaks in a more positive tone. He is convinced that even with respect to language and symbolism there exists a close relationship between man and the anthropoid apes. "This suggests," he writes, "that we may have happened upon an early phylogenetic stage in the evolution of symbolic process. There is abundant evidence that various other types of sign process than the symbolic are of frequent occurrence and function effectively in the chimpanzee." [10] Yet all this remains definitely prelinguistic. Even in the judgment of Yerkes all these functional expressions are exceedingly rudimentary, simple, and of limited usefulness by comparison with human cognitive processes.[11] The genetic question is not to be confused here with the analytical and phenomenological question. The logical analysis of human speech always leads us to an element of prime importance which has no parallel in the animal world. The general theory of evolution in no sense stands in the way of the acknowledgment of this fact. Even in the field of the phenomena of organic nature we have learned that evolution does not exclude a sort of original creation. The fact of sudden mutation and of emergent evolution has to be admitted. Modern biology no longer speaks of evolution in terms of earlier Darwinism; nor does it explain the causes of evolution in the same way. We may readily admit that the anthropoid apes, in the develop-

8. Koehler, The Mentality of Apes, p. 277.
9. Révész, op. cit., XLIII, Pt. II (1940), 33.
10. Yerkes and Nissen, "Pre-linguistic Sign Behavior in Chimpanzee," Science, LXXXIX, 587.
11. Yerkes, Chimpanzees, p. 189.

ment of certain symbolic processes, have made a significant forward step. But again we must insist that they did not reach the threshold of the human world. They entered, as it were, a blind alley.

For the sake of a clear statement of the problem we must carefully distinguish between *signs* and *symbols*. That we find rather complex systems of signs and signals in animal behavior seems to be an ascertained fact. We may even say that some animals, especially domesticated animals, are extremely susceptible to signs.[12] A dog will react to the slightest changes in the behavior of his master; he will even distinguish the expressions of a human face or the modulations of a human voice.[13] But it is a far cry from these phenomena to an under-

12. This susceptibility has, for instance, been proved in the famous case of "clever Hans" which a few decades ago created something of a sensation among psychobiologists. Clever Hans was a horse which appeared to possess an astounding intelligence. He could even master rather complicated arithmetical problems, extract cube roots, and so on, stamping on the ground as many times as the solution of the problem required. A special committee of psychologists and other scientists was called on to investigate the case. It soon became clear that the animal reacted to certain involuntary movements of its owner. When the owner was absent or did not understand the question, the horse could not answer it.

13. To illustrate this point I should like to mention another very revealing example. The psychobiologist, Dr. Pfungst, who had developed some new and interesting methods for the study of animal behavior, once told me that he had received a letter from a major about a curious problem. The major had a dog which accompanied him on his walks. Whenever the master got ready to go out the animal showed signs of great joy and excitement. But one day the major decided to try a little experiment. Pretending to go out, he put on his hat, took his cane, and made the customary preparations—without, however, any intention of going for a walk. To his great surprise the dog was not in the least deceived; he remained quietly in his corner. After a brief period of observation Dr. Pfungst was able to solve the mystery. In the major's room there was a desk with a drawer which contained some valuable and important documents. The major had formed the habit of rattling this drawer before leaving the house in order to make sure that it was safely locked. He did not do so the day he did not intend to go out. But for the dog this had become a signal, a necessary element of the walk-situation. Without this signal the dog did not react.

standing of symbolic and human speech. The famous experiments of Pavlov prove only that animals can easily be trained to react not merely to direct stimuli but to all sorts of mediate or representative stimuli. A bell, for example, may become a "sign for dinner," and an animal may be trained not to touch its food when this sign is absent. But from this we learn only that the experimenter, in this case, has succeeded in changing the food-situation of the animal. He has complicated this situation by voluntarily introducing into it a new element. All the phenomena which are commonly described as conditioned reflexes are not merely very far from but even opposed to the essential character of human symbolic thought. Symbols—in the proper sense of this term—cannot be reduced to mere signals. Signals and symbols belong to two different universes of discourse: a signal is a part of the physical world of being; a symbol is a part of the human world of meaning. Signals are "operators"; symbols are "designators." [14] Signals, even when understood and used as such, have nevertheless a sort of physical or substantial being; symbols have only a functional value.

Bearing this distinction in mind, we can find an approach to one of the most controverted problems. The question of the *intelligence of animals* has always been one of the greatest puzzles of anthropological philosophy. Tremendous efforts, both of thought and observation, have been expended on answers to this question. But the ambiguity and vagueness of the very term "intelligence" has always stood in the way of a clear solution. How can we hope to answer a question whose import we do not understand? Metaphysicians and scientists, naturalists and theologians have used the word intelligence in varying and contradictory senses. Some psychologists and psychobiologists have flatly refused to speak of the intelligence of animals. In all animal behavior they saw only the play of a certain automatism. This thesis had behind it the authority of Descartes; yet it has been reasserted in modern psychology. "The animal," says E. L. Thorndike in his work on animal

14. For the distinction between operators and designators see Charles Morris, "The Foundation of the Theory of Signs," *Encyclopedia of the Unified Sciences* (1938).

intelligence, "does not think one is like the other, nor does it, as is so often said, mistake one for the other. It does not think *about* it at all; it just thinks *it* . . . The idea that animals react to a particular and absolutely defined and realized sense-impression, and that a similar reaction to a sense-impression which varies from the first proves an association by similarity, is a myth." [15] Later and more exact observations led to a different conclusion. In the case of the higher animals it became clear that they were able to solve rather difficult problems and that these solutions were not brought about in a merely mechanical way, by trial and error. As Koehler points out, the most striking difference exists between a mere chance solution and a genuine solution, so that the one can easily be distinguished from the other. That at least some of the reactions of the higher animals are not merely a product of chance but guided by insight appears to be incontestable.[16] If by intelligence we understand either adjustment to the immediate environment or adaptive modification of environment, we must certainly ascribe to animals a comparatively highly developed intelligence. It must also be conceded that not all animal actions are governed by the presence of an immediate stimulus. The animal is capable of all sorts of detours in its reactions. It may learn not only to use implements but even to invent tools for its purposes. Hence some pyschobiologists do not hesitate to speak of a creative or constructive imagination in animals.[17] But neither this intelligence nor this imagination is of the specifically human type. In short, we may say that the animal possesses a practical imagination and intelligence whereas man alone has developed a new form: a *symbolic imagination and intelligence*.

Moreover, in the mental development of the individual mind the transition from one form to the other—from a merely practical attitude to a symbolic attitude—is evident. But here this step is the final result of a slow and continuous

15. Edward L. Thorndike, *Animal Intelligence* (New York, Macmillan, 1911), pp. 119 ff.

16. See Koehler, *op. cit.*, chap. vii, " 'Chance' and 'Imitation.' "

17. See R. M. and A. W. Yerkes, *The Great Apes* (New Haven, Yale University Press, 1929), pp. 368 ff., 520 ff.

process. By the usual methods of psychological observation it is not easy to distinguish the individual stages of this complicated process. There is, however, another way to obtain full insight into the general character and paramount importance of this transition. Nature itself has here, so to speak, made an experiment capable of throwing unexpected light upon the point in question. We have the classical cases of Laura Bridgman and Helen Keller, two blind deaf-mute children, who by means of special methods learned to speak. Although both cases are well known and have often been treated in psychological literature,[18] I must nevertheless remind the reader of them once more because they contain perhaps the best illustration of the general problem with which we are here concerned. Mrs. Sullivan, the teacher of Helen Keller, has recorded the exact date on which the child really began to understand the meaning and function of human language. I quote her own words: "I must write you a line this morning because something very important has happened. Helen has taken the second great step in her education. She has learned that *everything has a name, and that the manual alphabet is the key to everything she wants to know.*

". . . This morning, while she was washing, she wanted to know the name for 'water.' When she wants to know the name of anything, she points to it and pats my hand. I spelled 'w-a-t-e-r' and thought no more about it until after breakfast. . . . [Later on] we went out to the pump house, and I made Helen hold her mug under the spout while I pumped. As the cold water gushed forth, filling the mug, I spelled 'w-a-t-e-r' in Helen's free hand. The word coming so close upon the sensation of cold water rushing over her hand seemed to startle her. She dropped the mug and stood as one transfixed. A new light came into her face. She spelled 'water' several times. Then she dropped on the ground and asked for its name and pointed to the pump and the trellis and suddenly turning round she asked

18. For Laura Bridgman see Maud Howe and Florence Howe Hall, *Laura Bridgman* (Boston, 1903); Mary Swift Lamson, *Life and Education of Laura Dewey Bridgman* (Boston, 1881); Wilhelm Jerusalem, *Laura Bridgman. Erziehung einer Taubstumm-Blinden* (Berlin, 1905).

for my name. I spelled 'teacher.' All the way back to the house she was highly excited, and learned the name of every object she touched, so that in a few hours she had added thirty new words to her vocabulary. The next morning she got up like a radiant fairy. She has flitted from object to object, asking the name of everything and kissing me for very gladness. . . . Everything must have a name now. Wherever we go, she asks eagerly for the names of things she has not learned at home. She is anxious for her friends to spell, and eager to teach the letters to everyone she meets. She drops the signs and panto-mime she used before, as soon as she has words to supply their place, and the acquirement of a new word affords her the liveliest pleasure. And we notice that her face grows more expressive each day." [19]

The decisive step leading from the use of signs and panto-mime to the use of words, that is, of symbols, could scarcely be described in a more striking manner. What was the child's real discovery at this moment? Helen Keller had previously learned to combine a certain thing or event with a certain sign of the manual alphabet. A fixed association had been established between these things and certain tactile impres-sions. But a series of such associations, even if they are re-peated and amplified, still does not imply an understanding of what human speech is and means. In order to arrive at such an understanding the child had to make a new and much more significant discovery. It had to understand that *everything has a name*—that the symbolic function is not restricted to par-ticular cases but is a principle of *universal* applicability which encompasses the whole field of human thought. In the case of Helen Keller this discovery came as a sudden shock. She was a girl seven years of age who, with the exception of defects in the use of certain sense organs, was in an excellent state of health and possessed of a highly developed mind. By the neglect of her education she had been very much retarded. Then, suddenly, the crucial development takes place. It works like an intellectual revolution. The child begins to see the

19. See Helen Keller, *The Story of My Life* (New York, Doubleday, Page & Co., 1902, 1903), Supplementary Account of Helen Keller's Life and Education, pp. 315 ff.

world in a new light. It has learned the use of words not merely as mechanical signs or signals but as an entirely new instrument of thought. A new horizon is opened up, and henceforth the child will roam at will in this incomparably wider and freer area.

The same can be shown in the case of Laura Bridgman, though hers is a less spectacular story. Both in mental ability and in intellectual development Laura Bridgman was greatly inferior to Helen Keller. Her life and education do not contain the same dramatic elements we find in Helen Keller. Yet in both cases the same typical elements are present. After Laura Bridgman had learned the use of the finger-alphabet she, too, suddenly reached the point at which she began to understand the symbolism of human speech. In this respect we find a surprising parallelism between the two cases. "I shall never forget," writes Miss Drew, one of the first teachers of Laura Bridgman, "the first meal taken after she appreciated the use of the finger-alphabet. Every article that she touched must have a name; and I was obliged to call some one to help me wait upon the other children, while she kept me busy in spelling the new words." [20]

The principle of symbolism, with its universality, validity, and general applicability, is the magic word, the Open Sesame! giving access to the specifically human world, to the world of human culture. Once man is in possession of this magic key further progress is assured. Such progress is evidently not obstructed or made impossible by any lack in the sense material. The case of Helen Keller, who reached a very high degree of mental development and intellectual culture, shows us clearly and irrefutably that a human being in the construction of his human world is not dependent upon the quality of his sense material. If the theories of sensationalism were right, if every idea were nothing but a faint copy of an original sense impression, then the condition of a blind, deaf, and dumb child would indeed be desperate. For it would be deprived of the very sources of human knowledge; it would

20. See Mary Swift Lamson, *Life and Education of Laura Dewey Bridgman, the Deaf, Dumb, and Blind Girl* (Boston, Houghton, Mifflin Co., 1881), pp. 7 f.

be, as it were, an exile from reality. But if we study Helen Keller's autobiography we are at once aware that this is untrue, and at the same time we understand why it is untrue. Human culture derives its specific character and its intellectual and moral values, not from the material of which it consists, but from its form, its architectural structure. And this form may be expressed in any sense material. Vocal language has a very great technical advantage over tactile language; but the technical defects of the latter do not destroy its essential use. The free development of symbolic thought and symbolic expression is not obstructed by the use of tactile signs in the place of vocal ones. If the child has succeeded in grasping the meaning of human language, it does not matter in which particular material this meaning is accessible to it. As the case of Helen Keller proves, man can construct his symbolic world out of the poorest and scantiest materials. The thing of vital importance is not the individual bricks and stones but their general *function* as architectural form. In the realm of speech it is their general symbolic function which vivifies the material signs and "makes them speak." Without this vivifying principle the human world would indeed remain deaf and mute. With this principle, even the world of a deaf, dumb, and blind child can become incomparably broader and richer than the world of the most highly developed animal.

Universal applicability, owing to the fact that everything has a name, is one of the greatest prerogatives of human symbolism. But it is not the only one. There is still another characteristic of symbols which accompanies and complements this one, and forms its necessary correlate. A symbol is not only universal but extremely variable. I can express the same meaning in various languages; and even within the limits of a single language a certain thought or idea may be expressed in quite different terms. A sign or signal is related to the thing to which it refers in a fixed and unique way. Any one concrete and individual sign refers to a certain individual thing. In Pavlov's experiments the dogs could easily be trained to reach for food only upon being given special signs; they would not eat until they heard a particular sound which could be chosen at the discretion of the experimenter. But this bears no analogy, as it has often been interpreted, to human symbolism; on the contrary, it is in opposition to symbolism. A genuine human symbol is characterized not by its uniformity but by its versatility. It is not rigid or inflexible but mobile. It is true that the full *awareness* of this mobility seems to be a rather late achievement in man's intellectual and cultural development. In primitive mentality this awareness is very seldom attained. Here the symbol is still regarded as a property of the thing like other physical properties. In mythical thought the name of a god is an integral part of the nature of the god. If I do not call the god by his right name, then the spell or prayer becomes ineffective. The same holds good for symbolic actions. A religious rite, a sacrifice, must always be performed in the same invariable way and in the same order if it is to have its effect.[21] Children are often greatly confused when they first learn that not every name of an object is a "proper name," that the same thing may have quite different names in different languages. They tend to think that a thing "is" what it is called. But this is only a first step. Every normal child will learn very soon that it can use various symbols to express the same wish or thought. For this variability and mobility there is apparently no parallel in the animal world.[22] Long before Laura Bridgman had learned to speak, she had developed a very curious mode of expression, a language of her own. This language did not consist of articulated sounds but only of various noises, which are described as "emotional noises." She was in the habit of uttering these sounds in the presence of certain persons. Thus they became entirely individualized; every person in her environment was greeted by a special noise. "Whenever she met unexpectedly an acquaintance," writes Dr. Lieber, "I found that she repeatedly uttered the word for that person before she began to speak.

21. For further details see Cassirer, *Sprache und Mythos* (Leipzig, 1925).
22. For this problem see W. M. Urban, *Language and Reality*, Pt. I, iii, 95 ff.

It was the utterance of pleasurable recognition." [23] But when by means of the finger alphabet the child had grasped the meaning of human language the case was altered. Now the sound really became a name: and this name was not bound to an individual person but could be changed if the circumstances seemed to require it. One day, for instance, Laura Bridgman had a letter from her former teacher, Miss Drew, who, in the meantime, by her marriage had become a Mrs. Morton. In this letter she was invited to visit her teacher. This gave her great pleasure, but she found fault with Miss Drew because she had signed the letter with her old name instead of using the name of her husband. She even said that now she must find another noise for her teacher, as the one for Drew must not be the same as that for Morton.[24] It is clear that the former "noises" have here undergone an important and very interesting change in meaning. They are no longer special utterances, inseparable from a particular concrete situation. They have become abstract names. For the new name invented by the child did not designate a new individual but the same individual in a new relationship.

Another important aspect of our general problem now emerges—the problem of the *dependence of relational thought upon symbolic thought*. Without a complex system of symbols relational thought cannot arise at all, much less reach its full development. It would not be correct to say that the mere *awareness* of relations presupposes an intellectual act, an act of logical or abstract thought. Such an awareness is necessary even in elementary acts of perception. The sensationalist theories used to describe perception as a mosaic of simple sense data. Thinkers of this persuasion constantly overlooked the fact that sensation itself is by no means a mere aggregate or bundle of isolated impressions. Modern Gestalt psychology has corrected this view. It has shown that the very simplest perceptual processes imply fundamental structural elements, certain patterns or configurations. This principle holds both

23. See Francis Lieber, "A Paper on the Vocal Sounds of Laura Bridgman," *Smithsonian Contributions to Knowledge*, II, Art. 2, p. 27.
24. See Mary Swift Lamson, *op. cit.*, p. 84.

for the human and the animal world. Even in comparatively low stages of animal life the presence of these structural elements—especially of spatial and optical structures—has been experimentally proved.[25] The mere awareness of relations cannot, therefore, be regarded as a specific feature of human consciousness. We do find, however, in man a special type of relational thought which has no parallel in the animal world. In man an ability to isolate relations—to consider them in their abstract meaning—has developed. In order to grasp this meaning man is no longer dependent upon concrete sense data, upon visual, auditory, tactile, kinesthetic data. He considers these relations "in themselves"—*auto kath' hauto,* as Plato said. Geometry is the classic example of this turning point in man's intellectual life. Even in elementary geometry we are not bound to the apprehension of concrete individual figures. We are not concerned with physical things or perceptual objects, for we are studying universal spatial relations for whose expression we have an adequate symbolism. Without the preliminary step of human language such an achievement would not be possible. In all the tests which have been made of the processes of abstraction or generalization in animals, this point has become evident. Koehler succeeded in showing the ability of chimpanzees to respond to the *relation* between two or more objects instead of to a particular object. Confronted by two food-containing boxes, the chimpanzee by reason of previous general training would constantly choose the larger—even though the particular object selected might in a previous experiment have been rejected as the smaller of the pair. Similar capacity to respond to the nearer object, the brighter, the bluer, rather than to a particular box was demonstrated. Koehler's results were confirmed and extended by later experiments. It could be shown that the higher animals are capable of what has been called the "isolation of perceptual factors." They have the potentiality for singling out a particular perceptual quality of the experimental situation and

25. See Wolfgang Koehler, "Optische Untersuchungen am Schimpansen und am Haushuhn; Nachweis einfacher Strukturfunktionen beim Schimpansen und beim Haushuhn," *Abhandlungen der Berliner Akademie der Wissenschaften* (1915, 1918).

reacting accordingly. In this sense animals are able to abstract color from size and shape or shape from size and color. In some experiments made by Mrs. Kohts a chimpanzee was able to select from a collection of objects varying extremely in visual qualities those which had some one quality in common; it could, for instance, pick out all objects of a given color and place them in a receiving box. These examples seem to prove that the higher animals are capable of that process which Hume in his theory of knowledge terms making a *"distinction of reason."* [26] But all the experimenters engaged in these investigations have also emphasized the rarity, the rudimentariness, and the imperfection of these processes. Even after they have learned to single out a particular quality and to reach toward this, animals are liable to all sorts of curious mistakes.[27] If there are certain traces of a *distinctio rationis* in the animal world, they are, as it were, nipped in the bud. They cannot develop because they do not possess that invaluable and indeed indispensable aid of human speech, of a system of symbols.

The first thinker to have clear insight into this problem was Herder. He spoke as a philosopher of humanity who wished to pose the question in entirely "human" terms. Rejecting the metaphysical or theological thesis of a supernatural or divine origin of language, Herder begins with a critical revision of the question itself. Speech is not an object, a physical thing for which we may seek a natural or a supernatural cause. It is a process, a general function of the human mind. Psychologically we cannot describe this process in the terminology which was used by all the psychological schools of the eighteenth century. According to Herder speech is not an artificial creation of reason, nor is it to be accounted for by a special mechanism of associations. In his own attempt to set forth the nature of language Herder lays the whole stress upon what he calls *"reflection."* Reflection or reflective thought is the ability of man to single out from the whole undiscriminated

26. Hume's theory of the "distinction of reason" is explained in his *Treatise of Human Nature,* Pt. I, sec. 7 (London, Green and Grose, 1874), I, 332 ff.
27. Examples are given by Yerkes in *Chimpanzees,* pp. 103 ff.

mass of the stream of floating sensuous phenomena certain fixed elements in order to isolate them and to concentrate attention upon them.

"Man evinces reflection when the power of his soul acts so freely that it can segregate from the whole ocean of sensation surging through all his senses one wave, as it were; and that it can stay this wave, draw attention to it, and be aware of this attention. He evinces reflection when from the whole wavering dream of images rushing through his senses he can collect himself into a moment of waking, dwell on one image spontaneously, observe it clearly and more quietly, and abstract characteristics showing him that this and no other is the object. Thus he evinces reflection when he can not only perceive all the qualities vividly or clearly but when he can recognize one or several of them as distinctive qualities. . . . Now by what means did this recognition come about? Through a characteristic which he had to abstract, and which, as an element of consciousness, presented itself clearly. Well then, let us exclaim: Eureka! This initial character of consciousness was the language of the soul. With this, human language is created." [28]

This has more the appearance of a poetical portrait than of a logical analysis of human speech. Herder's theory of the origin of language remained entirely speculative. It did not proceed from a general theory of knowledge, nor from an observation of empirical facts. It was based on his ideal of humanity and on his profound intuition of the character and development of human culture. Nevertheless it contains logical and psychological elements of the most valuable sort. All the processes of generalization or abstraction in animals that have been investigated and described with accuracy [29] clearly lack the distinctive mark enphasized by Herder. Later on, however, Herder's view found a rather unexpected clarification and confirmation from a quite different quarter. Recent research in the field of the psychopathology of language has led

28. Herder, Über den Ursprung der Sprache (1772), "Werke," ed. Suphan, V, 34 f.
29. See, for instance, the remarks of R. M. Yerkes about "generalized responses" in the chimpanzee, op. cit., pp. 130 ff.

to the conclusion that the loss, or severe impairment, of speech caused by brain injury is never an isolated phenomenon. Such a defect alters the whole character of human behavior. Patients suffering from aphasia or other kindred diseases have not only lost the use of words but have undergone corresponding changes in personality. Such changes are scarcely observable in their outward behavior, for here they tend to act in a perfectly normal manner. They can perform the tasks of everyday life; some of them even develop considerable skill in all tests of this sort. But they are at a complete loss as soon as the solution of the problem requires any specific theoretical or reflective activity. They are no longer able to think in general concepts or categories. Having lost their grip on universals, they stick to the immediate facts, to concrete situations. Such patients are unable to perform any task which can be executed only by means of a comprehension of the abstract.[30] All this is highly significant, for it shows us to what degree that type of thought which Herder called reflective is dependent on symbolic thought. Without symbolism the life of man would be like that of the prisoners in the cave of Plato's famous simile. Man's life would be confined within the limits of his biological needs and his practical interests; it could find no access to the "ideal world" which is opened to him from different sides by religion, art, philosophy, science.

4 The Human World of Space and Time

Space and time are the framework in which all reality is concerned. We cannot conceive any real thing except under the conditions of space and time. Nothing in the world, according to Heraclitus, can exceed its measures—and these

30. A detailed and highly interesting account of these phenomena will be found in various publications of K. Goldstein and A. Gelb. Goldstein has given a general survey of his theoretical views in *Human Nature in the Light of Psychopathology*, the William James Lectures delivered at Harvard University, 1937–38 (Cambridge, Mass., Harvard University Press, 1940). I have discussed the question from a general philosophical point of view in *Philosophie der symbolischen Formen*, III, vi, 237–323.

measures are spatial and temporal limitations. In mythical thought space and time are never considered as pure or empty forms. They are regarded as the great mysterious forces which govern all things, which rule and determine not only our mortal life but also the life of the gods.

To describe and analyze the specific character which space and time assume in human experience is one of the most appealing and important tasks of an anthropological philosophy. It would be a naïve and unfounded assumption to consider the appearance of space and time as necessarily one and the same for all organic beings. Obviously we cannot ascribe to the lower organisms the same kind of space perception as to man. And even between the human world and the world of the higher anthropoids there remains in this respect an unmistakable and ineffaceable difference. Yet it is not easy to account for this difference if we merely apply our usual psychological methods. We must follow an indirect way: we must analyze the forms of human *culture* in order to discover the true character of space and time in our human world.

The first thing that becomes clear by such an analysis is that there are fundamentally different *types* of spatial and temporal experience. Not all the forms of this experience are on the same level. There are lower and higher strata arranged in a certain order. The lowest stratum may be described as *organic space and time*. Every organism lives in a certain environment and must constantly adapt itself to the conditions of this environment in order to survive. Even in the lower organisms adaptation requires a rather complicated system of reactions, a differentiation between physical stimuli and an adequate response to these stimuli. All this is not learned by individual experience. Newborn animals seem to have a very nice and accurate sense of spatial distance and direction. A young chicken that has just broken out of its shell gets its bearings and picks up the grains spread in its path. The special conditions on which this process of spatial orientation depends have been carefully studied by biologists and psychologists. Although we are unable to answer all the intricate questions concerning the power of orientation in bees, ants, and birds of passage, we can at least give a negative answer. We cannot assume that the animals when performing these very complicated reactions are guided by any *ideational* processes. On the contrary they seem to be led by bodily impulses of a special kind; they have no mental picture or idea of space, no prospectus of spatial relations.

As we approach the higher animals we meet with a new form of space which we may term *perceptual space*. This space is not a simple sense datum; it is of a very complex nature, containing elements of all the different kinds of sense experience—optical, tactual, acoustic, and kinesthetic. The manner in which all these elements coöperate in the construction of perceptual space has proved to be one of the most difficult questions of the modern psychology of sensation. A great scientist, Hermann von Helmholtz, found it necessary to inaugurate an entirely new branch of knowledge, to create the science of physiological optics, in order to solve the problems which confront us here. Nevertheless there still remain many questions which cannot for the present be decided in a clear and unambiguous manner. In the history of modern psychology the strife "on the dark battlefield of nativism and empiricism" has seemed interminable.[1]

We are not concerned here with this aspect of the problem. The *genetic* question, the question of the origin of spatial perception, which for a long time has overshadowed and eclipsed all the other problems, is not the only question; nor is it the most important one. From the point of view of a general theory of knowledge and of anthropological philosophy another issue now takes our interest and must be brought into focus. Rather than investigate the origin and development of perceptual space, we must analyze *symbolic space*. In approaching this issue we are on the borderline between the human and animal worlds. With regard to organic space, the *space of action*, man seems in many respects very much inferior to the animals. A child has to learn many skills which the animal was born with. But for this deficiency man is compensated by another gift which he alone develops and

1. See William Stern's observations in his *Psychology of Early Childhood*, trans. by Anna Barwell (2d ed. New York, Holt & Co., 1930), pp. 114 ff.

which bears no analogy to anything in organic nature. Not immediately, but by a very complex and difficult process of thought, he arrives at the idea of *abstract space*—and it is this idea which clears the way for man not only to a new field of knowledge but to an entirely new direction of his cultural life.

The greatest difficulties have from the first been encountered by the philosophers themselves in accounting for and describing the real nature of abstract or symbolic space. The fact of the existence of such a thing as abstract space was one of the first and most important discoveries of Greek thought. Materialists and idealists alike emphasized the significance of this discovery. But thinkers of both persuasions were hard put to it to elucidate its logical character. They tended to take refuge in paradoxical assertions. Democritus declares that space is nonbeing (*mê on*) but that this nonbeing has, nevertheless, true reality. Plato in the *Timaeus* refers to the concept of space as a *logismos nothos*—a "hybrid concept" which is hardly describable in adequate terms. And even in modern science and philosophy these early difficulties are still unsolved. Newton warns us not to confound abstract space—the true mathematical space—with the space of our sense experience. Common people, he says, think of space, time, and motion according to no other principle than the relations these concepts bear to sensible objects. But we must abandon this principle if we wish to achieve any real scientific or philosophic truth: in philosophy we have to abstract from our sense data.[2] This Newtonian view became the stumbling block for all the systems of sensationalism. Berkeley concentrated all his critical attacks on this point. He maintained that Newton's "true mathematical space" was in fact no more than an imaginary space, a fiction of the human mind. And if we admit the general principles of Berkeley's theory of knowledge we can scarcely refute this view. We must admit that abstract space has no counterpart and no foundation in any physical or psychological reality. The points and lines of the geometer are neither physical nor psychological objects; they are nothing

2. See Newton's *Principia*, Bk. I, Definition 8, Scholium.

but symbols for abstract relations. If we ascribe "truth" to these relations, then the sense of the term truth will henceforth require redefinition. For we are concerned in the case of abstract space not with the truth of things but with the truth of propositions and judgments.

But before this step could be taken and could be systematically grounded, philosophy and science had to travel a long way and to pass through many intermediate stages. The history of this problem has not yet been written, though it would be a very attractive task to trace the individual steps of this development. They yield an insight into the very character and general tendency of man's cultural life. I must content myself here with selecting a few typical stages. In primitive life and under the conditions of primitive society we find scarcely any trace of the idea of an abstract space. Primitive space is a space of action; and the action is centered around immediate practical needs and interests. So far as we can speak of a primitive "conception" of space, this conception is not of a purely theoretical character. It is still fraught with concrete personal or social feelings, with emotional elements. "So far as the primitive man carries out technical activities in space," writes Heinz Werner, "so far as he measures distances, steers his canoe, hurls his spear at a certain target, and so on, his space as a field of action, as a pragmatic space, does not differ in its structure from our own. But when primitive man makes this space a subject of representation and of reflective thought, there arises a specifically primordial idea differing radically from any intellectualized version. The idea of space, for primitive man, even when systematized, is syncretically bound up with the subject. It is a notion much more affective and concrete than the abstract space of the man of advanced culture . . . It is not so much objective, measurable, and abstract in character. It exhibits egocentric or anthropomorphic characteristics, and is physiognomic-dynamic, rooted in the concrete and substantial." [3]

From the point of view of primitive mentality and primitive culture it is indeed an almost impossible task to make that

3. Heinz Werner, Comparative Psychology of Mental Development (New York, Harper & Bros., 1940), p. 167.

decisive step which alone can lead us from the space of action
to a theoretical or scientific concept of space—to the space of
geometry. In the latter all the concrete differences of our immediate sense experience are wiped out. We no longer have a
visual, a tactile, an acoustic, or olfactory space. Geometrical
space abstracts from all the variety and heterogeneity imposed
upon us by the disparate nature of our senses. Here we have
a homogeneous, a universal space. And it was only by the
medium of this new and characteristic form of space that man
could arrive at the concept of a unique, systematic *cosmic*
order. The idea of such an order, of the unity and the lawfulness of the universe, never could have been reached without
the idea of a uniform space. But it was a very long time before
this step could be made. Primitive thought is not only incapable of thinking of a system of space; it cannot even conceive
a scheme of space. Its concrete space cannot be brought into
a *schematic* shape. Ethnology shows us that primitive tribes
usually are gifted with an extraordinarily sharp perception of
space. A native of these tribes has an eye for all the nicest
details of his environment. He is extremely sensitive to every
change in the position of the common objects of his surroundings. Even under very difficult circumstances he will be able
to find his way. When rowing or sailing he follows with the
greatest accuracy all the turns of the river that he goes up and
down. But upon closer examination we discover to our surprise that in spite of this facility there seems to be a strange
lack in his apprehension of space. If you ask him to give you
a general description, a delineation of the course of the river
he is not able to do so. If you wish him to draw a map of the
river and its various turns he seems not even to understand
your question. Here we grasp very distinctly the difference between the concrete and the abstract apprehension of space
and spatial relations. The native is perfectly acquainted with
the course of the river, but this acquaintance is very far from
what we may call knowledge in an abstract, a theoretical sense.
Acquaintance means only presentation; knowledge includes
and presupposes representation. The representation of an object is quite a different act from the mere handling of the object. The latter demands nothing but a definite series of

actions, of bodily movements coördinated with each other or following each other. It is a matter of habit acquired by a constantly repeated unvarying performance of certain acts. But the representation of space and spatial relations means much more. To represent a thing it is not enough to be able to manipulate it in the right way and for practical uses. We must have a general conception of the object, and regard it from different angles in order to find its relations to other objects. We must locate it and determine its position in a general system.

In the history of human culture this great generalization, which led to the conception of a cosmic order, seems first to have been made in Babylonian astronomy. Here we find the first definite evidence of a thought which transcends the sphere of man's concrete practical life, which dares to embrace the whole universe in a comprehensive view. It is for this reason that Babylonian culture has been looked upon as the cradle of all cultural life. Many scholars have maintained that all the mythological, religious, and scientific conceptions of mankind derived from this source. I shall not discuss here these Pan-Babylonian theories,[4] for I wish to raise another question. Is it possible to allege a reason for the fact that the Babylonians were not only the first to observe the celestial phenomena but the first to lay the foundations for a scientific astronomy and cosmology? The importance of the phenomena of the sky had never been completely overlooked. Man must very soon have become aware of the fact that his whole life was dependent on certain general cosmic conditions. The rising and setting of the sun, the moon, the stars, the cycle of the seasons—all these natural phenomena are well-known facts that play an important role in primitive mythology. But in order to bring them into a system of thought, another condition was requisite which could only be fulfilled under special circumstances. These favorable circumstances

4. For these theories see the writings of Hugo Winckler, especially *Himmelsbild und Weltenbild der Babylonier als Grundlage der Weltanschauung und Mythologie aller Völker* (Leipzig, 1901) and *Die babylonische Geisteskultur in ihren Beziehungen zur Kulturentwicklung der Menschheit* (Leipzig, 1901).

prevailed at the origin of Babylonian culture. Otto Neugebauer has written a very interesting study of the history of
ancient mathematics in which he corrects many of the former
views regarding this matter. The traditional view was that before the time of the Greeks no evidences of a scientific mathematics are to be found. The Babylonians and Egyptians—it
was generally assumed—had made great practical and technical progress; but they had not yet discovered the first elements
of a theoretical mathematics. According to Neugebauer a critical analysis of all the available sources leads to a different interpretation. It has become clear that the progress made in
Babylonian astronomy was not an isolated phenomenon. It
depended upon a more fundamental fact—upon the discovery
and the use of a new intellectual instrument. The Babylonians had discovered a *symbolic algebra*. In comparison with
later developments of mathematical thought this algebra was
still of course very simple and elementary. Nevertheless it contained a new and extremely fertile conception. Neugebauer
traces this conception down to the very beginnings of Babylonian culture. In order to understand the characteristic form
of Babylonian algebra, he tells us, we have to take into account
the historical background of Babylonian civilization. This civilization evolved under special conditions. It was the product
of a meeting and collision between two different races—the
Sumerians and the Akkadians. The two races are of different
origin and speak languages which bear no relation to one another. The language of the Akkadians belongs to the Semitic
type; that of the Sumerians to another group which is neither
Semitic nor Indo-European. When these two peoples met,
when they came to share in a common political, social, and
cultural life, they had new problems to solve, problems for
which they found it necessary to develop new intellectual
powers. The original language of the Sumerians could not be
understood; their written texts could not be deciphered by the
Akkadians without great difficulty and constant mental effort.
It was by this effort that the Babylonians first learned to understand the meaning and uses of an abstract symbolism. "Every
algebraic operation," says Neugebauer, "presupposes that one
possesses certain fixed symbols both for the mathematical

operation and for the quantities to which these operations are applied. Without such a conceptual symbolism it would not be possible to combine quantities that are not numerically determined and designated and it would not be possible to derive new combinations from them. But such a symbolism presented itself immediately and necessarily in the writing of Akkadian texts. . . . From the very beginning the Babylonians could, therefore, dispose of the most important groundwork of an algebraic development—of an appropriate and adequate symbolism." [5]

In Babylonian astronomy we find, however, only the first phases of that great process which finally led to the intellectual conquest of space and to the discovery of a cosmic order, of a system of the universe. Mathematical thought as such could not lead to an immediate solution of the problem, for in the dawn of human civilization mathematical thought never appears in its true logical shape. It is, as it were, wrapped in the atmosphere of mythical thought. The first discoverers of a scientific mathematics could not break through this veil. The Pythagoreans spoke of number as a magical and mysterious power, and even in their theory of space they use a mythical language. This interpenetration of seemingly heterogeneous elements becomes especially conspicuous in all the primitive systems of cosmogony. Babylonian astronomy in its entirety is still a mythical interpretation of the universe. It was no longer restricted within the narrow sphere of concrete, corporeal, primitive space. Space is, so to speak, transposed from the earth to the heavens. But when turning to the order of the celestial phenomena mankind could not forget its terrestrial needs and interests. If man first directed his eyes to the heavens, it was not to satisfy a merely intellectual curiosity. What man really sought in the heavens was his own reflection and the order of his human universe. He felt that his world was bound by innumerable visible and invisible ties to the general order of the universe—and he tried to penetrate into this mysterious connection. The celestial phenomena could

5. Otto Neugebauer, "Vorgriechische Mathematik," in *Vorlesungen über die Geschichte der antiken Mathematischen Wissenschaften* (Berlin, J. Springer, 1934), I, 68 ff.

not, therefore, be studied in a detached spirit of abstract meditation and pure science. They were regarded as the masters and rulers of the world and the governors of human life. In order to organize the political, the social, and the moral life of man it proved to be necessary to turn to the heavens. No human phenomenon seemed to explain itself; it had to be explained by referring it to a corresponding heavenly phenomenon on which it depends. From these considerations it becomes clear that and why the space of the first astronomical systems could not be a mere theoretical space. It did not consist of points or lines, of superficies in the abstract geometrical sense of these terms. It was filled with magical, with divine and demonic powers. The first and essential aim of astronomy was to win an insight into the nature and activity of these powers in order to foresee and to evade their dangerous influences. Astronomy could not arise except in this mythical and magical shape—in the shape of *astrology*. It preserved this character for many thousands of years; in a certain sense it was still prevalent in the first centuries of our own age, in the culture of the Renaissance. Even Kepler, the real founder of our own scientific astronomy, had to struggle throughout his life with this problem. But finally this last step had to be made. Astronomy supersedes astrology; geometrical space takes the place of mythical and magical space. It was a false and erroneous form of symbolic thought that first paved the way to a new and true symbolism, the symbolism of modern science.

One of the first and most difficult tasks of modern philosophy was to understand this symbolism in its true sense and in its full significance. If we study the evolution of Cartesian thought we find that Descartes did not begin with his *Cogito ergo sum*. He began with his concept and ideal of a *mathesis universalis*. His ideal was founded upon a great mathematical discovery—analytical geometry. In this symbolic thought took another step forward which was to have the most important systematic consequences. It became clear that all our knowledge of space and spatial relations could be translated into a new language, that of numbers, and that by this translation and transformation the true logical character of geometrical thought could be conceived in a much clearer and more adequate way.

We find the same characteristic progress when we pass from the problem of space to the *problem of time*. It is true that there are not only strict analogies but also characteristic differences in the development of both concepts. According to Kant space is the form of our "outer experience," time the form of our "inner experience." In the interpretation of his inner experience man had new problems to confront. Here he could not use the same methods as in his first attempt to organize and systematize his knowledge of the physical world. There is, however, a common background for both questions. Even time is first thought of not as a specific form of human life but as a general condition of organic life. Organic life exists only so far as it evolves in time. It is not a thing but a process—a never-resting continuous stream of events. In this stream nothing ever recurs in the same identical shape. Heraclitus' saying holds good for all organic life: "You cannot step twice into the same river." When dealing with the problem of organic life we have, first and foremost, to free ourselves from what Whitehead has called the prejudice of "simple location." The organism is never located in a single instant. In its life the three modes of time—the past, the present, and the future—form a whole which cannot be split up into individual elements. "Le présent est chargé du passé, et gros de l'avenir," said Leibniz. We cannot describe the momentary state of an organism without taking its history into consideration and without referring it to a future state for which this state is merely a point of passage.

One of the most distinguished physiologists of the nineteenth century, Ewald Hering, defended the theory that *memory* is to be regarded as a general function of all organic matter.[6] It is not only a phenomenon of our conscious life but it is spread over the whole domain of living nature. This theory was accepted and further developed by R. Semon, who, upon this basis, developed a new general scheme of psychology.

6. See Ewald Hering, *Über das Gedächtnis als eine allgemeine Funktion der organischen Materie* (1870).

According to Semon the only approach to a scientific psychology is by way of a *"mnemic biology."* "Mneme" was defined by Semon as the principle of conservation in the mutability of all organic happenings. Memory and heredity are two aspects of the same organic function. Every stimulus which acts upon an organism leaves in it an "engram," a definite physiological trace; and all the future reactions of the organism are dependent upon the chain of these engrams, upon the connected "engram complex." [7] But even if we admit the general thesis of Hering and Semon we are still very far from having explained the role and significance of memory in our human world. The anthropological concept of mneme or memory is something quite different. If we understand memory as a general function of all organic matter we mean merely that the organism preserves some traces of its former experience and that these traces have a definite influence upon its later reactions. But in order to have memory in the human sense of the word it is not enough that there remains "a latent remnant of the former action of a stimulus." [8] The mere presence, the sum total of these remnants, cannot account for the phenomenon of memory. Memory implies a process of recognition and identification, an ideational process of a very complex sort. The former impressions must not only be repeated; they must also be ordered and located, and referred to different points in time. Such a location is not possible without conceiving time as a general scheme—as a *serial order* which comprises all the individual events. The awareness of time necessarily implies the concept of such a serial order corresponding to that other schema which we call space.

Memory as a simple reproduction of a former event occurs also in the life of the higher animals. To what degree it depends on ideational processes comparable to those we find in man is a difficult and much controverted problem. Robert M.

7. For details see Semon's *Mneme* (1909) and *Die mnemischen Empfindungen* (1909). An abridged English version of these books, edited by Bella Duffy, has been published under the title *Mnemic Psychology* (New York, 1923).

8. "Der latente Rest einer früheren Reizwirkung" (Semon).

Yerkes in his latest book devotes a special chapter to the investigation and clarification of the problem. Do these animals, he asks with reference to the chimpanzees, "act as if able to remember, recall, recognize previous experiences, or is out of sight really out of mind? Can they anticipate, expect, imagine, and on the basis of such awareness prepare for future events? . . . Can they solve problems and generally adapt to environmental situations by the aid of symbolic processes analogous to our verbal symbols as well as by dependence on associations which function as signs?" [9] Yerkes is inclined to answer all these questions in the affirmative. But even if we accept all his evidence the crucial question still remains. For what matters here is not so much the *fact* of ideational processes in men and animals as the *form* of these processes. In man we cannot describe recollection as a simple return of an event, as a faint image or copy of former impressions. It is not simply a repetition but rather a rebirth of the past; it implies a creative and constructive process. It is not enough to pick up isolated data of our past experience; we must really *re-collect* them, we must organize and synthesize them, and assemble them into a focus of thought. It is this kind of recollection which gives us the characteristic human shape of memory, and distinguishes it from all the other phenomena in animal or organic life.

To be sure, in our ordinary experience we find many forms of recollection or memory which obviously do not correspond to this description. Many, perhaps most, cases of memory may quite adequately be accounted for according to the usual approach of the schools of sensationalism, that is, explained by a simple mechanism of the "association of ideas." Many psychologists have been convinced that there is no better way to test the memory of a person than to find out how many meaningless words or syllables he can keep in mind and repeat after a certain lapse of time. The experiments made upon this presupposition seemed to give the only exact measure of human memory. One of Bergson's contributions to psychology consists in his attacks on all these mechanical theories of memory.

9. Yerkes, *Chimpanzees*, p. 145.

According to Bergson's view, developed in *Matière et mémoire*, memory is a much deeper and more complex phenomenon. It means "internalization" and intensification; it means the interpenetration of all the elements of our past life. In Bergson's work this theory became a new metaphysical starting point, which proved to be the cornerstone of his philosophy of life.

We are not concerned here with this metaphysical aspect of the problem. Our objective is a *phenomenology of human culture*. We must try, therefore, to illustrate and to elucidate the issue by concrete examples taken from man's cultural life. A classical illustration is Goethe's life and works. Symbolic memory is the process by which man not only repeats his past experience but also reconstructs this experience. Imagination becomes a necessary element of true recollection. This was the reason why Goethe entitled his autobiography *Poetry and Truth* (*Dichtung und Wahrheit*). He did not mean that he had inserted into the narrative of his life any imaginary or fictitious elements. He wanted to discover and describe the truth about his life; but this truth could only be found by giving to the isolated and dispersed facts of his life a poetical, that is a symbolic, shape. Other poets have viewed their work in similar fashion. To be a poet, declared Henrik Ibsen, means to preside as judge over oneself.[10] Poetry is one of the forms in which a man may give the verdict on himself and his life. It is self-knowledge and self-criticism. Such criticism is not to be understood in a moral sense. It does not mean appraisal or blame, justification or condemnation, but a new and deeper understanding, a reinterpretation of the poet's personal life. The process is not restricted to poetry; it is possible in every other medium of artistic expression. If we look at the self-portraits of Rembrandt painted in the different epochs of his life we find in the features the whole story of Rembrandt's life, of his personality, of his development as an artist.

Yet poetry is not the only, and perhaps not the most characteristic, form of symbolic memory. The first great example

10. "At leve er—krig med trolde i hjertets og hjernens hvaelv.
   Att digte,—det er at holde dommedag over sig selv."
   Ibsen, *Digte* (5th ed. Copenhagen, 1886), p. 203.

of what an autobiography is and means was given in Augustine's *Confessions*. Here we find quite a different type of self-examination. Augustine does not relate the events of his own life, which were to him scarcely worthy of being remembered or recorded. The drama told by Augustine is the religious drama of mankind. His own conversion is but the repetition and reflection of the universal religious process—of man's fall and redemption. Every line in Augustine's book has not merely a historical but also a hidden symbolic meaning. Augustine could not understand his own life or speak of it except in the symbolic language of the Christian faith. By this procedure he became both a great religious thinker and the founder of a new psychology, of a new method of introspection and self-examination.

So far we have taken under consideration only one aspect of time—the relation of the present to the past. But there is yet another aspect which seems to be even more important to, and more characteristic of, the structure of human life. This is what might be called the third dimension of time, the dimension of the future. In our consciousness of time the future is an indispensable element. Even in the earliest stages of life this element begins to play a dominant role. "It is characteristic of the whole early development of the life of ideas," writes William Stern, "that they do not appear so much as memories pointing to something in the past, but as expectations directed to the future—even though only to a future immediately at hand. We meet here for the first time a general law of development. Reference to the future is grasped by the consciousness sooner than that to the past." [11] In our later life this tendency becomes even more pronounced. We live much more in our doubts and fears, our anxieties and hopes about the future, than in our recollections or in our present experiences. This would appear at first glance as a questionable human endowment, for it introduces an element of uncertainty into human life which is alien to all other creatures. It seems as though man would be wiser and happier if he got rid of this fantastic idea, of this mirage of the future. Philoso-

11. Stern, *op. cit.*, pp. 112 f.

phers, poets, and great religious teachers have at all times warned man against this source of constant self-deception. Religion admonishes man not to be fearful of the day to come, and human wisdom advises him to enjoy the present day, not caring for the future. "Quid sit futurum cras fuge quaerere," says Horace. But man never could follow this advice. To think of the future and to live in the future is a necessary part of his nature.

In a certain sense this tendency appears not to exceed the limits of all organic life. It is characteristic of all organic processes that we cannot describe them without reference to the future. Most of the animal instincts must be interpreted in this way. Instinctive actions are not prompted by immediate needs; they are impulses directed to the future, and often to a very remote future. The effect of these actions will not be seen by the animal which performs them, since it belongs to the life of the generation to come. If we study a book like Jules Fabre's *Souvenirs entomologiques*, we find on nearly every page striking examples of this characteristic of animal instincts.

All this does not require, and does not prove, any "idea," any conception or awareness of the future in the lower animals. As soon as we approach the life of the higher animals the case becomes doubtful. Many competent observers have spoken of the foresight of higher animals; and it would seem as if, without this assumption, we could hardly give an adequate description of their behavior. If in Wolfe's experiments an animal accepts token-rewards for real ones, this seems to imply a conscious anticipation of future facts; the animal "expects" that the tokens may later on be exchanged for food. "The number of observations is small," writes Wolfgang Koehler, "in which any reckoning upon a future contingency is recognizable, and it seems to me of theoretical importance that the clearest consideration of a future event occurs then when the anticipated event is a planned act *of the animal itself*. In such a case it may really happen that an animal will spend considerable time in preparatory work (in an unequivocal sense) . . . Where such preliminary work, obviously undertaken with a view to the final goal, lasts a long time, but in itself affords no visible approach to that end, there we have the signs of at least some sense of future." [12]

On the basis of this evidence it seems to follow that the anticipation of future events and even the planning of future actions are not entirely beyond the reach of animal life. But in human beings the awareness of the future undergoes the same characteristic change of meaning which we have noted with regard to the idea of the past. The future is not only an image; it becomes an "ideal." The meaning of this transformation manifests itself in all the phases of man's cultural life. So long as he remains entirely absorbed in his practical activities the difference is not clearly observable. It appears to be merely a difference of degree, not a specific difference. To be sure the future envisaged by man extends over a much wider area, and his planning is much more conscious and careful. But all this still belongs to the realm of prudence, not to that of wisdom. The term "prudence" (*prudentia*) is etymologically connected with "providence" (*providentia*). It means the ability to foresee future events and to prepare for future needs. But the *theoretical* idea of the future—that idea which is a prerequisite of all man's higher cultural activities—is of a quite different sort. It is more than mere expectation; it becomes an imperative of human life. And this imperative reaches far beyond man's immediate practical needs—in its highest form it reaches beyond the limits of his empirical life. This is man's *symbolic future,* which corresponds to and is in strict analogy with his symbolic past. We may call it "prophetic" future because it is nowhere better expressed than in the lives of the great religious prophets. These religious teachers were never content simply to foretell future events or to warn against future evils. Nor did they speak like augurs and accept the evidence of omens or presages. Theirs was another aim—in fact the very opposite of that of the soothsayers. The future of which they spoke was not an empirical fact but an ethical and religious task. Hence prediction was transformed into prophecy. Prophecy does not mean simply foretelling; it means a promise. This is the new feature which first becomes

12. Koehler, *The Mentality of Apes*, p. 282.

clear in the prophets of Israel—in Isaiah, Jeremiah, and Ezekiel. Their ideal future signifies the negation of the empirical world, the "end of all days"; but it contains at the same time the hope and the assurance of "a new heaven and a new earth." Here too man's symbolic power ventures beyond all the limits of his finite existence. But this negation implies a new and great act of integration; it marks a decisive phase in man's ethical and religious life.

5   Facts and Ideals

In his *Critique of Judgment* Kant raises the question whether it is possible to discover a general criterion by which we may describe the fundamental structure of the human intellect and distinguish this structure from all other possible modes of knowing. After a penetrating analysis he is led to the conclusion that such a criterion is to be sought in the character of human knowledge, which is such that the understanding is under the necessity of making a sharp distinction between the reality and the possibility of things. It is this character of human knowledge which determines the place of man in the general chain of being. A difference between "real" and "possible" exists neither for the beings below man nor for those above him. The beings below man are confined within the world of their sense perceptions. They are susceptible to actual physical stimuli and react to these stimuli. But they can form no idea of "possible" things. On the other hand the superhuman intellect, the divine mind, knows no distinction between reality and possiblity. God is *actus purus*. Everything he conceives is real. God's intelligence is an *intellectus archetypus* or *intuitus originarius*. He cannot think of a thing without, by this very act of thinking, creating and producing the thing. It is only in man, in his "derivative intelligence" (*intellectus ectypus*) that the problem of possibility arises. The difference between actuality and possibility is not metaphysical but epistemological. It does not denote any character of the things in themselves; it applies only to our knowledge of things. Kant did not mean to assert in a positive and dogmatic manner that a divine intellect, an *intuitus originarius*, really exists. He merely employed the concept of such an "intuitive understanding" in order to describe the nature and limits of the human intellect. The latter is a "discursive understanding," dependent upon two heterogeneous elements. We cannot think without images, and we cannot intuit without concepts. "Concepts without intuitions are empty; intuitions without concepts are blind." It is this dualism in the fundamental conditions of knowledge which, according to Kant, lies at the bottom of our distinction between possibility and actuality.[1]

From the point of view of our present problem this Kantian passage—one of the most important and most difficult in Kant's critical works—is of special interest. It indicates a problem crucial to any anthropological philosophy. Instead of saying that the human intellect is an intellect which is "in need of images" [2] we should rather say that it is in need of symbols. Human knowledge is by its very nature symbolic knowledge. It is this feature which characterizes both its strength and its limitations. And for symbolic thought it is indispensable to make a sharp distinction between real and possible, between actual and ideal things. A symbol has no actual existence as a part of the physical world; it has a "meaning." In primitive thought it is still very difficult to differentiate between the two spheres of being and meaning. They are constantly being confused: a symbol is looked upon as if it were endowed with magical or physical powers. But in the further progress of human culture the difference between things and symbols becomes clearly felt, which means that the distinction between actuality and possibility also becomes more and more pronounced.

This interdependence may be proved in an indirect way. We find that under special conditions in which the function of symbolic thought is impeded or obscured, the difference between actuality and possibility also becomes uncertain. It can no longer be clearly perceived. The pathology of speech has

1. See Kant, *Critique of Judgment*, secs. 76, 77.
2. ". . . ein der Bilder bedürftiger Verstand" (Kant).

thrown interesting light on this problem. In cases of aphasia it has very often been found that the patients had not only lost the use of special classes of words but at the same time exhibited a curious deficiency in their general intellectual attitude. Practically speaking, many of these patients did not deviate very much from the behavior of normal persons. But when they were confronted with a problem that required a more abstract mode of thinking, when they had to think of mere possibilities rather than actualities, they immediately experienced great difficulty. They could not think or speak of "unreal" things. A patient who was suffering from a hemiplegia, from a paralysis of his right hand, could not, for instance, utter the words: "I can write with my right hand." He even refused to repeat these words when they were pronounced for him by the physician. But he could easily say: "I can write with my left hand" because this was to him the statement of a fact, not of a hypothetical or unreal case.[3] "These and similar examples," declares Kurt Goldstein, "show that the patient is unable to deal with any merely 'possible' situation at all. Thus we may also describe the deficiency in these patients as a lack of capacity for approaching a 'possible' situation. . . . Our patients have the greatest difficulty in starting any performance which is not determined directly by external stimuli. . . . They have great trouble in

---

3. Also children sometimes seem to have great difficulty in imagining hypothetical cases. This becomes particularly clear when the development of a child is retarded by special circumstances. A striking parallel to the above-mentioned pathological cases may, for instance, be quoted from the life and education of Laura Bridgman. "It has been remarked," writes one of her teachers, "that it was very difficult in the beginning to make her understand figures of speech, fables, or supposititious cases of any kind, and this difficulty is not yet entirely overcome. If any sum in arithmetic is given to her, the first impression is, that what is supposed did actually happen. For instance, a few mornings ago, when her teacher took an arithmetic to read a sum, she asked: 'How did the man who wrote that book know I was here?' The sum given her was this: 'If you can buy a barrel of cider for four dollars, how much can you buy for one dollar?' upon which her first comment was, 'I cannot give much for cider, because it is very sour.'" See Maud Howe and Florence Howe Hall, Laura Bridgman, p. 112.

voluntary shifting, in switching over voluntarily from one topic to another. Consequently they fail in performances in which such a shift is necessary. . . . Shifting presupposes that I have in mind simultaneously the object to which I am reacting at the moment and the one to which I am going to react. One is in the foreground, the other in the background. But it is essential that the object in the background be there as a possible object for future reaction. Only then can I change from one to the other. This presupposes the capacity for approaching things that are only imagined, 'possible' things, things which are not given in the concrete situation. . . . The mentally sick man is incapable of this because of his inability to grasp what is abstract. Our patients are unable to imitate or copy anything that is not a part of their immediate concrete experience. It is a very interesting expression of this incapacity that they have the greatest difficulty in repeating a sentence which is meaningless for them—that is, the contents of which do not correspond to the reality they are capable of grasping. . . . To say such things apparently requires the assumption of a very difficult attitude. It demands, so to speak, the ability to live in two spheres, the concrete sphere where real things take place and the non-concrete, the merely 'possible' sphere. . . . This the patient is unable to do. He can live and act only in the concrete sphere." [4]

Here we have our finger on a universal problem, a problem of paramount importance for the whole character and development of human culture. Empiricists and positivists have always maintained that the highest task of human knowledge is to give us the facts and nothing but the facts. A theory not based on facts would indeed be a castle in the air. But this is no answer to the problem of a true scientific method; it is, on the contrary, the problem itself. For what is the meaning of a "scientific fact"? Obviously no such fact is given in any haphazard observation or in a mere accumulation of sense data. The facts of science always imply a theoretical, which means a symbolic, element. Many, if not most, of those

4. Kurt Goldstein, *Human Nature in the Light of Psychopathology*, pp. 49 ff., 210.

scientific facts which have changed the whole course of the history of science have been hypothetical facts before they became observable facts. When Galileo founded his new science of dynamics he had to begin with the conception of an entirely isolated body, a body which moves without the influence of any external force. Such a body had never been observed and could never be observed. It was not an actual but a possible body—and in a sense it was not even possible, for the condition upon which Galileo based his conclusion, the absence of all external forces, is never realized in nature.[5] It has been rightly emphasized that all the conceptions which led to the discovery of the principle of inertia are by no means evident or natural; that to the Greeks, as well as to men of the Middle Ages, these conceptions would have appeared as evidently false, and even absurd.[6] Nevertheless, without the aid of these quite unreal conceptions Galileo could not have proposed his theory of motion; nor could he have developed "a new science dealing with a very ancient subject." And the same holds for almost all the other great scientific theories. Upon first appearance they were invariably great paradoxes that it took unusual intellectual courage to propound and to defend.

There is perhaps no better way to prove this point than to consider the *history of mathematics*. One of the most fundamental concepts of mathematics is number. Since the time of the Pythagoreans number has been recognized as the central theme of mathematical thought. Finding a comprehensive and adequate theory of number became the greatest and most urgent task of students in this field. But at every step in this direction mathematicians and philosophers faced the same difficulty. They were constantly under the necessity of enlarging their field and of introducing "new" numbers. All these new numbers were of a highly paradoxical character. Their first appearance aroused the deepest suspicions of mathematicians and logicians. They were thought to be absurd or impossible.

5. For a more detailed treatment of the problem see Cassirer, *Substanzbegriff und Funktionsbegriff*. English trans. by W. C. and M. C. Swabey, *Substance and Function* (Chicago and London, 1923).

6. See A. Koyré, "Galileo and the Scientific Revolution of the Seventeenth Century," *Philosophical Review*, LII (1943), 392 ff.

We can trace this development in the history of negative, irrational, and imaginary numbers. The very term "irrational" (*árrêton*) means a thing not to be thought of and not to be spoken of. Negative numbers first appear in the sixteenth century in Michael Stifel's *Arithmetica integra*—and here they are called "fictitious numbers" (*numeri ficti*). For a long time even the greatest mathematicians looked upon the idea of imaginary numbers as an insoluble mystery. The first to give a satisfactory explanation and sound theory of these numbers was Gauss. The same doubts and hesitations recurred in the field of geometry when the first non-Euclidean systems—those of Lobatschevski, Bolyai, and Riemann—began to appear. In all the great systems of rationalism mathematics had been considered the pride of human reason—the province of "clear and distinct" ideas. But this reputation seemed suddenly called in question. Far from being clear and distinct the fundamental mathematical concepts proved to be fraught with pitfalls and obscurities. These obscurities could not be removed until the general character of mathematical concepts had been clearly recognized—until it had been acknowledged that mathematics is not a theory of things but a theory of symbols.

The lesson we derive from the history of mathematical thought may be supplemented and confirmed by other considerations which at first sight seem to belong to a different sphere. Mathematics is not the only subject in which the general function of symbolic thought may be studied. The real nature and full force of this thought become even more evident if we turn to the development of our *ethical ideas and ideals*. Kant's observation that for the human understanding it is both necessary and indispensable to distinguish between the reality and possibility of things expresses not only a general characteristic of theoretical reason but a truth about practical reason as well. It is characteristic of all the great ethical philosophers that they do not think in terms of mere actuality. Their ideas cannot advance a single step without enlarging and even transcending the limits of the actual world. Possessed of great intellectual and moral power, the ethical teachers of mankind were endowed too with a profound imagination.

Their imaginative insight permeates and animates all their assertions.

The writings of Plato and of his followers have always been liable to the objection that they refer to a completely unreal world. But the great ethical thinkers did not fear this objection. They accepted it and proceeded openly to defy it. "The Platonic Republic," writes Kant in the *Critique of Pure Reason*, "has been supposed to be a striking example of purely imaginary perfection. It has become a byword, as something that could exist only in the brain of an idle thinker. . . . We should do better, however, to follow up his thought and endeavor to place it in a clearer light by our own efforts, rather than to throw it aside as useless, under the miserable and very dangerous pretext of its impracticability. . . . For nothing can be more mischievous and more unworthy of a philosopher than the vulgar appeal to what is called adverse experience, which possibly might never have existed if at the proper time institutions had been formed according to those ideas, and not according to crude conceptions which, because they were derived from experience only, have marred all good intentions."

All modern ethical and political theories which have been molded after Plato's *Republic* have been conceived in the same vein of thought. When Thomas More wrote his *Utopia* he expressed this view in the very title of his work. A Utopia is not a portrait of the real world, or of the actual political or social order. It exists at no moment of time and at no point in space; it is a "nowhere." But just such a conception of a nowhere has stood the test and proved its strength in the development of the modern world. It follows from the very nature and character of ethical thought that it can never condescend to accept "the given." The ethical world is never given; it is forever in the making. "To live in the ideal world," said Goethe, "is to treat the impossible as if it were possible." [7] The great political and social reformers are indeed constantly under the necessity of treating the impossible as though it were possible. In his first political writings Rousseau

7. "In der Idee leben heisst das Unmögliche so behandeln als wenn es möglich wäre." Goethe, *Sprüche in Prosa*, "Werke" (Weimar ed.), XLII, Pt. II, 142.

seems to speak as a determined naturalist. He wishes to restore the natural rights of man and to bring him back to his original state, to the state of nature. The natural man (*l'homme de nature*) is to replace the conventional, social man (*l'homme de l'homme*). But if we pursue the further development of Rousseau's thought it becomes clear that even this "natural man" is far from a physical concept, that it is in fact a symbolic concept. Rousseau himself could not forbear admitting this fact. "Let us begin," he says in the Introduction to his *Discours sur l'origine et les fondements de l'inégalité parmi les hommes*, "by laying aside facts [*par écarter tous les faits*]; for they do not affect the question. The researches, in which we may engage on this occasion, are not to be taken for historical truths, but merely as hypothetical and conditional reasonings, fitter to illustrate the nature of things than to show their true origin; like those systems which our naturalists daily make of the formation of the world." In these words Rousseau attempts to introduce that hypothetical method which Galileo had employed for the study of natural phenomena into the field of the moral sciences; and he is convinced that only by way of such "hypothetical and conditional reasoning" (*des raisonnements hypothétiques et conditionelles*) can we arrive at a true understanding of the nature of man. Rousseau's description of the state of nature was not intended as a historical narrative of the past. It was a symbolic construct designed to portray and to bring into being a new future for mankind. In the history of civilization the Utopia has always fulfilled this task. In the philosophy of the Enlightenment it became a literary genre by itself, and proved one of the most powerful weapons in all attacks on the existing political and social order. To this end it was used by Montesquieu, by Voltaire, and by Swift. In the nineteenth century Samuel Butler made similar use of it. The great mission of the Utopia is to make room for the possible as opposed to a passive acquiescence in the present actual state of affairs. It is symbolic thought which overcomes the natural inertia of man and endows him with a new ability, the ability constantly to reshape his human universe.

II MAN AND CULTURE

6 The Definition of Man in Terms of Human Culture

It was a turning point in Greek culture and Greek thought
when Plato interpreted the maxim "Know thyself" in an entirely new sense. This interpretation introduced a problem
which was not only alien to pre-Socratic thought but also went
far beyond the limits of the Socratic method. In order to obey
the demand of the Delphic god, in order to fulfil the religious
duty of self-examination and self-knowledge, Socrates had approached the individual man. Plato recognized the limitations
of the Socratic way of inquiry. In order to solve the problem,
he declared, we must project it upon a larger plan. The
phenomena we encounter in our individual experience are so
various, so complicated and contradictory that we can scarcely
disentangle them. Man is to be studied not in his individual
life but in his political and social life. Human nature, according to Plato, is like a difficult text, the meaning of which has
to be deciphered by philosophy. But in our personal experience this text is written in such small characters that it
becomes illegible. The first labor of philosophy must be to enlarge these characters. Philosophy cannot give us a satisfactory
theory of man until it has developed a theory of the state.
The nature of man is written in capital letters in the nature
of the state. Here the hidden meaning of the text suddenly
emerges, and what seemed obscure and confused becomes
clear and legible.

But political life is not the only form of a communal human
existence. In the history of mankind the state, in its present
form, is a late product of the civilizing process. Long before

man had discovered this form of social organization he had made other attempts to organize his feelings, desires, and thoughts. Such organizations and systematizations are contained in language, in myth, in religion, and in art. We must accept this broader basis if we wish to develop a theory of man. The state, however important, is not all. It cannot express or absorb all the other activities of man. To be sure, these activities in their historical evolution are closely connected with the development of the state; in many respects they are dependent upon the forms of political life. But, while not possessing a separate historical existence, they have nevertheless a purport and value of their own.

In modern philosophy Comte was one of the first to approach this problem and to formulate it in a clear and systematic way. It is something of a paradox that in this respect we must regard the positivism of Comte as a modern parallel to the Platonic theory of man. Comte was of course never a Platonist. He could not accept the logical and metaphysical presuppositions upon which Plato's theory of ideas is based. Yet, on the other hand, he was strongly opposed to the views of the French ideologists. In his hierarchy of human knowledge two new sciences, the science of social ethics and that of social dynamics, occupy the highest rank. From this sociological viewpoint Comte attacks the psychologism of his age. One of the fundamental maxims of his philosophy is that our method of studying man must, indeed, be subjective, but that it cannot be individual. For the subject we wish to know is not the individual consciousness but the universal subject. If we refer to this subject by the term "humanity," then we must affirm that humanity is not to be explained by man, but man by humanity. The problem must be reformulated and re-examined; it must be put on a broader and sounder basis. Such a basis we have discovered in sociological and historical thought. "To know yourself," says Comte, "know history." Henceforth historical psychology supplements and supersedes all previous forms of individual psychology. "The so-called observations made on the mind, considered in itself and *a priori*," wrote Comte in a letter, "are pure illusions. All that we call *logic, metaphysics, ideology,* is an idle fancy and a dream when it is not an absurdity." [1]

In Comte's *Cours de philosophie positive* we can trace step by step the nineteenth-century transition in methodological ideals. Comte began merely as a scientist, his interest being apparently wholly absorbed in mathematical, physical, and chemical problems. In his hierarchy of human knowledge the scale goes from astronomy through mathematics, physics, and chemistry to biology. Then comes what looks like a sudden reversal of this order. As we approach the human world the principles of mathematics or of the natural sciences do not become invalid, but they are no longer sufficient. Social phenomena are subject to the same rules as physical phenomena, yet they are of a different and much more complicated character. They are not to be described merely in terms of physics, chemistry, and biology. "In all social phenomena," says Comte, "we perceive the working of the physiological laws of the individual; and moreover something which modifies their effects, and which belongs to the influence of individuals over each other—singularly complicated in the case of the human race by the influence of generations on their successors. Thus it is clear that our social science must issue from that which relates to the life of the individual. On the other hand, there is no occasion to suppose, as some eminent physiologists have done, that Social Physics is only an appendage to Physiology. The phenomena of the two are not identical, though they are homogeneous; and it is of high importance to hold the two sciences separate. As social conditions modify the operation of physiological laws, Social Physics must have a set of observations of its own." [2]

The disciples and followers of Comte were not, however, inclined to accept this distinction. They denied the difference

1. Comte, *Lettres à Valat,* p. 89; cited from L. Lévy-Bruhl, *La philosophie d'Auguste Comte.* For further details see Lévy-Bruhl, *op. cit.* English trans., *The Philosophy of Comte* (New York and London, 1903), pp. 247 ff.

2. Comte, *Cours de philosophie positive.* English trans. by Harriet Martineau, *Positive Philosophy* (New York, 1855), Intro., chap. ii, 45 f.

between physiology and sociology because they feared that acknowledging it would lead back to a metaphysical dualism. Their ambition was to establish a purely naturalistic theory of the social and cultural world. To this end they found it necessary to negate and destroy all those barriers which seem to separate the human from the animal world. The theory of evolution had evidently effaced all these differences. Even before Darwin the progress of natural history had frustrated all attempts at such differentiation. In the earlier stages of empirical observation it was still possible for the scientist to cherish the hope of finding eventually an anatomical character reserved for man. As late as the eighteenth century it was still a generally accepted theory that there is a marked difference, in some respects a sharp contrast, between the anatomical structure of man and that of the other animals. It was one of Goethe's great merits in the field of comparative anatomy that he vigorously combated this theory. The same homogeneity, not merely in the anatomical and physiological but also in the mental structure of man, remained to be demonstrated. For this purpose all the attacks on the older way of thinking had to be concentrated upon one point. The thing to be proved was that what we call the intelligence of man is by no means a self-dependent, original faculty. Proponents of the naturalistic theories could appeal for proof to the principles of psychology established by the older schools of sensationalism. Taine developed the psychological basis for his general theory of human culture in a work on the intelligence of man.[3] According to Taine, what we call "intelligent behavior" is not a special principle or privilege of human nature; it is only a more refined and complicated play of the same associative mechanism and automatism which we find in all animal reactions. If we accept this explanation the difference between intelligence and instinct becomes negligible; it is a mere difference of degree, not of quality. Intelligence itself becomes a useless and scientifically meaningless term.

The most surprising and paradoxical feature of the theories of this type is the striking contrast between what they promise

3. De l'intelligence (Paris, 1870). 2 vols.

and what they actually give us. The thinkers who built up these theories were very severe with respect to their methodological principles. They were not content to speak of human nature in terms of our common experience, for they were striving after a much higher ideal, an ideal of absolute scientific exactness. But if we compare their results with this standard we cannot help being greatly disappointed. "Instinct" is a very vague term. It may have a certain descriptive value but it has obviously no explanatory value. By reducing some classes of organic or human phenomena to certain fundamental instincts, we have not alleged a new cause; we have only introduced a new name. We have put a question, not answered one. The term "instinct" gives us at best an *idem per idem*, and in most cases it is an *obscurum per obscurius*. Even in the description of animal behavior most modern biologists and psycho-biologists have become very cautious about using it. They warn us against the fallacies which appear to be inextricably connected with it. They try rather to avoid or to abandon "the error-freighted concept of instinct and the oversimple concept of intelligence." In one of his most recent publications Robert M. Yerkes declares that the terms "instinct" and "intelligence" are outmoded and that the concepts for which they stand are sadly in need of redefining.[4] But in the field of anthropological philosophy we are still, apparently, far from any such redefinition. Here these terms are very often accepted quite naïvely without critical analysis. When used in this way the concept of instinct becomes an example of that typical methodological error which was described by William James as the psychologist's fallacy. The word "instinct," which may be useful for the description of animal or human behavior, is hypostatized into a sort of natural power. Curiously enough this error was often committed by thinkers who, in all other respects, felt secure against relapses into scholastic realism or "faculty-psychology." A very clear and impressive criticism of this mode of thinking is contained in John Dewey's *Human Nature and Conduct*. "It is unscientific," writes Dewey, "to try to restrict original ac-

4. *Chimpanzees*, p. 110.

tivities to a definite number of sharply demarcated classes of instincts. And the practical result of this attempt is injurious. To classify is, indeed, as useful as it is natural. The indefinite multitude of particular and changing events is met by the mind with acts of defining, inventorying, and listing, reducing to common heads and tying up in bunches. . . . But when we assume that our lists and bunches represent fixed separations and collections *in rerum natura,* we obstruct rather than aid our transactions with things. We are guilty of a presumption which nature promptly punishes. We are rendered incompetent to deal effectively with the delicacies and novelties of nature and life. . . . The tendency to forget the office of distinctions and classifications, and to take them as marking things in themselves is the current fallacy of scientific specialism. . . . This attitude which once flourished in physical science now governs theorizing about human nature. Man has been resolved into a definite collection of primary instincts which may be numbered, catalogued and exhaustively described one by one. Theorists differ only or chiefly as to their number and ranking. Some say one, self-love; some two, egoism and altruism; some three, greed, fear and glory; while today writers of a more empirical turn run the number up to fifty and sixty. But in fact there are as many specific reactions to differing stimulating conditions as there is time for, and our lists are only classifications for a purpose." [5]

After this brief survey of the different methods that have hitherto been employed in answering the question: What is man? we now come to our central issue. Are these methods sufficient and exhaustive? Or is there still another approach to an anthropological philosophy? Is any other way left open besides that of psychological introspection, biological observation and experiment, and of historical investigation? I have endeavored to discover such an alternative approach in my *Philosophy of Symbolic Forms.*[6] The method of this work

5. John Dewey, *Human Nature and Conduct* (New York, Holt & Co., 1922), Pt. II, sec. 5, p. 131.

6. *Philosophie der symbolischen Formen.* Vol. I, *Die Sprache* (1923); Vol. II, *Das mythische Denken* (1925); Vol. III, *Phaenomenologie der Erkenntnis* (1929).

is by no means a radical innovation. It is not designed to abrogate but to complement former views. The philosophy of symbolic forms starts from the presupposition that, if there is any definition of the nature or "essence" of man, this definition can only be understood as a functional one, not a substantial one. We cannot define man by any inherent principle which constitutes his metaphysical essence—nor can we define him by any inborn faculty or instinct that may be ascertained by empirical observation. Man's outstanding characteristic, his distinguishing mark, is not his metaphysical or physical nature—but his work. It is this work, it is the system of human activities, which defines and determines the circle of "humanity." Language, myth, religion, art, science, history are the constituents, the various sectors of this circle. A "philosophy of man" would therefore be a philosophy which would give us insight into the fundamental structure of each of these human activities, and which at the same time would enable us to understand them as an organic whole. Language, art, myth, religion are no isolated, random creations. They are held together by a common bond. But this bond is not a *vinculum substantiale*, as it was conceived and described in scholastic thought; it is rather a *vinculum functionale*. It is the basic function of speech, of myth, of art, of religion that we must seek far behind their innumerable shapes and utterances, and that in the last analysis we must attempt to trace back to a common origin.

It is obvious that in the performance of this task we cannot neglect any possible source of information. We must examine all the available empirical evidence, and utilize all the methods of introspection, biological observation, and historical inquiry. These older methods are not to be eliminated but referred to a new intellectual center, and hence seen from a new angle. In describing the structure of language, myth, religion, art, and science, we feel the constant need of a psychological terminology. We speak of religious "feeling," of artistic or mythical "imagination," of logical or rational thought. And we cannot enter into all these worlds without a sound scientific psychological method. Child psychology gives us valuable clues for the study of the general development of human speech.

Even more valuable seems to be the help we get from the study of general sociology. We cannot understand the form of primitive mythical thought without taking into consideration the forms of primitive society. And more urgent still is the use of historical methods. The question as to what language, myth, and religion "are" cannot be answered without a penetrating study of their historical development.

But even if it were possible to answer all these psychological, sociological, and historical questions, we should still be in the precincts of the properly "human" world; we should not have passed its threshold. All human works arise under particular historical and sociological conditions. But we could never understand these special conditions unless we were able to grasp the general structural principles underlying these works. In our study of language, art, and myth the problem of meaning takes precedence over the problem of historical development. And here too we can ascertain a slow and continuous change in the methodological concepts and ideals of empirical science. In linguistics, for instance, the conception that the history of language covers the whole field of linguistic studies was for a long time an accepted dogma. This dogma left its mark upon the whole development of linguistics during the nineteenth century. Nowadays, however, this one-sidedness appears to have been definitely overcome.

The necessity of independent methods of descriptive analysis is generally recognized.[7] We cannot hope to measure the depth of a special branch of human culture unless such measurement is preceded by a descriptive analysis. This structural view of culture must precede the merely historical view. History itself would be lost in the boundless mass of disconnected facts if it did not have a general structural scheme by means of which it can classify, order, and organize these facts. In the field of the history of art such a scheme was developed, for instance, by Heinrich Wölfflin. As Wölfflin insists, the historian of art would be unable to characterize the art of different epochs or of different individual artists if

7. For a fuller discussion of the problem see Chap. 8, pp. 155–158.

he were not in possession of some fundamental *categories* of artistic description. He finds these categories by studying and analyzing the different modes and possibilities of artistic expression. These possibilities are not unlimited; as a matter of fact they may be reduced to a small number. It was from this point of view that Wölfflin gave his famous description of classic and baroque. Here the terms "classic" and "baroque" were not used as names for definite historical phases. They were intended to designate some general structural patterns not restricted to a particular age. "It is not the art of the sixteenth and seventeenth centuries," says Wölfflin at the end of his *Principles of Art History*, "which was to be analyzed—only the schema and the visual and creative possibilities within which art remained in both cases. To illustrate this, we could naturally only proceed by referring to the individual work of art, but everything which was said of Raphael and Titian, of Rembrandt and Velasquez, was only intended to elucidate the general course of things. . . . Everything is transition and it is hard to answer the man who regards history as an endless flow. For us, intellectual self-preservation demands that we should classify the infinity of events with reference to a few results." [8]

If the linguist and the historian of art require fundamental structural categories for their "intellectual self-preservation," such categories are even more necessary to a philosophical description of human civilization. Philosophy cannot be content with analyzing the individual forms of human culture. It seeks a universal synthetic view which includes all individual forms. But is not such an all-embracing view an impossible task, a mere chimera? In human experience we by no means find the various activities which constitute the world of culture existing in harmony. On the contrary, we find the perpetual strife of diverse conflicting forces. Scientific thought contradicts and suppresses mythical thought. Religion in its highest theoretical and ethical development is under the necessity of defending the purity of its own ideal against the extravagant fancies of myth or art. Thus the unity and harmony of human culture appear to be little more than a *pium*

8. Wölfflin, *Kunstgeschichtliche Grundbegriffe*. English trans. by M. D. Hottinger (London, G. Bell & Sons, 1932), pp. 226 f.

desiderium—a pious fraud—which is constantly frustrated by the real course of events.

But here we must make a sharp distinction between a material and a formal point of view. Undoubtedly human culture is divided into various activities proceeding along different lines and pursuing different ends. If we content ourselves with contemplating the results of these activities—the creations of myth, religious rites or creeds, works of art, scientific theories—it seems impossible to reduce them to a common denominator. But a philosophic synthesis means something different. Here we seek not a unity of effects but a unity of action; not a unity of products but a unity of the *creative process*. If the term "humanity" means anything at all it means that, in spite of all the differences and oppositions existing among its various forms, these are, nevertheless, all working toward a common end. In the long run there must be found an outstanding feature, a universal character, in which they all agree and harmonize. If we can determine this character the divergent rays may be assembled and brought into a focus of thought. As has been pointed out, such an organization of the facts of human culture is already getting under way in the particular sciences—in linguistics, in the comparative study of myth and religion, in the history of art. All of these sciences are striving for certain principles, for definite "categories," by virtue of which to bring the phenomena of religion, of art, of language into a systematic order. Were it not for this previous synthesis effected by the sciences themselves philosophy would have no starting point. Philosophy cannot, on the other hand, stop here. It must seek to achieve an even greater condensation and centralization. In the boundless multiplicity and variety of mythical images, of religious dogmas, of linguistic forms, of works of art, philosophic thought reveals the unity of a general function by which all these creations are held together. Myth, religion, art, language, even science, are now looked upon as so many variations on a common theme—and it is the task of philosophy to make this theme audible and understandable.

7 Myth and Religion

Of all the phenomena of human culture myth and religion are most refractory to a merely logical analysis. Myth appears at first sight to be a mere chaos—a shapeless mass of incoherent ideas. To seek after the "reasons" of these ideas seems to be vain and futile. If there is anything that is characteristic of myth it is the fact that it is "without rhyme and reason." As to religious thought, it is by no means necessarily opposed to rational or philosophic thought. To determine the true relation between these two modes of thought was one of the principal tasks of medieval philosophy. In the systems of high scholasticism the problem appeared to be solved. According to Thomas Aquinas religious truth is supra-natural and supra-rational; but it is not "irrational." By reason alone we cannot penetrate into the mysteries of faith. Yet these mysteries do not contradict, they complete and perfect reason.

Nevertheless there were always deep religious thinkers who took issue with all these attempts to reconcile the two opposite forces. They maintained a much more radical and uncompromising thesis. Tertullian's dictum *Credo quia absurdum* never lost its force. Pascal declared obscurity and incomprehensibility to be the very elements of religion. The true God, the God of Christian religion, always remains a *Deus absconditus*, a hidden God.[1] Kierkegaard describes religious life as the great "paradox." To him an attempt to lessen this paradox meant the negation and destruction of religious life. And religion remains a riddle not only in a theoretical but also in an ethical sense. It is fraught with theoretical antinomies and with ethical contradictions. It promises us a communion with nature, with men, with supra-natural powers and the gods themselves. Yet its effect is the very opposite. In its concrete appearance it becomes the source of the most profound dissensions and fanatic struggles among men. Religion claims to be in possession of an absolute truth; but its history

1. See above, Chap. 1, p. 29.

is a history of errors and heresies. It gives us the promise and prospect of a transcendent world—far beyond the limits of our human experience—and it remains human, all too human.

The problem appears however in a new perspective as soon as we decide to change our point of view. A philosophy of human culture does not ask the same question as a metaphysical or theological system. Here we are not inquiring into the subject matter but into the form of mythical imagination and religious thought. The subjects, the themes, and motives of mythical thought are unmeasurable. If we approach the mythical world from this side it always remains—to use Milton's words—

> a dark illimitable ocean,
> without bound, without dimension, where length, breadth and height,
> And Time and place are lost.

There is no natural phenomenon and no phenomenon of human life that is not capable of a mythical interpretation, and which does not call for such an interpretation. All the attempts of the various schools of comparative mythology to unify the mythological ideas, to reduce them to a certain uniform type were bound to end in complete failure. Yet notwithstanding this variety and discrepancy of the mythological productions the myth-making function does not lack a real homogeneity. Anthropologists and ethnologists were often very much surprised to find the same elementary thoughts spread over the whole world and under quite different social and cultural conditions. The same holds good for the history of religion. The articles of faith, the dogmatic creeds, the theological systems are engaged in an interminable struggle. Even the ethical ideals of different religions are widely divergent and scarcely reconcilable with each other. Yet all this does not affect the specific form of religious feeling and the inner unity of religious thought.[2] The religious symbols change incessantly, but the underlying principle, the symbolic activity

2. An excellent description of this inner unity has been given in the work of Archibald Allan Bowman, *Studies in the Philosophy of Religion* (London, 1938). 2 vols.

as such, remains the same: *una est religio in rituum varietate*.

A *theory* of myth is, however, from the beginning laden with difficulties. Myth is nontheoretical in its very meaning and essence. It defies and challenges our fundamental categories of thought. Its logic—if there is any logic—is incommensurate with all our conceptions of empirical or scientific truth. But philosophy could never admit such a bifurcation. It was convinced that the creations of the myth-making function must have a philosophical, an understandable "meaning." If myth hides this meaning under all sorts of images and symbols, it became the task of philosophy to unmask it. Since the time of the Stoics philosophy has developed a special, very elaborate technique of allegorical interpretation. For many centuries this technique was regarded as the only possible access to the mythical world. It prevailed throughout the Middle Ages, and it was still in full vigor at the beginning of our modern era. Bacon wrote a special treatise on the "Wisdom of the Ancients" in which he displayed a great sagacity in the interpretation of ancient mythology.

If we study this treatise we are inclined to smile at these allegorical interpretations that to a modern reader in most cases seem to be extremely naïve. Nevertheless our own much more refined and sophisticated methods are to a large degree liable to the same objection. Their "explanation" of the mythical phenomena becomes in the end an entire negation of these phenomena. The mythical world appears as an artificial world, as a pretense for something else. Instead of being a belief, it is a mere make-believe. What distinguishes these modern methods from the earlier forms of allegorical interpretation is the fact that they no longer regard myth as a mere invention made for a special purpose. Though myth is fictitious, it is an unconscious, not a conscious fiction. The primitive mind was not aware of the meaning of its own creations. But it is for us, it is for our scientific analysis, to reveal this meaning—to detect the true face behind these innumerable masks. This analysis may proceed in a double direction. It may apply an objective or subjective method. In the former case it will try to classify the *objects* of mythical thought; in the latter it will try to classify its *motives*. A theory seems to be so much the more perfect the farther it goes in this process of simplification. If in the end it should succeed in discovering *one* single object or *one* simple motive that contains and comprises all the others, it would have attained its aim and fulfilled its task. Modern ethnology and modern psychology have attempted both these ways. Many ethnological and anthropological schools started from the presupposition that first and foremost we have to seek an objective center of the mythical world. "To writers of this school," says Malinowski, "every myth possesses as its kernel or ultimate reality some natural phenomenon or other, elaborately woven into a tale to an extent which sometimes almost masks and obliterates it. There is not much agreement among these students as to what type of natural phenomenon lies at the bottom of most mythological productions. There are extreme lunar mythologists so completely moonstruck with their idea that they will not admit that any other phenomenon could lend itself to a savage rhapsodic interpretation except that of earth's nocturnal satellite. . . . Others . . . regard the sun as the only subject around which primitive man has spun his symbolic tales. Then there is the school of meteorological interpreters who regard wind, weather, and colors of the skies as the essence of myth. . . . Some of these departmental mythologists fight fiercely for their heavenly body or principle; others have a more catholic taste, and prepare to agree that primeval man has made his mythological brew from all the heavenly bodies taken together." [3] In Freud's psychoanalytic theory of myth, on the other hand, all its productions were declared to be variations and disguises of one and the same psychological theme—sexuality. We need not enter here into the details of all these theories. However divergent in their contents all of them show us the same methodological attitude. They hope to make us understand the mythical world by a process of intellectual reduction. But none of them can reach its goal without constantly pressing and stretching the facts for the sake of rendering the theory a homogeneous whole.

Myth combines a theoretical element and an element of

3. Malinowski, *Myth in Primitive Psychology* (New York, Norton, 1926), pp. 12 f.

artistic creation. What first strikes us is its close kinship with poetry. "Ancient myth," it has been said, "is the 'mass' from which modern poetry has slowly grown by the processes which evolutionists call differentiation and specialization. The myth-maker's mind is the prototype; and the mind of the poet . . . is still essentially mythopoeic."[4] But in spite of this genetic connection we cannot fail to recognize the specific difference between myth and art. A clue to this is to be found in Kant's statement that aesthetic contemplation is "entirely indifferent to the existence or nonexistence of its object." Precisely such an indifference, however, is entirely alien to mythical imagination. In mythical imagination there is always implied an act of *belief*. Without the belief in the reality of its object, myth would lose its ground. By this intrinsic and necessary condition we seem to be led on to the opposite pole. In this respect it seems to be possible and even indispensable to compare myth-ical with scientific thought. Of course they do not follow the same ways. But they seem to be in quest of the same thing: reality. In modern anthropology this relationship was empha-sized by Sir James Frazer. Frazer propounds the thesis that there is no sharp boundary separating magical art from our modes of scientific thought. Magic, too, however imaginary and fantastic in its means, is scientific in its aim. Theoretically speaking, magic is science, although practically speaking it is an elusive science—a pseudo science. For even magic argues and acts upon the presupposition that in nature one event follows another necessarily and invariably without the inter-vention of any spiritual or personal agency. The conviction here is "that the course of nature is determined not by the passions or caprice of personal beings, but by the operation of immutable laws acting mechanically." Hence magic is a faith, implicit, but real and firm in the order and uniformity of nature.[5] This thesis could not, however, stand a critical test; modern anthropology seems entirely to have given up the views

4. F. C. Prescott, *Poetry and Myth* (New York, Macmillan, 1927), p. 10.
5. See Frazer, *The Magic Art and the Evolution of Kings*, Vol. I of *The Golden Bough* (2d ed. Macmillan, 1900), pp. 61 ff., 220 ff.

of Frazer.[6] It is now generally admitted that it is a very inadequate conception of myth and magic to look upon them as typically aetiological or explanatory. We cannot reduce myth to certain fixed static elements; we must strive to grasp it in its inner life, in its mobility and versatility, in its dynamic principle.

It is easier to describe this principle if we approach the problem from a different angle. Myth has, as it were, a double face. On the one hand it shows us a conceptual, on the other hand a perceptual structure. It is not a mere mass of unorganized and confused ideas; it depends upon a definite mode of perception. If myth did not *perceive* the world in a different way it could not judge or interpret it in its specific manner. We must go back to this deeper stratum of perception in order to understand the character of mythical thought. What interests us in empirical thought are the constant features of our sense experience. Here we always make a distinction between what is substantial or accidental, necessary or contingent, invariable or transient. By this discrimination we are led on to the concept of a world of physical objects endowed with fixed and determinate qualities. But all this involves an analytical process that is opposed to the fundamental structure of mythical perception and thought. The mythical world is, as it were, at a much more fluid and fluctuating stage than our theoretical world of things and properties, of substances and accidents. In order to grasp and to describe this difference we may say that what myth primarily perceives are not objective but *physiognomic* characters. Nature, in its empirical or scientific sense, may be defined as "the existence of things as far as it is determined by general laws." [7] Such a "nature" does not exist for myths. The world of myth is a dramatic world—a world of actions, of forces, of conflicting powers. In every phenomenon of nature it sees the collision of these powers. Mythical perception is always impregnated with these emotional qualities. Whatever is seen or felt is surrounded by a special atmosphere—an atmosphere of joy or grief, of an-

6. For a criticism of Frazer's thesis see R. R. Marett, *The Threshold of Religion* (2d ed. London, Methuen, 1914), pp. 47 ff., 177 ff.
7. Cf. Kant, *Prolegomena to Every Future Metaphysics*, sec. 14.

guish, of excitement, of exultation or depression. Here we cannot speak of "things" as a dead or indifferent stuff. All objects are benignant or malignant, friendly or inimical, familiar or uncanny, alluring and fascinating or repellent and threatening. We can easily reconstruct this elementary form of human experience, for even in the life of the civilized man it has by no means lost its original power. If we are under the strain of a violent emotion we have still this dramatic conception of all things. They no longer wear their usual faces; they abruptly change their physiognomy; they are tinged with the specific color of our passions, of love or hate, of fear or hope. There can scarcely be a greater contrast than between this original direction of our experience and the ideal of truth that is introduced by science. All the efforts of scientific thought are directed to the aim of obliterating every trace of this first view. In the new light of science mythical perception has to fade away. But that does not mean that the data of our physiognomic experience as such are destroyed and annihilated. They have lost all objective or cosmological value, but their anthropological value persists. In our human world we cannot deny them and we cannot miss them; they maintain their place and their significance. In social life, in our daily intercourse with men, we cannot efface these data. Even in the genetic order the distinction between physiognomic qualities seems to precede the distinction between perceptual qualities. A child seems to be sensitive to them in the first stages of his development.[8] While science has to abstract from these qualities in order to fulfil its task, it cannot completely suppress them. They are not extirpated root and branch; they are only restricted to their own field. It is this restriction of the subjective qualities that marks the general way of science. Science delimits their objectivity but it cannot completely destroy their reality. For every feature of our human experience has a claim to reality. In our scientific concepts we reduce the difference between two colors, let us say red and blue, to a numeric difference. But it is a very inadequate way of speaking if we declare num-

8. With regard to this problem see Cassirer, *Philosophie der symbolischen Formen*, Vol. III, Pt. I, chaps. ii and iii.

ber to be more real than color. What is really meant is that it is more general. The mathematical expression gives us a new and more comprehensive view, a freer and larger horizon of knowledge. But to hypostatize number as did the Pythagoreans, to speak of it as the ultimate reality, the very essence and substance of things, is a metaphysical fallacy. If we argue upon this methodological and epistemological principle even the lowest stratum of our sense experience—the stratum of our "feeling-qualities"—appears in a new light. The world of our sense perceptions, of the so-called "secondary qualities," is in an intermediate position. It has abandoned and overcome the first rudimentary stage of our physiognomic experience, without having reached that form of generalization that is attained in our scientific concepts—our concepts of the physical world. But all these three stages have their definite functional value. None of them is a mere illusion; every one is, in its measure, a step on our way to reality.

The best and clearest statement of this problem has to my mind been given by John Dewey. He was one of the first to recognize and to emphasize the relative right of those feeling-qualities which prove their full power in mythical perception and which are here regarded as the basic elements of reality. It was precisely his conception of the task of a genuine empiricism that led him to this conclusion. "Empirically," says Dewey, "things are poignant, tragic, beautiful, humorous, settled, disturbed, comfortable, annoying, barren, harsh, consoling, splendid, fearful; are such immediately and in their own right and behalf. . . . These traits stand in themselves on precisely the same level as colors, sounds, qualities of contact, taste and smell. Any criterion that finds the latter to be ultimate and 'hard' data will, impartially applied, come to the same conclusion about the former. Any quality as such is final; it is at once initial and terminal; just what it is as it exists. It may be referred to other things, it may be treated as an effect or as a sign. But this involves an extraneous extension and use. It takes us beyond quality in its immediate qualitativeness. . . . The surrender of immediate qualities, sensory and significant, as objects of science, and as proper forms of classification and understanding, left in reality these immediate qualities just as they were; since they are *had* there is no need to *know* them. But . . . the traditional view that the object of knowledge is reality *par excellence* led to the conclusion that the object of science was preëminently metaphysically real. Hence, immediate qualities, being extended from the object of science, were left thereby hanging loose from the 'real' object. Since their *existence* could not be denied, they were gathered together into a psychic realm of being, set over against the object of physics. Given this premise, all the problems regarding the relation of mind and matter, the psychic and the bodily, necessarily follow. Change the metaphysical premise; restore, that is to say, immediate qualities to their rightful position as qualities of inclusive situations, and the problems in question cease to be epistemological problems. They become specifiable scientific problems; questions, that is to say, of how such and such an event having such and such qualities actually occurs." [9]

Hence if we wish to account for the world of mythical perception and mythical imagination we must not begin with a criticism of both of them from the point of view of our theoretical ideals of knowledge and truth. We must take the qualities of mythical experience on their "immediate qualitativeness." For what we need here is not an explanation of mere thoughts or beliefs but an interpretation of mythical life. Myth is not a system of dogmatic creeds. It consists much more in actions than in mere images or representations. It is a mark of definite progress in modern anthropology and modern history of religion that this view has become more and more prevalent. That ritual is prior to dogma, both in a historical and in a psychological sense, seems now to be a generally adopted maxim. Even if we should succeed in analyzing myth into ultimate conceptual elements, we could, by such an analytical process, never grasp its vital principle, which is a dynamic not a static one; it is describable only in terms of action. Primitive man expresses his feelings and emotions not in mere abstract symbols but in a concrete and immediate way; and

9. *Experience and Nature* (Chicago, Open Court Publishing Co., 1925), pp. 96, 264 f.

we must study the whole of this expression in order to become aware of the structure of myth and primitive religion.

One of the clearest and most consistent theories of this structure has been given by the French sociological school, in the work of Durkheim and his disciples and followers. Durkheim starts from the principle that we can give no adequate account of myth as long as we seek its sources in the physical world, in an intuition of natural phenomena. Not nature but society is the true model of myth. All its fundamental motives are projections of man's social life. By these projections nature becomes the image of the social world; it reflects all its fundamental features, its organization and architecture, its divisions and subdivisions.[10] The thesis of Durkheim has come to its full development in the work of Lévy-Bruhl. But here we meet with a more general characteristic. Mythical thought is described as *"prelogical thought."* If it asks for causes, these are neither logical nor empirical; they are "mystic causes." "Our daily activity implies unruffled, perfect confidence in the invariability of natural laws. The attitude of primitive man is very different. To him the nature amid which he lives presents itself under an entirely different aspect. All things and all creatures therein are involved in a network of mystic participations and exclusions." According to Lévy-Bruhl this mystic character of primitive religion follows from the very fact that its representations are "collective representations." To these we cannot apply the rules of our own logic that are intended for quite different purposes. If we approach this field, even the law of contradiction, and all the other laws of rational thought, become invalid.[11] To my mind the French sociological school has given full and conclusive proof of the first

10. Cf. Durkheim, Les formes élémentaires de la vie religieuse (Paris, 1912); English trans., Elementary Forms of the Religious Life (New York, 1915).

11. Cf. Lévy-Bruhl, Les fonctions mentales dans les sociétés inférieures (Paris, 1910); English trans., How Natives Think (London and New York, 1926); La mentalité primitive (Paris, 1922); English trans., Primitive Mentality (New York, 1923); L'Ame primitive (Paris, 1928); English trans., The "Soul" of the Primitive (New York, 1928).

part of its thesis but not of the second part. The fundamental social character of myth is uncontroverted. But that all primitive mentality necessarily is prelogical or mystical seems to be in contradiction with our anthropological and ethnological evidence. We find many spheres of primitive life and culture that show the well-known features of our own cultural life. As long as we assume an absolute heterogeneity between our own logic and that of the primitive mind, as long as we think them specifically different from and radically opposed to each other, we can scarcely account for this fact. Even in primitive life we always find a secular or profane sphere outside the holy sphere. There is a secular tradition that consists of customary or legal rules, determining the manner in which social life is conducted. "The rules which we find here," says Malinowski, "are completely independent of magic, of supernatural sanctions, and they are never accompanied by any ceremonial or ritual elements. It is a mistake to assume that, at an early stage of development, man lived in a confused world, where the real and the unreal formed a medley, where mysticism and reason were as interchangeable as forged and real coin in a disorganized country. To us the most essential point about magic and religious ritual is that it steps in only where knowledge fails. Supernaturally founded ceremonial grows out of life, but it never stultifies the practical efforts of man. In his ritual of magic or religion, man attempts to enact miracles, not because he ignores the limitations of his mental powers, but, on the contrary, because he is fully cognizant of them. To go one step farther, the recognition of this seems to me indispensable if we want once and for ever to establish the truth that religion has its own subject-matter, its own legitimate field of development." [12]

And even in the latter field, in the legitimate field of myth and religion, the conception of nature and of human life is by no means devoid of any rational meaning. What we, from our own point of view, may call irrational, prelogical, mystical, are the premises from which mythical or religious inter-

12. Malinowski, *The Foundations of Faith and Morals* (London, Oxford University Press, 1936; published for the University of Durham), p. 34.

pretation starts, but not the mode of interpretation. If we accept these premises and if we understand them aright— if we see them in the same light that primitive man does—the inferences drawn from them cease to appear illogical or antilogical. To be sure all attempts to intellectualize myth— to explain it as an allegorical expression of a theoretical or moral truth—have completely failed.[13] They ignored the fundamental facts of mythical experience. The real substratum of myth is not a substratum of thought but of feeling. Myth and primitive religion are by no means entirely incoherent, they are not bereft of sense or reason. But their coherence depends much more upon unity of feeling than upon logical rules. This unity is one of the strongest and most profound impulses of primitive thought. If scientific thought wishes to describe and explain reality it is bound to use its general method, which is that of classification and systematization. Life is divided into separate provinces that are sharply distinguished from each other. The boundaries between the kingdoms of plants, of animals, of man—the differences between species, families, genera—are fundamental and ineffaceable. But the primitive mind ignores and rejects them all. Its view of life is a synthetic, not an analytical one. Life is not divided into classes and subclasses. It is felt as an unbroken continuous whole which does not admit of any clean-cut and trenchant distinctions. The limits between the different spheres are not insurmountable barriers; they are fluent and fluctuating. There is no specific difference between the various realms of life. Nothing has a definite, invariable, static shape. By a sudden metamorphosis everything may be turned into everything. If there is any characteristic and outstanding feature of the mythical world, any law by which it is governed —it is this law of metamorphosis. Even so we can scarcely explain the instability of the mythical world by the incapacity of primitive man to grasp the empirical differences of things. In this regard the savage very often proves his superiority to the civilized man. He is susceptible to many distinctive fea-

13. Even in modern literature we still find many traces of this intellectualistic tendency. See, for instance, F. Langer, *Intellectualmythologie* (Leipzig, 1916).

tures that escape our attention. The animal drawings and paintings that we find in the lowest stages of human culture, in paleolithic art, have often been admired for their naturalistic character. They show an astounding knowledge of all sorts of animal forms. The whole existence of primitive man depends in great part upon his gifts of observation and discrimination. If he is a hunter he must be familiar with the smallest details of animal life; he must be able to distinguish the traces of various animals. All this is scarcely in keeping with the assumption that the primitive mind, by its very nature and essence, is undifferentiated or confused, a prelogical or mystical mind.

What is characteristic of primitive mentality is not its logic but its general sentiment of life. Primitive man does not look at nature with the eyes of a naturalist who wishes to classify things in order to satisfy an intellectual curiosity. He does not approach it with merely pragmatic or technical interest. It is for him neither a mere object of knowledge nor the field of his immediate practical needs. We are in the habit of dividing our life into the two spheres of practical and theoretical activity. In this division we are prone to forget that there is a lower stratum beneath them both. Primitive man is not liable to such forgetfulness. All his thoughts and his feelings are still embedded in this lower original stratum. His view of nature is neither merely theoretical nor merely practical; it is *sympathetic*. If we miss this point we cannot find the approach to the mythical world. The most fundamental feature of myth is not a special direction of thought or a special direction of human imagination. Myth is an offspring of emotion and its emotional background imbues all its productions with its own specific color. Primitive man by no means lacks the ability to grasp the empirical differences of things. But in his conception of nature and life all these differences are obliterated by a stronger feeling: the deep conviction of a fundamental and indelible *solidarity of life* that bridges over the multiplicity and variety of its single forms. He does not ascribe to himself a unique and privileged place in the scale of nature. The consanguinity of all forms of life seems to be a general presupposition of mythical thought. Totemistic creeds are among the most characteristic features of primitive culture. The whole religious and social life of the most primitive tribes —as, for instance, those aboriginal Australian tribes that have been carefully studied and described by Spencer and Gillen[14]—is governed by totemistic conceptions. And even in a much more advanced stage, in the religion of highly cultivated nations, we find a very complex and elaborate system of animal worship. In totemism man does not merely regard himself as a descendant of certain animal species. A bond that is present and actual as well as genetic connects his whole physical and social existence with his totemistic ancestors. In many cases this connection is felt and expressed as identity. The ethnologist Karl von den Steinen relates that the members of certain totemistic clans of an Indian tribe asserted they were one with the animals from which they derived their origin: they expressly declared themselves to be aquatic animals or red parrots.[15] Frazer relates that among the Dieri tribe in Australia the head man of a totem consisting of a particular sort of seed was spoken of by his people as being the plant itself which yields the seed.[16]

We see from these examples how the firm belief in the unity of life eclipses all those differences that, from our own point of view, seem to be unmistakable and ineffaceable. We need by no means assume that these differences are completely overlooked. They are not denied in an empirical sense but they are declared to be irrelevant in a religious sense. To mythical and religious feeling nature becomes one great society, the society of life. Man is not endowed with outstanding rank in this society. He is a part of it but he is in no respect higher than any other member. Life possesses the same religious dignity in its humblest and in its highest forms. Men and animals, animals and plants are all on the same level. In totemistic societies we find totem-plants side by side with

14. Sir Baldwin Spencer and F. J. Gillen, The Native Tribes of Central Australia, The Northern Tribes of Central Australia.

15. Cf. Karl von den Steinen, Unter den Naturvölkern Zentral-Brasiliens (Berlin, 1897), p. 307.

16. Frazer, Lectures on the Early History of Kingship (London, Macmillan, 1905), p. 109.

totem-animals. And we find the same principle—that of the solidarity and unbroken unity of life—if we pass from space to time. It holds not only in the order of simultaneity but also in the order of succession. The generations of men form a unique and uninterrupted chain. The former stages of life are preserved by reincarnation. The soul of the grandparent appears in a newborn child in a rejuvenated state. Present, past, and future blend into each other without any sharp line of demarcation; the limits between the generations of man became uncertain.

The feeling of the indestructible unity of life is so strong and unshakable as to deny and to defy the fact of death. In primitive thought death is never regarded as a natural phenomenon that obeys general laws. Its occurrence is not necessary but accidental. It always depends upon individual and fortuitous causes. It is the work of witchcraft or magic or some other personal inimical influence. In their description of the aboriginal tribes of Australia Spencer and Gillen point out that no such thing as natural death is ever realized by the native. A man who dies has of necessity been killed by some other man or perhaps even by a woman; and sooner or later that man or woman will be attacked.[17] Death has not always been; it came into being by a particular event, by a failure of man or some accident. Many mythical tales are concerned with the origin of death. The conception that man is mortal, by his nature and essence, seems to be entirely alien to mythical and primitive religious thought. In this regard there is a striking difference between the mythical belief in immortality and all the later forms of a pure philosophical belief. If we read Plato's *Phaedo* we feel the whole effort of philosophical thought to give clear and irrefutable proof of the immortality of the human soul. In mythical thought the case is quite different. Here the burden of proof always lies on the opposite side. If anything is in need of proof it is not the fact of immortality but the fact of death. And myth and primitive religion never admit these proofs. They emphatically deny the very possibility of death. In a certain sense the whole of mythi-

17. Spencer and Gillen, *The Native Tribes of Central Australia*, p. 48.

cal thought may be interpreted as a constant and obstinate negation of the phenomenon of death. By virtue of this conviction of the unbroken unity and continuity of life myth has to clear away this phenomenon. Primitive religion is perhaps the strongest and most energetic affirmation of life that we find in human culture. In a description of the oldest Pyramid texts Breasted says that the chief and dominant note throughout is insistent, even passionate, protest against death. "They may be said to be the record of humanity's earliest supreme revolt against the great darkness and silence from which none returns. The word 'death' never occurs in the Pyramid Texts except in the negative or applied to a foe. Over and over again we hear the indomitable assurance that the dead lives." [18]

In his individual and social feeling primitive man is filled with this assurance. The life of man has no definite limits in space or time. It extends over the whole realm of nature and over the whole of man's history. Herbert Spencer has propounded the thesis that ancestor worship is to be regarded as the first source and the origin of religion. At any rate it is one of the most general religious motives. There seem to be few races in the world which do not practice, in one or another form, a sort of death cult. It is one of the highest religious duties of the survivor, after the death of a parent, to provide him with food and other necessaries needed to maintain him in the new state on which he has entered.[19] In many cases ancestor worship appears as the all-pervading trait that characterizes and determines the whole religious and social life. In China this worship of the ancestors, sanctioned and regulated by the state religion, is conceived to be the only religion that people may have. It signifies, says de Groot in his description of Chinese religion, "that the family ties with the dead are by no means broken, and that the dead continue to exercise their authority and protection. They are the natural patron divinities of the Chinese people, their household-gods,

18. James Henry Breasted, *Development of Religion and Thought in Ancient Egypt* (New York, Charles Scribner's Sons, 1912), p. 91.

19. Rich ethnological material illustrating this point is to be found in the article on Ancestor-Worship in Hastings' *Encyclopedia of Religion and Ethics*, I, 425 ff.

affording protection against specters, and thus creating felicity. . . . It is ancestral worship which, by bestowing on man the protection of the deceased member of his family endows him with wealth and prosperity. Therefore his possessions actually are those of the dead; indeed these continue to dwell and live with him and the laws of paternal and patriarchal authority will have it that parents are the owners of everything a child possesses . . . We have, then, to consider the worship of parents and ancestors as the very core of the religious and social life of the Chinese people." [20]

China is the classical country of ancestor worship in which we can study all its fundamental features and all its special implications. Nevertheless the general religious motives that lie at the bottom of the cult of the ancestors do not depend on particular cultural or social conditions. We find them in entirely different cultural environments. If we look at classical antiquity we meet with the same motives in Roman religion—and there, too, they have marked the whole character of Roman life. In his well-known book, La cité antique, Fustel de Coulanges has given a description of Roman religion in which he tries to show that the whole social and political life of the Romans bears the impress of their worship of the Manes. The cult of the ancestors always remained one of the basic and prevalent characteristics of Roman religion.[21] On the other hand one of the most marked features of the religion of the Americans Indians, shared by nearly all of the many tribes from Alaska to Patagonia, is their belief in life after death based upon the equally general belief in communication between mankind and the spirits of the dead.[22] All this shows in a clear and unmistakable manner that we have here come to a really universal, an irreducible and essential characteristic of primitive religion. And it is impossible to understand this element in its true sense so long as we start from the pre-

20. J. J. M. de Groot, The Religion of the Chinese (New York, Macmillan, 1910), pp. 67, 82. For further information see de Groot, The Religious System of China (Leyden, 1892 ff.), Vols. IV–VI.

21. Fustel de Coulanges, La cité antique; Wissowa, Religion der Römer (1902), pp. 187 ff.

22. Cf. Ancestor-Worship, in Hastings' Encyclopedia, I, 433.

supposition that all religion originates in fear. We must seek for another and deeper source if we wish to understand the common band that unites the phenomenon of totemism with the phenomenon of ancestor worship. It is true that the Holy, the Sacred, the Divine, always contains an element of fear: it is, at the same time, a *mysterium fascinosum* and a *mysterium tremendum*.[23] But if we follow our general device—if we judge the mentality of primitive man by his actions as well as by his representations or creeds—we find that these actions imply a different and stronger motive. From all sides and at every moment the life of primitive man is threatened by unknown dangers. The old saying *Primus in orbe deos fecit timor* contains, therefore, an inner psychological verisimilitude. But it seems as if even in the earliest and lowest stages of civilization man had found a new force by which he could resist and banish the fear of death. What he opposed to the fact of death was his confidence in the solidarity, the unbroken and indestructible unity of life. Even totemism expresses this deep conviction of a community of all living beings—a community that must be preserved and reinforced by the constant efforts of man, by the strict performance of magical rites and religious observances. It is one of the great merits of W. Robertson-Smith's book on the religion of the Semites that it emphasizes this point. He was thus able to connect the phenomena of totemism with other phenomena of religious life that, at first sight, seem to be of quite a different type. Even the crudest and most cruel superstitions appear in a different light when looked at from this angle. "Some of the most notable and constant features of all ancient heathenism," says Robertson-Smith, "from the totemism of savages upwards, find their sufficient explanation in the physical kinship that unites the human and superhuman members of the same religious and social community. . . . The indissoluble bond that unites men to their god is the same bond of blood-fellowship which in early society is the one binding link between man and man, and the one sacred principle of moral obligation. And thus we see that even in its rudest forms religion was a moral force.

23. Cf. Rudolf Otto, *Das Heilige* (Göttingen, 1912).

. . . From the earliest times religion, as distinct from magic or sorcery, addresses itself to kindred and friendly beings, who may indeed be angry with their people for a time, but are always placable except to the enemies of their worshippers or to renegade members of the community. . . . Religion in this sense is not the child of terror, and the difference between it and the savage's dread of unseen foes is as absolute and fundamental in the earliest as in the latest stages of development." [24]

The funeral rites that we find in all parts of the world tend to the same point. Fear of death is undoubtedly one of the most general and most deeply rooted human instincts. The first reaction of man toward the dead body must have been to leave it to its fate and to fly from it in terror. But such a reaction is to be found only in a few exceptional cases. It is very soon superseded by the opposite attitude, by the wish to detain or to recall the spirit of the dead. Our ethnological material shows us the struggle between these two impulses. It is, however, the latter one that usually seems to get the upper hand. To be sure, we find many attempts to prevent the spirit of the dead from returning to its house. Ashes are strewed behind the coffin as it is being borne to the grave so that the ghost may miss the road. The custom of closing the eyes of a dead person has been explained as an attempt to blindfold the corpse and prevent it from seeing the way by which it is borne to its grave.[25] In most cases, however, the opposite tendency prevails. With all their powers the survivors strive to detain the spirit in their neighborhood. Very often the corpse is buried in the house itself where it maintains its permanent dwelling place. The ghosts of the deceased become the household gods; and the life and prosperity of the family depend on their assistance and favor. At his death the parent is implored not to go away. "We ever loved and cherished you," says a song quoted by Tylor, "and have lived long together

24. W. Robertson-Smith, *Lectures on the Religion of the Semites* (Edinburgh, A. & C. Black, 1889), Lecture II, pp. 53 ff. Cf. Lecture X, pp. 334 ff.

25. For the ethnological material see Sir Edward Burnett Tylor, *Primitive Culture* (New York, Henry Holt & Co., 1874), chap. xiv.

under the same roof; Desert it not now! Come to your home! It is swept for you, and clean; and we are there who loved you ever; and there is rice put for you; and water; Come home, come home, come to us again." [26]

There is no radical difference in this respect between mythical and religious thought. Both of them originate in the same fundamental phenomena of human life. In the development of human culture we cannot fix a point where myth ends or religion begins. In the whole course of its history religion remains indissolubly connected and penetrated with mythical elements. On the other hand myth, even in its crudest and most rudimentary forms, contains some motives that in a sense anticipate the higher and later religious ideals. Myth is from its very beginning potential religion. What leads from one stage to the other is no sudden crisis of thought and no revolution of feeling. In *Les deux sources de la morale et de la religion* Henri Bergson tries to convince us that there is an irreconcilable opposition between what he describes as "Static Religion" and "Dynamic Religion." The former is a product of social pressure; the latter is based on freedom. In dynamic religion we yield not to a pressure but to an attraction—and by this attraction we break all the former social bonds of a static, conventional, and traditional morality. We do not come to the highest form of religion, to a religion of humanity, by degrees, through the stages of the family and the nation. "We must," says Bergson, "in a single bound, be carried far beyond it, and without having made it our goal, reach it by outstripping it. . . . Whether we speak the language of religion or the language of philosophy, whether it be a question of love or respect, a different morality, another kind of obligation supervenes, above and beyond the social pressure. . . . Whereas natural obligation is a pressure or propulsive force, complete and perfect morality has the effect of an appeal . . . It is not by a process of expansion of the self that we can pass from the first state to the second. . . . When we dispel appearances to get at reality, . . . then at the two extremes we find pressure and aspiration: the former the more perfect as it becomes

26. Tylor, *op. cit.* (3d ed.), II, 32 f.

more impersonal, closer to those natural forces which we call habit or even instinct, the latter the more powerful according as it is more obviously aroused in us by definite persons and the more it apparently triumphs over nature." [27]

It is rather surprising that Bergson, whose doctrine has often been described as a biological philosophy, as a philosophy of life and nature, in his last work seems to be led to a moral and religious ideal that goes far beyond this field.

"Man outwits nature when he extends social solidarity into the brotherhood of man; but he is deceiving her nevertheless; for those societies whose design was prefigured in the original structure of the human soul . . . required that the group be closely united, but that between group and group there should be virtual hostility. . . . Man, fresh from the hands of nature, was a being both intelligent and social, his sociability being devised to find its scope in small communities, his intelligence being designed to further individual and group life. But intelligence, expanding through its own efforts, has developed unexpectedly. It has freed men from restrictions to which they were condemned by the limitations of their nature. This being so, it was not impossible that some of them, specially gifted, should reopen that which was closed and do, at least for themselves, what nature could not possibly have done for mankind." [28]

Bergson's ethics is a consequence and a corollary of his metaphysics. The task he set to himself was to interpret man's ethical life in terms of his metaphysical system. In his philosophy of nature the organic world had been described as the result of a struggle between two contrary forces. On the one hand we find the mechanism of matter, on the other hand the creative and the constructive power of the *élan vital*. The pendulum of life constantly swings from one pole to the other. The inertia of matter resists the energy of the vital impulse.

27. Bergson, *Les deux sources de la morale et de la religion*. English trans. by R. Ashley Audra and Cloudesley Brereton, *The Two Sources of Morality and Religion* (New York, Holt & Co., 1935), ii, 25, 26, 30, 42.

28. Bergson, *op. cit.*, pp. 48 f.

According to Bergson man's ethical life reflects the same meta-physical strife between an active and a passive principle. Social life repeats and mirrors the universal process which we find in organic life. It is divided between two opposite forces. The one tends to maintaining and making eternal the present state of affairs; the other is striving for new forms of human life which never existed before. The first tendency is characteristic of static religion, the second of dynamic religion. The two can never be reduced to the same denominator. Mankind could only come by a sudden jump from one point to the other; from passivity to activity, from social pressure to an individual, self-dependent, ethical life.

I do not deny that there is a fundamental difference between the two forms of religion described by Bergson as those of "pressure" and "appeal." His book gives a very clear and impressive analysis of both these forms. Yet a metaphysical system cannot content itself with a mere analytic description of phenomena; it must try to trace them back to their ultimate causes. Bergson had, therefore, to derive the two types of moral and religious life from two divergent forces: the one governing primitive social life, the other breaking the chain of society in order to create a new ideal of a free personal life. If we accept this thesis there exists no continuous process which can lead from one form to the other. It is a sudden crisis of thought and a revolution of feeling that marks the transition from static to dynamic religions.

Yet a closer study of the history of religion is scarcely apt to corroborate this conception. From a historical point of view it is very difficult to maintain the trenchant distinction between the two sources of religion and morality. Surely Bergson did not mean to found his ethical and religious theory on mere metaphysical reasons. He always refers to the empirical evidence contained in the works of sociologists and anthropologists. Among the students of anthropology it was, indeed, long a current opinion that, under the conditions of primitive social life, we cannot speak of any activity on the part of the individual. In primitive society—it was assumed—the individual had not yet entered the lists. The feelings, the thoughts, the acts of man did not proceed from himself; they were impressed on him by an external force. Primitive life is characterized by a rigid, uniform, inexorable mechanism. Tradition and custom were obeyed slavishly and unwittingly through mere mental inertia or through a pervading group instinct. This automatic submission of every member of the tribe to its laws was long regarded as the fundamental axiom underlying the inquiry into primitive order and adherence to rule. Recent anthropological research has done much to shake this dogma of the complete mechanism and automatism of primitive social life. According to Malinowski this dogma has placed the reality of native life in a false perspective. As he points out, the savage has undoubtedly the greatest respect for his tribal custom and tradition as such; but the force of custom or tradition is not the only one in savage life. Even on a very low level of human culture there are definite traces of a different force.[29] A life of mere pressure, a human life in which all individual activities were completely suppressed and eliminated, seems to be rather a sociological or metaphysical construction than a historical reality.

In the history of Greek culture we find a period in which the old gods, the gods of Homer and Hesiod, began to decline. The popular conceptions of these gods are vigorously attacked. There arises a new religious ideal formed by individual men. The great poets and the great thinkers—Aeschylus and Euripides, Xenophanes, Heraclitus, Anaxagoras—create new intellectual and moral standards. When measured by these standards the Homeric gods lose their authority. Their anthropomorphic character is clearly seen and severely criticized. Nevertheless this anthropomorphism of Greek popular religion was by no means devoid of a positive value and significance. The humanization of the gods was an indispensable step in the evolution of religious thought. In many local Greek cults we still find definite traces of animal worship and even totemistic creeds.[30] "The progress of Greek religion," says

29. See Malinowski, *Crime and Custom in Savage Society* (London and New York, 1926).

30. For further details see Jane Ellen Harrison, *Prolegomena to the Study of Greek Religion* (Cambridge, 1903), chap. i.

Gilbert Murray, "falls naturally into three stages, all of them historically important. First there is the primitive *Euetheia* or Age of Ignorance before Zeus came to trouble men's minds, a stage to which our anthropologists and explorers have found parallels in every part of the world . . . In some ways characteristically Greek, in others it is so typical of similar stages of thought elsewhere that one is tempted to regard it as the normal beginning of all religion, or almost as the normal raw material out of which religion is made." [31] Then comes that process which in the work of Gilbert Murray is described as the "Olympian conquest." After this conquest man conceived nature and his own place in nature in a different sense. The general feeling of the solidarity of life gave way to a new and stronger motive—to the specific sense of man's individuality. There was no longer a natural kinship, a consanguinity that connects man with plants or animals. In his personal gods man began to see his own personality in a new light. This progress is clearly to be felt in the development of the highest god, of the Olympian Zeus. Even Zeus is a god of nature, a god worshiped on the mountain tops, holding sway over the clouds, the rain, the thunder. But gradually he assumes new shape. In Aeschylus he has become the expression of the highest ethical ideals, the guardian and protector of justice. "The Homeric religion," says Murray, "is a step in the self-realization of Greece. . . . The world was conceived as neither quite without external governance, nor as merely subject to the incursions of *mana* snakes and bulls and thunder-stones and monsters, but as governed by an organized body of personal and reasoning rulers, wise and bountiful fathers, like man in mind and shape, only unspeakably higher." [32]

In this progress of religious thought we become cognizant of the awakening of a new strength and a new activity of the human mind. Philosophers and anthropologists have often told us that the true and ultimate source of religion is man's feeling of dependency. According to Schleiermacher religion

31. Gilbert Murray, *Five Stages of Greek Religion*, Columbia University Lectures (New York, Columbia University Press, 1930), p. 16.
32. *Idem*, p. 82.

has arisen from "the feeling of absolute dependence on the Divine." In *The Golden Bough* J. G. Frazer adopted this thesis. "Thus religion," he says, "beginning as a slight and partial acknowledgment of powers superior to man, tends with the growth of knowledge to deepen into a confession of man's entire and absolute dependence on the divine; his old free bearing is exchanged for an attitude of lowliest prostration before the mysterious powers of the unseen." [33] But if this description of religion contains any truth it gives us only half the truth. In no one field of human culture can an "attitude of lowliest prostration" be thought to be the genuine and decisive impulse. From an entirely passive attitude there cannot develop any productive energy. In this regard even magic is to be taken as an important step in the development of human consciousness. Faith in magic is one of the earliest and most striking expressions of man's awakening self-confidence. Here he no longer feels himself at the mercy of natural or supernatural forces. He begins to play his own part, he becomes an actor in the spectacle of nature. Every magical practice is based upon the conviction that natural effects to a large degree depend on human deeds. The life of nature depends on the right distribution and coöperation of human and superhuman forces. A strict and elaborate ritual regulates this coöperation. Every particular field has its own magic rules. There are special rules for agriculture, for hunting, for fishing. In totemistic societies the different clans possess different magical rites that are their privilege and their secret. They become so much the more necessary the more difficult and dangerous a special performance is. Magic is not used for practical purposes, for supporting man in his needs of everyday life. It is destined for higher aims, for bold and dangerous enterprises. In his description of the mythology of the natives of the Trobriand Islands in Melanesia Malinowski reports that in all those tasks that need no particular and exceptional efforts, no special courage or endurance, we find no magic and no mythology. But a highly developed magic and, connected with it, a mythology always occur if a pursuit is dangerous and its is-

33. Frazer, *The Golden Bough*, I, 78.

sues uncertain. In minor economic pursuits such as arts and crafts, hunting, the collection of roots and the gathering of fruit man is not in need of magic.[34] It is only under a strong emotional strain that he takes recourse to magical rites. But it is precisely the performance of these rites that gives him a new feeling of his own powers—his will power and his energy. What man wins by magic is the highest concentration of all his efforts which under other commonplace circumstances are dispersed or incoherent. It is the technique of magic itself that requires such intense concentration. Every magical art needs the highest attention. If it is not performed in the right order and according to the same invariable rules it fails of its effect. In this regard magic may be said to be the first school through which primitive man had to pass. Even if it cannot lead to the desired practical ends, if it cannot fulfil the wishes of man, it teaches him to have confidence in his own powers— to regard himself as a being who need not simply submit to the forces of nature but is able by spiritual energy to regulate and control them.

The relation between magic and religion is one of the most obscure and most controversial subjects. Philosophical anthropologists have over and over again attempted to clarify this question. But their theories are widely divergent and often in flagrant contradiction with each other. It is natural to desire a clear-cut definition that would enable us to trace a sharp line of demarcation between magic and religion. Theoretically speaking, we are convinced that they cannot mean the same thing and we are loath to trace them to a common origin. We think of religion as the symbolic expression of our highest moral ideals; we think of magic as a crude aggregate of superstitions. Religious belief seems to become mere superstitious credulity if we admit any relationship with magic. On the other hand the character of our anthropological and ethnographical material makes it extremely difficult to separate the two fields. The attempts made in this direction have become more and more questionable. It seems to be one of the postulates of modern anthropology that there is complete continuity

34. Malinowski, *The Foundations of Faith and Morals*, p. 22.

betweeen magic and religion.[35] Frazer was one of the first to try to prove that even from an anthropological point of view magic and religion cannot be subsumed under a common heading. According to him they are entirely different in psychological origin and they tend to opposite aims. The failure and breakdown of magic paved the way to religion. Magic had to collapse that religion might arise. "Man saw that he had taken for causes what were no causes, and that all his efforts to work by means of these imaginary causes had been vain. His painful toil had been wasted, his curious ingenuity had been squandered to no purpose. He had been pulling at strings to which nothing was attached." It was in despairing of magic that man found religion and that he discovered its true sense. "If the great world went on its way without the help of him or his fellows, it must surely be because there were other beings, like himself, but far stronger, who, unseen themselves, directed its course and brought about all the varied series of events which he had hitherto believed to be dependent on his own magic." [36]

This distinction, however, seems to be rather artificial both from a systematic point of view and from that of the ethnological facts. We have no empirical evidence at all that there ever was an age of magic that has been followed and superseded by an age of religion.[37] And even the psychological analysis, on which this distinction between the two ages is based, is questionable. Frazer regards magic as the offspring of a theoretical or scientific activity, as a result of the curiosity of man. This curiosity incited man to inquire into the causes of things; but since he was unable to discover the real causes he had to satisfy himself with fictitious causes.[38] Religion, on the other hand, has no theoretical aims; it is an ex-

35. See, for instance, R. R. Marett, *Faith, Hope, and Charity in Primitive Religion*, the Gifford Lectures (Macmillan, 1932), Lecture II, pp. 21 ff.

36. Frazer, *op. cit.*, I, 76 f.

37. See the criticism of Frazer's theory in Marett, *The Threshold of Religion*, pp. 29 ff.

38. See above, p. 75 f.

pression of ethical ideals. But both of these views seem to be untenable if we look at the facts of primitive religion. From the first religion had to fulfil a theoretical and a practical function. It contains a cosmology and an anthropology; it answers the question of the origin of the world and the origin of human society. And from this origin it derives man's duties and obligations. These two aspects are not sharply distinguished; they are combined and fused together in that fundamental feeling that we have tried to describe as the feeling of the solidarity of life. Here we find a common source of magic and religion. Magic is not a kind of science—a pseudo science. Nor is it to be derived from that principle which in modern psychoanalysis has been described as the "omnipotence of thought" (*Allmacht des Gedankens*).[39] Neither the mere wish to know nor the mere wish to possess and to master nature can account for the facts of magic. Frazer makes a sharp distinction between two forms of magic that he designates as "imitative magic" and "sympathetic magic." [40] But all magic is "sympathetic" in its origin and in its significance; for man would not think of coming into a magical contact with nature if he had not the conviction that there is a common bond that unites all things —that the separation between himself and nature and between the different kinds of natural objects is, after all, an artificial, not a real one.

In philosophical language this conviction has been expressed by the Stoic maxim, *sympatheia tôn holôn*, which in a certain sense expresses very concisely that fundamental belief which is at the bottom of all magic rituals. It is true that it seems to be dangerous and arbitrary to apply a conception of Greek philosophy to the most rudimentary beliefs of mankind. But the Stoics, who coined this concept of the "sympathy of the Whole," had by no means completely outgrown the views of popular religion. By virtue of their principle of the *notitiae communes*—of those common notions that are found the world over and at all times—they strove to reconcile mythi-

39. Cf. Freud, *Totem und Tabu* (Vienna, 1920).
40. Cf. Frazer, *op. cit.*, I, 9.

cal and philosophical thought; they admitted that even the latter contains some elements of truth. They themselves did not hesitate to use the argument of the "sympathy of the Whole" to interpret and justify popular beliefs. As a matter of fact the Stoic doctrine of an all-pervading *pneuma*—of a breath diffused throughout the universe which imparts to all things the tension by which they are held together—still shows very striking analogies with primitive concepts, with the mana of the Polynesians, the Iroquois orenda, the Sioux wakan, the Algonquian manitu.[41] Of course to put the philosophical interpretation on the same level as the mythico-magical interpretation would be preposterous. Nevertheless we can trace both of them back to a common root, to a very deep stratum of religious feeling. In order to penetrate into this stratum we must not try to construct a theory of magic based on the principles of our empirical psychology, especially on the principles of the association of ideas.[42] We must approach the problem from the side of magic ritual. Malinowski has given a very impressive description of tribal festivities of the natives of the Trobriand Islands. They are always accompanied by mythical tales and magical ceremonies. During the sacred season, the season of harvest rejoicing, the younger generation are reminded by their elders that the spirits of their ancestors are about to return from the underworld. The spirits come for a few weeks and settle again in the villages, perched in the trees, sitting on high platforms specially erected for them, watching the magical dances.[43] Such a magical rite gives us a clear and concrete impression of the true sense of "sympathetic magic," and of its social and religious function. The men who celebrate such a festivity, who perform their magical dances, are fused with each other and fused with all things in nature. They are not isolated; their joy is felt by the whole of nature and shared by their ancestors. Space and time have vanished;

41. For a more detailed description of these concepts and their significance in mythical thought see *Philosophie der symbolischen Formen*, II, 98 ff.

42. Such a theory has been developed by Frazer, *Lectures on the Early History of Kingship*, pp. 52 ff.

43. Cf. Malinowski, *op. cit.*, p. 14.

the past has become the present; the golden age of mankind has come back.[44]

Religion had not the power, nor could it ever tend, to suppress or eradicate these deepest instincts of mankind. It had to fulfil a different task—to use them and lead them into new channels. The belief in the "sympathy of the Whole" is one of the firmest foundations of religion itself. But religious sympathy is of a different kind from the mythical and magical. It gives scope for a new feeling, that of individuality. Yet we appear to be confronted here with one of the fundamental antinomies of religious thought. Individuality seems to be a negation or at least a restriction of that universality of feeling that is postulated by religion: *omnis determinatio est negatio.* It means finite existence—and as long as we do not break the barriers of this finite existence we cannot grasp the infinite. It was this difficulty and this riddle that had to be solved by the progress of religious thought. We can follow this progress in a threefold direction. We can describe it in its psychological, its sociological, and its ethical implications. The development of the individual, the social, the moral consciousness tends to the same point. It shows a progressive differentiation that finally leads to a new integration. The conceptions of primitive religion are much more vague and indeterminate than our own conceptions and ideals. The mana of the Polynesians, like the corresponding conceptions that we find in other parts of the world, shows this vague and fluctuating character. It has no individuality, either subjective or objective. It is conceived as a common mysterious stuff that permeates all things. According to the definition of Codrington, who was the first to describe the concept of mana, it is "a power or influence, not

44. The Arunta people of the central deserts of Australia, says Marett, "set up by means of their dramatic rites a sort of timeless Alcheringa into which they can turn aside from the hardships of their present lot, so as to refresh themselves by communion with transcendent beings who are at once their forefathers and their ideal selves. For the rest it is to be noted that of distinctive individuality these supermen of the Alcheringa have almost none. The chorus seeks simply to glut its collective soul with the glamour of ancestry—with the consciousness of kind. The mana in which they participate is tribal." *Faith, Hope, and Charity in Primitive Religion,* p. 36.

physical, and in a way super-natural; but it shows itself in physical force, or in any kind of power or excellence which a man possesses." [45] It may be the attribute of a soul or spirit; but it is not in itself a spirit—it is not an animistic but a pre-animistic conception.[46] It is to be found in all things whatsoever regardless of their special nature and their generic distinction. A stone which attracts attention by its size or its singular shape is filled with mana and will exert magical powers.[47] It is not bound up with a special subject; the mana of a man may be stolen from him and transferred to a new possessor. We can distinguish in it no individual features, no personal identity. One of the first and most important functions of all the higher religions was to discover and to reveal such personal elements in what was called the Holy, the Sacred, the Divine.

But in order to attain this end religious thought had to come a long way. Man could not give his gods a definite individual shape before he had found a new principle of differentiation in his own existence and in his social life. He found this principle not in abstract thought but in his work. It was in fact the division of labor that introduced a new era of religious thought. Long before the appearance of the personal gods we meet with those gods that have been called functional gods. They are not as yet the personal gods of Greek religion, the Olympian gods of Homer. On the other hand they no longer have the vagueness of the primitive mythical conceptions. They are concrete beings; but they are concrete in their actions, not in their personal appearance or existence. They have, therefore, no proper names—like Zeus, Hera, Apollo—but adjectival names that characterize their special function or activity. In many cases they are bound up with a special place; they are local, not general gods. If we wish to understand the true character of these functional gods and the role they play in the development of religious thought we

45. R. H. Codrington, *The Melanesians* (Oxford, Clarendon Press, 1891), p. 118.
46. For this problem see Marett, "The Conception of Mana," *The Threshold of Religion*, pp. 99 ff.
47. Codrington, *op. cit.*, p. 119.

must look at Roman religion. There the differentiation has reached the highest degree. In the life of a Roman farmer every act, however specialized, had its specific religious meaning. There was one class of deities—of *Di Indigites*—that watched over the act of sowing, another that watched over the act of harrowing, of manuring; there was a Sator, an Occator, a Sterculinus.[48] In all agricultural work there was not a single act that was not under guidance and protection of functional deities, and each class had its own rites and observances.

In this religious system we see all the typical features of the Roman mind. It is a sober, practical, energetic mind endowed with a great power of concentration. To a Roman life meant active life. And he had the special gift of organizing this active life, of regulating and coördinating all its efforts. The religious expression of this tendency is to be found in the Roman functional gods. They have to fulfil definite practical tasks. They are not a product of religious imagination or inspiration; they are conceived as the rulers of particular activities. They are, so to speak, administrative gods who have shared among themselves the different provinces of human life. They have no definite personality; but they are clearly distinguished by their office, and upon this office their religious dignity depends.

Of a different type are those gods that were revered in every Roman house: the gods of the flame on the hearth. They do not originate in a special and restricted sphere of practical life. They express the deepest feelings of Roman family life; they are the sacred center of the Roman home. These gods arose from piety toward ancestors. But they too have no individual physiognomy. They are the *Di Manes*—the "good gods"—conceived in a collective, not in a personal sense. The term "manes" never appears in the singular. It was only in a later period, when the Greek influence became preponderant, that these gods assumed a more personal shape. In their earliest state the Di Manes are still an indefinite mass of spirits bound together by their common relation to the

48. For details see *Philosophie der symbolischen Formen*, II, 246 ff.

family. They have been described as mere potentialities thought of in groups rather than as individuals. "Subsequent centuries," it has been said, "saturated with Greek philosophy and filled with an idea of individuality which was totally lacking in the earlier days of Rome, identified this poor shadowy potentiality with the human soul, and read into the whole matter a belief in immortality." In Rome it was "the family *idea*, so fundamental in the social structure of Roman life, that triumphed over the grave and possessed an immortality which the individual failed to obtain." [49]

Quite a different tendency of thought and feeling seems to have prevailed from very early times in Greek religion. Here too we find definite traces of ancestor worship.[50] Greek classical literature has preserved many of these traces. Aeschylus and Sophocles describe the gifts—the libations of milk, the garlands of flowers, the locks of hair—that are offered at the tomb of Agamemnon by his children. But under the influence of the Homeric poems all these archaic features of Greek religion begin to fade away. They are overshadowed by a new direction of mythical and religious thought. Greek art paved the way to a new conception of the gods. As Herodotus says, Homer and Hesiod "gave the Greek gods their names and portrayed their shapes." And the work that had been begun by Greek poetry was completed in Greek sculpture: we can scarcely think of the Olympian Zeus without representing him in the shape that he received from Phidias. What was denied to the active and practical Roman mind was performed by the contemplative and artistic mind of the Greeks. It was no moral tendency which created the Homeric gods. The Greek philosophers were right in complaining of the character of these gods. "Homer and Hesiod," says Xenophanes, "have ascribed to the gods all deeds that are a shame and a disgrace among men: thieving, adultery, fraud." Yet this very lack and defect of the Greek personal gods was able to bridge the gap between the human and the divine nature. In the Homeric

49. See J. B. Carter in an article in Hastings' *Encyclopedia*, I, 462.
50. For this question see Erwin Rohde, *Psyche. The Cult of Souls and Belief in Immortality among the Greeks* (New York, Harcourt, Brace, 1925).

poems we find no definite barrier between the two worlds. What man portrays in his gods is himself, in all his variety and multiformity, his turn of mind, his temperament, even his idiosyncrasies. But it is not, as in Roman religion, the practical side of his nature that man projects upon the deity. The Homeric gods represent no moral ideals, but they express very characteristic mental ideals. They are not those functional and anonymous deities that have to watch over a special activity of man: they are interested in and favor individual men. Every god and goddess has his favorites who are appreciated, loved, and assisted, not on the ground of a mere personal predilection but by virtue of a kind of mental relationship that connects the god and the man. Mortals and immortals are the embodiments not of moral ideals but of special mental gifts and tendencies. In the Homeric poems we often find very clear and characteristic expressions of this new religious feeling. When Odysseus returns to Ithaca without knowing that he has come to his native country Athene appears to him in the form of a young shepherd and asks him his name. Odysseus who is anxious to keep his incognito immediately concocts a story full of lies and deceptions. The goddess smiles at this story, recognizing what she herself has bestowed upon him: "Cunning must he be and knavish who would go beyond thee in all manner of guile, aye, though it were a god that met thee. Bold man, crafty in counsel, insatiate in deceit, not even in thine own land, it seems, wast thou to cease from guile and deceitful tales, which thou lovest from the bottom of thine heart. But come, let us no longer talk of this, being both well versed in craft, since thou art far the best of all men in counsel and in speech, and I among all the gods am famed for wisdom and craft. . . . Ever such is the thought in thy breast, and therefore it is that I cannot leave thee in thy sorrow, for thou art soft of speech, keen of wit, and prudent." [51]

It is quite a different aspect of the Divine which we meet with in the great monotheistic religions. These religions are the offspring of moral forces; they concentrate upon a single

51. *The Odyssey*, Bk. XIII, vv. 291 ff. Trans. by A. T. Murray (Loeb Classical Library, Harvard University Press, Cambridge, Mass., 1930).

point, upon the problem of good and evil. In the religion of Zoroaster there is only one Supreme Being Ahura Mazda, the "wise lord." Beyond him, apart from him, and without him nothing exists. He is the first and foremost, the most perfect being, the absolute sovereign. Here we find no individualization, no plurality of gods that are the representatives of different natural powers or different mental qualities. Primitive mythology is attacked and overcome by a new force, a purely ethical force. In the first conceptions of the holy, the supernatural, such a force is entirely unknown. The mana, the wakan, or the orenda may be used for good or bad purposes—it always works in the same way. It acts, as Codrington says, "in all kinds of ways for good and evil." [52] Mana may be described as the first, or existential, dimension of the supernatural—but it has nothing to do with its moral dimension. Here the good manifestations of the all-pervading supernatural power are on the same level with the malign or destructive ones.[53] From its very beginnings the religion of Zoroaster is radically opposed to this mythical indifference or to that aesthetic indifference which is characteristic of Greek polytheism. This religion is not a product of mythical or aesthetic imagination; it is the expression of a great personal moral will. Even nature assumes a new shape, for it is seen exclusively in the mirror of ethical life. No religion could ever think of cutting or even loosening the bond between nature and man. But in the great ethical religions this bond is tied and fastened in a new sense. The sympathetic connection that we find in magic and in primitive mythology is not denied or destroyed; but nature is now approached from the rational instead of from the emotional side. If nature contains a divine element it appears not in the abundance of its life but in the simplicity of its order. Nature is not, as in polytheistic religion, the great and benign mother, the divine lap from which all life originates. It is conceived as the sphere of law and lawfulness. And by this feature alone it proves its divine origin. In Zoroastrian religion nature is described by the concept of

52. Codrington, op. cit., p. 118.
53. See Marett, "The Conception of Mana," op. cit., pp. 112 ff.

Asha. Asha is the wisdom of nature that reflects the wisdom of its creator, of Ahura Mazda, the "wise lord." This universal, eternal, inviolable order governs the world and determines all single events: the path of the sun, the moon, the stars, the growth of plants and animals, the way of winds and clouds. All this is maintained and preserved, not by mere physical forces but by the force of the Good. The world has become a great moral drama in which both nature and man have to play their roles.

Even in a very primitive stage of mythical thought we find a conviction that man, in order to attain a desired end, has to coöperate with nature and its divine or demonic powers. Nature does not bestow its gifts upon him without his active assistance. In the religion of Zoroaster we meet with the same conception. But here it points in an entirely new direction. The ethical meaning has replaced and superseded the magical meaning. The whole life of man becomes an uninterrupted struggle for the sake of righteousness. The triad of "good thoughts, good words, and good deeds" has the leading part in this struggle. The Divine is no longer sought or approached by magical powers but by the power of righteousness. From now on there is not a single step in man's everyday practical life that, in a religious and moral sense, is regarded as insignificant or indifferent. Nobody can stand aside in the combat between the divine and the demonic power, between Ahura Mazda and Angra Mainyu. The two primal spirits, says one of the texts, who revealed themselves in vision as twins are the Better and the Bad. Between these two the wise knew how to choose aright, the foolish not so. Every act, however common or humble, has its definite ethical worth and is tinged with a specific ethical color. It means order or disorder, preservation or destruction. The man who cultivates or waters the soil, who plants a tree, who kills a dangerous animal, performs a religious duty; he prepares and secures the final victory of the power of the good, of the "wise lord," over his demonic adversary. In all this we feel a heroic effort of mankind; an effort to get rid of the pressure and compulsion of magic forces, a new ideal of freedom. For here it is only by freedom, by a self-dependent decision, that man can come into contact with the divine. By such a decision man becomes the ally of the godhead.

"The decision between the two ways of life rests with the individual. Man is the arbiter of his destiny. He has the power and freedom to choose between truth and falsehood, righteousness and wickedness, good and evil. He is responsible for the moral choice he makes and is consequently responsible for his actions. If he makes the right choice and embraces righteousness, he will reap its reward, but if, as a free agent, he chooses wickedness, the accountability will be his and his own daena or self will lead him to retribution. . . . [In the end there will come] the period when every individual in his or her own capacity will embrace and act righteousness and will thus make the entire world of humanity gravitate towards Asha. . . . All . . . have to contribute to this mighty work. The righteous ones living in different ages and at different places form the members of one righteous group, inasmuch as they are all actuated by one and the same motive and work for the common cause." [54] It is this form of a universal ethical sympathy which in monotheistic religion gains the victory over the primitive feeling of a natural or magical solidarity of life.

When Greek philosophy approached the problem it could hardly surpass the greatness and sublimity of these religious thoughts. Greek philosophy, in later Hellenistic times, retained a great many religious and even mythical motives. In Stoic philosophy the concept of a universal providence (*pronoia*) that leads the world to its goal is central. And even here man, as a conscious and rational being, has to work for the sake of providence. The universe is a great society of God and men, "urbs Dis hominibusque communis." [55] To "live with the Gods" (*suzen theois*) means to work with them. Man is no mere spectator; he is, according to his measure, the creator of the world order. The wise man is a priest and minister of the gods.[56] Here too we find the conception of

54. M. N. Dhalla, *History of Zoroastrianism* (New York, Oxford University Press, 1938), pp. 52 ff.

55. Seneca, *Ad Marciam de consolatione*, 18.

56. Marcus Aurelius, *Ad se ipsum*, Bk. III, par. 4.

the "sympathy of the Whole," but it is now understood and interpreted in a new ethical sense.

All this could only be attained by a slow and continuous development of religious thought and feeling. The transition from the most rudimentary forms to the higher and highest forms could not be made by a sudden jump. Bergson declares that without such a jump mankind would not have been able to find its way to a pure dynamic religion—to a religion that is based not upon social pressure and obligation but upon freedom. But his own metaphysical thesis of "creative evolution" scarcely favors such a view. Without the great creative spirits, without the prophets that felt themselves inspired by the power of God and destined to reveal his will, religion would not have found its way. But even these individual powers could not change its fundamentally social character. They could not create a new religion out of nothing. The great individual religious reformers were not living in empty space, in the space of their own religious experience and inspiration. By a thousand bonds they were tied to their social environment. It is not by a sort of revolt that mankind passes from moral obligation to religious freedom. Even Bergson admits that, historically speaking, the mystic spirit that he thinks to be the spirit of true religion is no break in continuity. Mysticism reveals to us, or rather would reveal to us, if we actually willed it, a marvelous prospect; but we do not, and in most cases we could not, will it; we should collapse under the strain. Therefore we remain with a mixed religion. In history we find interposed transitions between two things which are as a matter of fact radically different in nature and which, at first sight, we can hardly believe deserve the same name.[57] For the philosopher, for the metaphysician these two forms of religion always remain antagonistic. He cannot derive them from the same origin, for they are expressions of totally different forces. One is entirely based on instinct; it is the instinct of life that has created the myth-making function. But religion does not arise from instinct nor from intelligence or reason. It

57. Bergson, *op. cit.*, pp. 201 ff.

needs a new impetus, a special kind of intuition and inspiration.

"To get at the very essence of religion and understand the history of mankind, one must needs pass at once from the static and outer religion to dynamic, inner religion. The first was designed to ward off the dangers to which intelligence might expose man; it was infra-intellectual. . . . Later, and by an effort which might easily never have been made, man wrenched himself free from this motion of his on his own axis. He plunged anew into the current of evolution, at the same time carrying it forward. Here was dynamic religion, coupled doubtless with higher intellectuality, but distinct from it. The first form of religion had been infra-intellectual . . . the second was supra-intellectual." [58]

Such a sharp dialectic distinction between three fundamental powers—instinct, intelligence, and mystical intuition—is, however, out of keeping with the facts of the history of religion. Even the thesis of Frazer that mankind began with an age of magic that later on was followed and superseded by an age of religion is untenable. Magic lost ground by a very slow process. If we look at the history of our own European civilization we find that even in the most advanced stages, in the stages of a highly developed and very refined intellectual culture, the belief in magic was not seriously shaken. Even religion could to a certain extent admit this belief. It forbade and condemned some magical practices, but there was a sphere of "white" magic that was thought to be innocuous. The thinkers of the Renaissance—Pomponazzi, Cardano, Campanella, Bruno, Giambattista della Porta, Paracelsus— gave their own philosophical scientific theories of the magic art. One of the noblest and most pious thinkers of the Renaissance, Giovanni Pico della Mirandola, was convinced that magic and religion are tied to each other by indissoluble bonds. "Nulla est scientia," he says, "quae nos magis certificet de divinitate Christi quam Magia et Cabala." We may infer from these examples what religious evolution really means. It does not mean the complete destruction of the first and funda-

58. Idem, pp. 175 f.

mental characteristics of mythical thought. If the great individual religious reformers wished to be heard and understood they had to speak not only the language of God but the language of man. But the great prophets of Israel no longer spoke merely to their own nations. Their God was a god of Justice and His message was not restricted to a special group. The prophets predicted a new heaven and a new earth. What is really new is not the contents of this prophetic religion but its inner tendency, its ethical meaning. One of the greatest miracles that all the higher religions had to perform was to develop their new character, their ethical and religious interpretation of life, out of the crude raw material of the most primitive conceptions, the grossest superstitions.

There is perhaps no better example of this transformation than the development of the concept of taboo. There are many stages of human civilization in which we find no definite ideas of divine powers and no definite animism—no theory of the human soul. But there seems to be no society, however primitive, that has not developed a system of taboo—and in most cases this system has a very complex structure. In the Polynesian islands from which the term "taboo" is derived the name stands for the whole system of religion.[59] And we find many primitive societies in which the only offense known is taboo breaking.[60] In the elementary stages of human civilization the term covers the whole field of religion and morality. In this sense many historians of religion have ascribed to the taboo system a very high value. In spite of its obvious defects it was declared to be the first and indispensable germ of a higher cultural life; it was even said to be an a priori principle of moral and religious thought. Jevons describes the taboo as a sort of categorical imperative, the only one that was known and accessible to primitive man. The sentiment that there are some things which "must not be done," he says, is purely formal and without content. The essence of taboo is that

59. Cf. Marett, "Is Taboo a Negative Magic?" *The Threshold of Religion*, p. 84.
60. Cf. F. B. Jevons, *An Introduction to the History of Religion* (London, Methuen, 1902), p. 70.

without consulting experience it pronounces a priori certain things to be dangerous.

"Those things, as a matter of fact, were in a sense not dangerous, and the belief in their danger was irrational. Yet had not that belief existed, there would be now no morality, and consequently no civilization. . . . The belief was a fallacy. . . . But this fallacy was the sheath which enclosed and protected a conception that was to blossom and bear a priceless fruit—the conception of Social Obligation." [61]

But how could such a conception develop from a conviction which, in itself, did not bear any relation to ethical values? In its original and literal sense taboo seems to mean only a thing that is marked off—that is not on the same level as other usual, profane, harmless things. It is surrounded by an atmosphere of dread and danger. This danger has often been described as a supernatural one, but it is by no means a moral one. If it is distinguished from other things, this distinction does not mean moral discrimination and does not imply a moral judgment. A man who commits a crime becomes taboo but the same holds for a woman in childbirth. The "infectious impurity" extends to all spheres of life. A touch of the Divine is just as dangerous as a touch of physically impure things; the sacred and the abominable are on the same level. The "infection of holiness" produces the same results as the "pollution of uncleanness." Who touches a corpse becomes unclean; but even a newborn child is feared in the same way. Among some peoples children on the day of birth were so taboo that they might not be put upon the ground. And in consequence of the principle of the transmissibility of the original infection there is no possible limit to its propagation. "A single thing taboo," it has been said, "might infect the whole universe." [62] There is not a shadow of any individual responsibility in this system. If a man commits a crime it is not he himself who is marked off—his family, his friends, his

61. *Idem*, pp. 86 f. Quoted by courtesy of Methuen & Co. and the Executors of F. B. Jevons.

62. For the anthropological material see Frazer, *The Golden Bough*, I, 169 ff. and Pt. VI, *The Scapegoat*; and Jevons, *op. cit.*, chaps. vi–viii.

whole tribe bears the same mark. They are stigmatized; they partake in the same miasma. And the rites of purification correspond to this conception. The ablution is to be attained by merely physical and external means. Running water may wash away the stain of the crime. Sometimes the sin is transferred to an animal, to a "scapegoat" or to a bird, which flies away with it.[63]

For all the higher religions it proved to be extremely difficult to overcome this system of a very primitive tabooism. But after many efforts they succeeded in accomplishing this task. They needed for it the same process of discrimination and individualization that we attempted to describe above. The first necessary step was to find a line of demarcation that separated the holy sphere from the unclean or the uncanny. There can be little doubt that all the Semitic religions, at their first appearance, were based on a very complicated system of taboos. In his investigations of the religion of the Semites W. Robertson-Smith declares that the first Semitic rules of holiness and uncleanness are in their origin indistinguishable from savage taboos. Even in those religions that are based upon the purest ethical motives, there are still maintained many features that point to an earlier stage of religious thought in which purity or impurity was understood in a merely physical sense. The religion of Zoroaster, for instance, contains very severe prescriptions against the pollution of the physical elements. To soil the pure element of fire by the touch of a corpse or any other unclean thing is regarded as a mortal sin. It is even a crime to bring back fire to a house in which a man has died, within nine nights in winter and a month in summer.[64] Even for the higher religion it was impossible to neglect or suppress all these lustrative rules and rites. What could be altered and what had to be altered in the progress of religious thought were not the material taboos themselves but the motives that lay behind them. In the original system these motives were entirely irrelevant. Beyond

63. For further details see Robertson-Smith, op. cit., Note G, pp. 427 ff.
64. For further details see Dhalla, op. cit., pp. 55, 221 ff.

the region of our common and familiar things lies another one, filled with unknown powers and unknown dangers. A thing belonging to this field is marked off but it is only the distinction itself, not the direction of the distinction, that gives it its special mark. It may be taboo by its superiority or its inferiority, by its virtue or vice, by its excellence or depravity. In its beginnings religion does not dare to reject the taboo itself, for by an attack on this sacred sphere it would risk loss of its own ground. But it begins with introducing a new element. "The fact that all the Semites have rules of uncleanness as well as rules of holiness," says Robertson-Smith, "that the boundary between the two is often vague, and that the former as well as the latter present the most startling agreement in point of detail with savage *taboos*, leaves no reasonable doubt as to the origin and ultimate relations of the idea of holiness. On the other hand the fact that the Semites . . . distinguish between the holy and the unclean, marks a real advance above savagery. All taboos are inspired by awe of the supernatural, but there is a great moral difference between precautions against the invasion of mysterious hostile powers and precautions founded on respect for the prerogative of a friendly god. The former belong to magical superstition . . . which being founded only on fear, acts merely as a bar to progress and an impediment to the free use of nature by human energy and industry. But the restrictions on individual licence which are due to respect for a known and friendly power allied to man, however trivial and absurd they may appear to us in their details, contain within them germinant principles of social progress and moral order." [65]

To develop these principles it was imperative to make a sharp distinction between the subjective and the objective violation of a religious law. To the primitive system of taboos such a distinction is entirely alien. What matters here is the action itself, not the motive of the action. The danger of becoming taboo is a physical danger. It is entirely beyond the reach of our moral powers. The effect is quite the same in the case of an involuntary and a voluntary act. The infection

65. Robertson-Smith, *op. cit.*, pp. 143 f.

is entirely impersonal and it is transmitted in a merely passive way. Generally speaking the meaning of a taboo may be described as a sort of *Noli me tangere*—it is the untouchable, a thing not to be lightly approached. The way or the intention of approach does not count. A taboo may be conveyed not only by touch but also by hearing or sight. And the consequences are the same whether I deliberately look at a tabooed object or incidentally and involuntarily catch sight of it. To be seen by a tabooed person, by a priest or king, is as dangerous as to look at him. ". . . the action of taboo is always mechanical; contact with the tabooed object communicates the taboo infection as certainly as contact with water communicates moisture, or an electric current an electric shock. The intentions of the taboo-breaker have no effect upon the action of the taboo; he may touch in ignorance, or for the benefit of the person he touches, but he is tabooed as surely as if his motive were irreverent or his action hostile. Nor does the mood of the sacred persons, the Mikado, the Polynesian chief, the priestess of Artemis Hymnia, modify the mechanical action of taboo; their touch or glance is as fatal to friend as foe, to plant life as to human. Still less does the morality of the taboo-breaker matter; the penalty descends like rain alike upon the unjust and the just." [66] But here begins that slow process that we have tried to designate by the name of a religious "change of meaning." If we look at the development of Judaism we feel how complete and how decisive this change of meaning was. In the prophetic books of the Old Testament we find an entirely new direction of thought and feeling. The ideal of purity means something quite different from all the former mythical conceptions. To seek for purity or impurity in an object, in a material thing, has become impossible. Even human actions, as such, are no longer regarded as pure or impure. The only purity that has a religious significance and dignity is purity of the heart.

And by this first discrimination we are led to another one that is of no less importance. The taboo system imposes upon

66. Jevons, *op. cit.*, p. 91.

man innumerable duties and obligations. But all these duties have a common character. They are entirely negative; they include no positive ideal whatever. Some things have to be avoided; some actions have to be abstained from. What we find here are inhibitions and prohibitions, not moral or religious demands. For it is fear that dominates the taboo system; and fear knows only how to forbid, not how to direct. It warns against the danger but it cannot arouse a new active or moral energy in man. The more the taboo system develops the more it threatens to congeal the life of man to a complete passivity. He cannot eat or drink, he cannot stay or walk. Even speech becomes irksome; in every word man is threatened by unknown dangers. In Polynesia it is not only forbidden to utter the name of a chief or of a deceased person; even other words or syllables in which this name happens to appear may not be used in common conversation. It was here that religion, in its progress, found a new task. But the problem that it had to confront was extremely difficult, and in a certain sense it seemed to be insoluble. In spite of all its obvious defects the taboo system was the only system of social restriction and obligation that had been discovered by man. It was the cornerstone of the whole social order. There was no part of the social system that was not regulated and governed by special taboos. The relation between rulers and subjects, political life, sexual life, family life, possessed no other and no more sacred bond. The same holds for the whole economic life. Even property seems, in its very origin, to be a taboo institution. The first way to take possession of a thing or a person, to occupy a piece of ground or to betroth a woman, is to mark them by a taboo sign. It was impossible for religion to abrogate this complex system of interdictions. To suppress it would have meant complete anarchy. Yet the great religious teachers of mankind found a new impulse by which, henceforward, the whole life of man was led to a new direction. They discovered in themselves a positive power, a power not of inhibition but of inspiration and aspiration. They turned passive obedience into an active religious feeling. The taboo system threatens to make the life of man a burden that in the end becomes unbearable. Man's whole existence, physical and moral, is smothered under the continual pressure of this system. It is here that religion intervenes. All the higher ethical religions—the religion of the prophets of Israel, Zoroastrianism, Christianity—set themselves a common task. They relieve the intolerable burden of the taboo system; but they detect, on the other hand, a more profound sense of religious obligation that instead of being a restriction or compulsion is the expression of a new positive ideal of human freedom.

8 Language

1   Language and myth are near of kin. In the early stages of human culture their relation is so close and their coöperation so obvious that it is almost impossible to separate the one from the other. They are two different shoots from one and the same root. Whenever we find man we find him in possession of the faculty of speech and under the influence of the myth-making function. Hence, for a philosophical anthropology it is tempting to bring both of these specifically human characteristics under a common head. Attempts in this direction have often been made. F. Max Müller developed a curious theory by which myth was explained as a mere by-product of language. He regarded myth as a sort of disease of the human mind, the causes of which are to be sought in the faculty of speech. Language is, by its very nature and essence, metaphorical. Unable to describe things directly, it resorts to indirect modes of description, to ambiguous and equivocal terms. It is this inherent ambiguity of language to which, according to Max Müller, myth owes its origin and in which it has always found its mental nutriment. "The question of mythology," says Müller, "has become in fact a question of psychology, and, as our psyche becomes objective to us chiefly through language, a question of the Science of Language. This will explain why . . . I called [myth] a Disease of Language rather than of Thought. . . . Language and thought are inseparable, and . . . a disease of language is therefore the same as a disease of thought . . . To represent the su-

preme God as committing every kind of crime, as being deceived by men, as being angry with his wife and violent with his children, is surely proof of a disease, of an unusual condition of thought, or, to speak more clearly, of real madness. . . . It is a case of mythological pathology. . . .

"Ancient language is a difficult instrument to handle, particularly for religious purposes. It is impossible in human language to express abstract ideas except by metaphor, and it is not too much to say that the whole dictionary of ancient religion is made up of metaphors. . . . Here is a constant source of misunderstandings, many of which have maintained their place in the religion and in the mythology of the ancient world." [1]

But to regard a fundamental human activity as a mere monstrosity, as a sort of mental disease, can scarcely pass muster as an adequate interpretation of it. We need no such strange and farfetched theories in order to see that for the primitive mind myth and language are, as it were, twin brothers. Both are based on a very general and very early experience of mankind, an experience of a social rather than of a physical nature. Long before a child learns to talk it has discovered other and simpler means of communicating with other persons. The cries of discomfort, of pain and hunger, of fear or fright, which we find throughout the organic world begin to assume a new shape. They are no longer simple instinctive reactions, for they are employed in a more conscious and deliberate way. When left alone the child demands by more or less articulate sounds the presence of its nurse or mother, and it becomes aware that these demands have the desired effect. Primitive man transfers this first elementary social experience to the totality of nature. To him nature and society are not only interconnected by the closest bonds; they form a coherent and indistinguishable whole. No clear-cut line of demarcation separates the two realms. Nature itself is nothing but a great society—the society of life. From this point of view we can

1. F. Max Müller, *Contributions to the Science of Mythology* (London, Longmans, Green & Co., 1897), I, 68 f., and *Lectures on the Science of Religion* (New York, Charles Scribner's Sons, 1893), pp. 118 f.

easily understand the use and specific function of the magic word. The belief in magic is based upon a deep conviction of the solidarity of life.[2] To the primitive mind the social power of the word, experienced in innumerable cases, becomes a natural and even supernatural force. Primitive man feels himself surrounded by all sorts of visible and invisible dangers. He cannot hope to overcome these dangers by merely physical means. To him the world is not a dead or mute thing; it can hear and understand. Hence if the powers of nature are called upon in the right way they cannot refuse their aid. Nothing resists the magic word, *carmina vel coelo possunt deducere lunam.*

When man first began to realize that this confidence was vain—that nature was inexorable not because it was reluctant to fulfil his demands but because it did not understand his language—the discovery must have come to him as a shock. At this point he had to face a new problem which marked a turning point and a crisis in his intellectual and moral life. From that time on man must have found himself in a deep solitude, subject to feelings of utter loneliness and of absolute despair. He would scarcely have overcome these had he not developed a new spiritual force, which barred the way to magic but at the same time opened another and more promising road. All hope of subduing nature by the magic word had been frustrated. But as a result man began to see the relation between language and reality in a different light. The magic function of the word was eclipsed and replaced by its semantic function. The word is no longer endowed with mysterious powers; it no longer has an immediate physical or supernatural influence. It cannot change the nature of things and it cannot compel the will of gods or demons. Nevertheless it is neither meaningless nor powerless. It is not simply a *flatus vocis*, a mere breath of air. Yet the decisive feature is not its physical but its logical character. Physically the word may be declared to be impotent, but logically it is elevated to a higher, indeed to the highest rank. The *Logos* becomes the

2. See above, Chap. 7, pp. 111–117.

principle of the universe and the first principle of human knowledge.

This transition took place in early Greek philosophy. Heraclitus still belongs to that class of Greek thinkers who in Aristotle's *Metaphysics* are referred to as the "ancient physiologists" (*hoi archaioi physiologoi*). His whole interest is concentrated on the phenomenal world. He does not admit that above the phenomenal world, the world of "becoming," there exists a higher sphere, an ideal or eternal order of pure "being." Yet he is not content with the mere *fact* of change; he seeks the *principle* of change. According to Heraclitus this principle is not to be found in a material thing. Not the material but the human world is the clue to a correct interpretation of the cosmic order. In this human world the faculty of speech occupies a central place. We must, therefore, understand what speech means in order to understand the "meaning" of the universe. If we fail to find this approach—the approach through the medium of language rather than through physical phenomena—we miss the gateway to philosophy. Even in Heraclitus' thought the word, the Logos, is not a merely anthropological phenomenon. It is not confined within the narrow limits of our human world, for it possesses universal cosmic truth. But instead of being a magic power the word is understood in its semantic and symbolic function. "Don't listen to me," writes Heraclitus, "but to the Word and confess that all things are one."

Early Greek thought thus passed from a philosophy of nature to a philosophy of language. But here it encountered new and grave difficulties. There is perhaps no more bewildering and controversial problem than "the meaning of meaning." [3] Even in our own day linguists, psychologists, and philosophers entertain widely divergent views upon this subject. Ancient philosophy could not grapple directly with this intricate problem in all its aspects. It could only give a tentative solution. This solution was based upon a principle which in early Greek thought was generally accepted and which appeared to be firmly established. All the different schools—the physiologists

3. See C. K. Ogden and I. A. Richards, *The Meaning of Meaning* (1923; 5th ed. New York, 1938).

as well as the dialecticians—started from the assumption that without an identity between the knowing subject and the reality known the fact of knowledge would be unaccountable. Idealism and realism, although differing in the application of this principle, agreed in acknowledging its truth. Parmenides declared that we cannot separate being and thought, for they are one and the same. The nature philosophers understood and interpreted this identity in a strictly material sense. If we analyze man's nature we find the same combination of elements as occurs everywhere in the physical world. The microcosm being an exact counterpart of the macrocosm makes knowledge of the latter possible. "For it is with earth," says Empedocles, "that we see Earth, and Water with water; by air we see bright Air, by fire destroying Fire. By love do we see Love, and Hate by grievous hate." [4]

Accepting this general theory, what is the "meaning of meaning"? First and foremost meaning must be explained in terms of being; for being, or substance, is the most universal category which links and binds together truth and reality. A word could not "mean" a thing if there were not at least a partial identity between the two. The connection between the symbol and its object must be a natural, not a merely conventional one. Without such a natural connection a word of human language could not accomplish its task; it would become unintelligible. If we admit this presupposition, which originates in a general theory of knowledge rather than in a theory of language, we are immediately faced with the onomatopoetic doctrine. This doctrine alone seems capable of bridging the gap between names and things. On the other hand our bridge threatens to break down at our first attempt to use it. For Plato it was sufficient to develop the onomatopoetic thesis in all its consequences in order to refute it. In the Platonic dialogue Kratylus Socrates accepts the thesis in his ironical way. But his approval is only intended to destroy it by its own inherent absurdity. Plato's account of the theory that all language originated in sound imitation ends in a trav-

4. Empedocles, Fragment 335. See John Burnet, Early Greek Philosophy (London and Edinburgh, A. & C. Black, 1892), Bk. II, p. 232.

esty and caricature. Nevertheless the onomatopoetic thesis prevailed for many centuries. Even in recent literature it is by no means obliterated, though it no longer appears in the same naïve forms as in Plato's *Kratylus*.

The obvious objection to this thesis is the fact that when analyzing the words of common speech we are in most cases completely at a loss to discover the pretended similarity between sounds and objects. This difficulty could, however, be removed by pointing out that human language has from the first been subject to change and decay. Hence we cannot content ourselves with its present state. We must trace our terms back to their origins if we are to detect the bond uniting them with their objects. From derivative words we must go back to primary words; we must discover the etymon, the true and original form, of every term. According to this principle etymology became not only the center of linguistics but also one of the keystones of the philosophy of language. And the first etymologies used by Greek grammarians and philosophers suffered from no theoretical or historical scruples. No etymology based upon scientific principles appeared before the first half of the nineteenth century.[5] Up to this time everything was possible, and the most fantastic and bizarre explanations were readily admitted. Besides the positive etymologies there were the famous negative ones of the type *lucus a non lucendo*. As long as these schemes held the field the theory of a natural relation between names and things appeared to be philosophically justifiable and defensible.

But there were other general considerations which from the first militated against this theory. The Greek Sophists were in a sense the disciples of Heraclitus. In his dialogue *Theaetetus* Plato went so far as to say that the sophistic theory of knowledge had no claim to originality. He declared it to be an outgrowth and corollary of the Heraclitian doctrine of the "flux of all things." Yet there was an ineradicable difference between Heraclitus and the Sophists. To the former the word, the Logos, was a universal metaphysical principle. It possessed general truth, objective validity. But the Sophists

5. Cf. A. F. Pott, *Etymologische Forschungen aus dem Gebiete der indogermanischen Sprachen* (1833 ff.).

no longer admit that "divine word" which Heraclitus held to be the origin and first principle of all things, of the cosmic and moral order. Anthropology, not metaphysics, plays the leading role in the theory of language. Man has become the center of the universe. According to the dictum of Protagoras, "man is the measure of all things, of those which are, that they are—and of those which are not, that they are not." To look for any explanation of language in the world of physical things is, therefore, vain and useless. The Sophists had found a new and much simpler approach to human speech. They were the first to treat linguistic and grammatical problems in a systematic way. Yet they were not concerned with these problems in a merely theoretical sense. A theory of language has other and more urgent tasks to accomplish. It has to teach us how to speak and to act in our actual social and political world. In Athenian life of the fifth century language had become an instrument for definite, concrete, practical purposes. It was the most powerful weapon in the great political struggles. Nobody could hope to play a leading role without this instrument. It was of vital importance to use it in the right way and constantly to improve and sharpen it. To this end the Sophists created a new branch of knowledge. Rhetoric, not grammar or etymology, became their chief concern. In their definition of wisdom (*sophia*) rhetoric maintains a central position. All the disputes about the "truth" or "correctness" (*orthotês*) of terms and names became futile and superfluous. Names are not intended to express the nature of things. They have no objective correlates. Their real task is not to describe things but to arouse human emotions; not to convey mere ideas or thoughts but to prompt men to certain actions.

So far we have arrived at a threefold conception of the function and value of language: a mythological, a metaphysical, and a pragmatic one. But all these accounts appear in a sense beside the mark, for they all fail to note one of the most conspicuous features of language. The most elementary human utterances do not refer to physical things nor are they merely arbitrary signs. The alternative *physei on* or *thesei on* does not apply to them. They are "natural," not "artificial"; but they bear no relation to the nature of external objects.

They do not depend upon mere convention, upon custom or habit; they are much more deeply rooted. They are involuntary expressions of human feelings, interjections and ejaculations. It was not an accident that this interjectional theory was introduced by a natural scientist, the greatest scientist among the Greek thinkers. Democritus was the first to propound the thesis that human speech originates in certain sounds of a merely emotional character. Later on the same view was upheld by Epicurus and Lucretius on the authority of Democritus. It had a permanent influence on language theory. As late as the eighteenth century it still appears in almost the same shape in thinkers like Vico or Rousseau. From the scientific point of view it is easy to understand the great advantages of this interjectional thesis. Here, it seems, we no longer need to rely on speculation alone. We have uncovered some verifiable facts, and these facts are not restricted to the human sphere. Human speech can be reduced to a fundamental instinct implanted by nature in all living creatures. Violent outcries—of fear, of rage, of pain or joy—are not a specific property of man. We find them everywhere in the animal world. Nothing was more plausible than to trace the social fact of speech back to this general biological cause. If we accept the thesis of Democritus and his pupils and followers, semantics ceases to be a separate province; it becomes a branch of biology and physiology.

And yet the interjectional theory could not reach maturity until biology itself had found a new scientific basis. It was not enough to connect human speech with certain biological facts. The connection had to be grounded in a universal principle. Such a principle was provided by the theory of evolution. When Darwin's book appeared it was hailed with the greatest enthusiasm not merely by scientists and philosophers but also by linguists. August Schleicher, whose first writings show him to have been an adherent and pupil of Hegel, became a convert to Darwin.[6] Darwin himself had treated his subject strictly from the point of view of a naturalist. Yet his general method was easily applicable to linguistic phenomena, and

6. See August Schleicher, Die Darwin'sche Theorie und die Sprachwissenschaft (Weimar, 1873).

even in this field he seemed to open up an unexplored path. In *The Expression of the Emotions in Man and Animals* Darwin had shown that expressive sounds or acts are dictated by certain biological needs and used according to definite biological rules. Approached from this angle the old riddle of the origin of language could be treated in a strictly empirical and scientific manner. Human language ceased being "a state within the state" and became herewith a general natural gift.

There remained, however, a fundamental difficulty. The creators of the biological theories of the origin of language failed to see the wood for trees. They set out with the assumption that a direct path leads from interjection to speech. But this is to beg the question, not to solve it. It was not the mere fact but the structure of human speech which called for an explanation. An analysis of this structure discloses a radical difference between emotional and propositional language. The two types are not on the same level. Even if it were possible to connect them genetically, the passage from one type to the opposite must always remain logically a *metabasis eis allo genos*, a transition from one genus to another. So far as I can see, no biological theory ever succeeded in obliterating this logical and structural distinction. We have no psychological evidence whatever for the fact that any animal ever crossed the borderline separating propositional from emotional language. The so-called "animal language" always remains entirely subjective; it expresses various states of feeling but it does not designate or describe objects.[7] On the other hand there is no historical evidence that man, even in the lowest stages of his culture, ever was reduced to a merely emotional language or to the language of gestures. If we wish to pursue a strictly empirical method, we must exclude any such assumption as, if not quite improbable, at least dubious and hypothetical.

As a matter of fact a closer examination of these theories always brings us to a point where the very principle on which they rest becomes questionable. After a few steps in this argu-

7. See the views of W. Koehler and G. Révész quoted above, Chap. 3, p. 48.

ment the defenders of these theories are forced to admit
and to stress the same difference which they at first sight
seemed to deny or at least to minimize. To illustrate this
fact I shall choose two concrete examples, the first taken from
linguistics, the second from psychological and philosophical
literature. Otto Jespersen was perhaps the last modern linguist
to retain a keen interest in the old problem of the origin of
language. He did not deny that all the former solutions of
the problem had been very indequate; in fact he was convinced that he had discovered a new method which held forth
promise of better success. "The method I recommend," states
Jespersen, "and which I am the first to employ consistently is
to trace our modern languages as far back in time as history
and our materials will allow us. . . . If by this process we arrive finally at uttered sounds of such a description that they
can no longer be called a real language, but something antecedent to language—why then the problem will have been
solved; for transformation is something we can understand,
while a creation out of nothing never can be comprehended
by the human understanding." According to this theory such
a transformation took place when human utterances, which at
first were nothing but emotional cries or perhaps musical
phrases, were used as names. What originally had been a jum-
ble of meaningless sounds became in this manner suddenly
an instrument of thought. For instance, a combination of
sounds sung to a certain melody and employed in a chant of
triumph over a defeated and slain foe could be changed into
a proper name for that peculiar event or even for the man
who slew the enemy. And the development could now proceed by a metaphorical transference of the expression to
similar situations.[8] It is, however, precisely this "metaphorical
transference" which contains our whole problem in a nutshell.
Such a transference means that sound utterances, which
hitherto had been mere outcries, involuntary discharges of
strong emotions, were performing an entirely new task. They
were being used as symbols conveying a definite meaning.

8. This theory was first propounded by Jespersen in *Progress in Language* (London, 1894). See also his *Language, Its Nature, Development and Origin* (London and New York, 1922), pp. 418, 437 ff.

Jespersen himself quotes an observation by Benfey that between interjection and word there is a chasm wide enough to allow us to say that the interjection is the negation of language; for interjections are employed only when one either cannot or will not speak. According to Jespersen language arose when "communicativeness took precedence of exclamativeness." This very step, however, is not accounted for but presupposed by this theory.

The same criticism holds for the thesis developed in Grace de Laguna's book, *Speech. Its Function and Development.* Here we find a much more detailed and elaborate statement of the problem. The rather fantastic concepts which we sometimes find in Jespersen's book are eliminated. The transition from cry to speech is described as a process of gradual objectification. The primitive affective qualities attaching to the situation as a whole become diversified and at the same time distinguished from the perceived features of the situation. ". . . *objects* emerge, which are cognized rather than felt. . . . At the same time, this increased conditionality takes on systematic form . . . Finally, . . . the objective order of reality appears and the world becomes truly known." [9] This objectification and systematization is, indeed, the principal and most important task of human language. But I fail to see how a merely interjectional theory can account for this decisive step. And in Professor de Laguna's account the gap between interjections and names has not been bridged; on the contrary here it stands out all the more sharply. It is a remarkable fact that those authors who, generally speaking, have been inclined to believe that speech has developed from a state of mere interjections have been led to the conclusion that, after all, the difference between interjections and names is much greater and much more conspicuous than their supposed identity. Gardiner, for example, begins with the statement that, between human and animal language, there is an "essential homogeneity." But in developing his theory he has to admit that between the animal utterance and human speech there is a difference so vital as almost to eclipse the essential ho-

9. Grace de Laguna, *Speech. Its Function and Development* (New Haven, Yale University Press, 1927), pp. 260 f.

mogeneity.[10] The seeming similarity is in fact only a material connection which does not exclude, but, on the contrary, accentuates the formal, the functional heterogeneity.

2   The question of the origin of language has, at all times, exerted a strange fascination upon the human mind. With the first glimmerings of his intellect man began to wonder about this matter. In many mythical tales we are informed how man learned to talk from God himself or with the assistance of a divine teacher. This interest in the origin of language is easily understandable if we accept the first premises of mythical thought. Myth knows of no other mode of explanation than to go back to the remote past and to derive the present state of the physical and human world from this primeval stage of things. It is, however, surprising and paradoxical to find the same tendency still prevailing in philosophical thought. Yet here for many centuries the systematic question was overshadowed by the genetic. It was thought to be a foregone conclusion that, the genetic question once solved, all the other problems would readily follow suit. From a general epistemological point of view, however, this was a gratuitous assumption. The theory of knowledge has taught us that we must always draw a sharp line of demarcation between genetic and systematic problems. Confusion of these two types is misleading and perilous. How is it that this methodological maxim, which in other branches of knowledge appeared to be firmly established, was forgotten when dealing with linguistic problems? It would of course be of the greatest interest and importance to be in possession of the full historical evidence regarding language—to be able to answer the question whether all the languages of the world derive from a common stem or from different and independent roots, and to be able to trace step by step the development of individual idioms and linguistic types. Yet all this would not suffice to solve the fundamental problems of a philosophy of language. In philosophy we cannot content ourselves with the mere flux of things and with the chronology of events. Here we must in a sense always

10. Alan H. Gardiner, *The Theory of Speech and Language* (Oxford, 1932), pp. 118 f.

accept the Platonic definition according to which philosophical knowledge is a knowledge of "being," not of mere "becoming." To be sure language has no being outside and beyond time; it does not belong to the realm of eternal ideas. Change—phonetic, analogic, semantic change—is an essential element of language. Nevertheless the study of all these phenomena is not enough to make us understand the general function of language. For the analysis of every symbolic form we are dependent on historical data. The question as to what myth, religion, art, language "are" cannot be answered in a purely abstract way, by a logical definition. On the other hand when studying religion, art, and language we always meet with general structural problems belonging to a different type of knowledge. These problems must be treated separately; they cannot be dealt with and they cannot be solved by merely historical investigations.

In the nineteenth century it was still a current and generally accepted opinion that history is the only clue to a scientific study of human speech. All the great achievements of linguistics came from scholars whose historical interest prevailed to such a degree as almost to preclude any other tendency of thought. Jakob Grimm laid the first foundation for a comparative grammar of the Germanic languages. The comparative grammar of the Indo-European language was inaugurated by Bopp and Pott, and perfected by A. Schleicher, Karl Brugmann, and B. Delbrück. The first to raise the question of the principles of linguistic history was Hermann Paul. He was fully aware of the fact that historical research alone cannot solve all the problems of human speech. He insisted that historical knowledge always stands in need of a systematic complement. To every branch of historical knowledge, he declared, there corresponds a science which deals with the general conditions under which the historical objects evolve and inquiries into those factors which remain invariable in all the changes of human phenomena.[11] The nineteenth century was not only a historical but also a psychological century. It was, therefore, quite natural to assume, it even appeared self-evi-

11. Hermann Paul, *Prinzipien der Sprachgeschichte* (Halle, 1880), chap. i. English trans. by H. A. Strong (London, 1889).

dent, that the principles of linguistic history were to be sought in the field of psychology. These were the two cornerstones of linguistic studies. "Paul and most of his contemporaries," says Leonard Bloomfield, "dealt only with Indo-European languages and, what with their neglect of descriptive problems, refused to work with languages whose history was unknown. This limitation cut them off from a knowledge of foreign types of grammatical structure, which would have opened their eyes to the fact that even the fundamental features of Indo-European grammar . . . are by no means universal in human speech. . . . Alongside the great stream of historical research, there ran, however, a small but accelerating current of general linguistic study. . . . Some students saw more and more clearly the natural relation between descriptive and historical studies. . . . The merging of these two streams of study, the historical-comparative and the philosophical-descriptive, has made clear some principles that were not apparent to the great Indo-Europeanists of the nineteenth century . . . All historical study of language is based upon the comparison of two or more sets of descriptive data. It can be only as accurate and only as complete as these data permit it to be. In order to describe a language one needs no historical knowledge whatever; in fact, the observer who allows such knowledge to affect his description, is bound to distort his data. Our descriptions must be unprejudiced, if they are to give a sound basis for comparative work." [12]

This methodological principle had found its first and in a sense its classical expression in the work of a great linguist and a great philosophical thinker. Wilhelm von Humboldt took the first step toward classifying the languages of the world and reducing them to certain fundamental types. For this purpose he could not employ purely historical methods. The languages he studied were no longer solely the Indo-European types. His interest was truly comprehensive; it included the whole field of linguistic phenomena. He gave the first analytical description of the aboriginal American languages, utilizing the wealth of material which his brother, Alexander von Humboldt, had

12. Bloomfield, *Language* (New York, Holt & Co., 1933), pp. 17 ff.

brought back from his exploratory travels on the American continent. In the second volume of his great work on the varieties of human speech[13] W. von Humboldt wrote the first comparative grammar of the Austronesian languages, the Indonesian and Melanesian. Yet for this grammar no historical data were available, the history of these languages being completely unknown. Humboldt had to approach the problem from an entirely new angle and to pave his own way.

Yet his methods remained strictly empirical; they were based on observations, not on speculation. But Humboldt was not content with the description of particular facts. He immediately drew from his facts very far-reaching general inferences. It is impossible, he maintained, to gain a true insight into the character and function of human speech so long as we think of it as a mere collection of "words." The real difference between languages is not a difference of sounds or signs but one of "world-perspectives" (*Weltansichten*). A language is not simply a mechanical aggregate of terms. Splitting it up into words or terms means disorganizing and disintegrating it. Such a conception is detrimental, if not disastrous, to any study of linguistic phenomena. The words and rules which according to our ordinary notions make up a language, Humboldt asserted, really exist only in the act of connected speech. To treat them as separate entities is "nothing but a dead product of our bungling scientific analysis." Language must be looked upon as an *energeia* rather than as an *ergon*. It is not a ready-made thing but a continuous process; it is the ever-repeated labor of the human mind to utilize articulated sounds to express thought.[14]

Humboldt's work was more than a notable advance in linguistic thought. It marked also a new epoch in the history of the philosophy of language. Humboldt was neither a scholar who specialized in particular linguistic phenomena nor a metaphysician like Schelling or Hegel. He followed the "criti-

13. Berlin (1836–39). See Humboldt's *Gesammelte Schriften* (Berlin Academy), Vol. VII, Pt. I.

14. Humboldt, op. cit., pp. 46 f. A more detailed account of Humboldt's theory is given in my *Philosophie der symbolischen Formen*, I, 98 ff.

cal" method of Kant, not indulging in speculation as to the essence or the origin of language. The latter problem is never even mentioned in his work. It was the structural problems of language which came to the fore in his book. That these problems cannot be solved by merely historical methods is now generally admitted. Scholars of different schools and working in different fields are unanimous in stressing the fact that descriptive linguistics can never be rendered superfluous by historical linguistics, because the latter must always be based on the description of those stages of the development of language which are directly accessible to us.[15] From the point of view of the general history of ideas it is a very interesting and remarkable fact that linguistics, in this respect, underwent the same change as we find in other branches of knowledge. The former positivism was superseded by a new principle which we may call structuralism. Classical physics was convinced that, in order to discover the general laws of motion, we must always begin with the study of the movements of "material points." Lagrange's *Mécanique analytique* was based on this principle. Later on the laws of the electromagnetic field, as discovered by Faraday and Maxwell, tended to the opposite conclusion. It became clear that the electromagnetic field could not be split up into individual points. An electron was no longer regarded as an independent entity with an existence of its own; it was defined as a limit-point in the field as a whole. Thus arose a new type of "field physics" which in many respects diverged from the former conception of classical mechanics. In biology we find an analogous development. The new holistic theories, which have become prevalent since the beginning of the twentieth century, have gone back to the old Aristotelian definition of the organism. They have insisted that in the organic world "the whole is prior to the part." These theories do not deny the facts of evolution but they can no longer interpret them in the same sense as did Darwin and the orthodox Darwinians.[16] As for

15. See for instance Jespersen, *The Philosophy of Grammar* (New York, Holt & Co., 1924), pp. 30 f.
16. See J. B. S. Haldane, *The Causes of Evolution* (New York and London, 1932).

psychology, it had followed with a few exceptions the Humian way throughout the nineteenth century. The only method to account for a psychical phenomenon was to reduce it to its first elements. All complex facts were thought to be an accumulation, an aggregate of simple sense data. Modern Gestalt psychology has criticized and destroyed this conception; it has thus paved the way to a new type of structural psychology.

If linguistics now adopts the same method and concentrates more and more on structural problems, this does not of course mean that former views have lost anything in importance and interest. Yet instead of moving in a straight line, instead of being exclusively concerned with the chronological order of the phenomena of speech, linguistic research is describing an elliptical line having two different focal points. Some scholars went so far as to say that the combination of descriptive and historical views which was the distinctive mark of linguistics throughout the nineteenth century was, from a methodological viewpoint, a mistake. Ferdinand de Saussure declared in his lectures that the whole idea of a "historical grammar" would have to be given up. Historical grammar, he maintained, is a hybrid concept. It contains two disparate elements which cannot be reduced to a common denominator and fused into an organic whole. According to de Saussure the study of human speech is not the subject matter of *one* science but of two sciences. In such a study we always have to distinguish between two different axes, the "axis of simultaneity" and the "axis of succession." Grammar by its nature and essence belongs to the former type. De Saussure drew a sharp line between *la langue* and *la parole*. Language (*la langue*) is universal, whereas the process of speech (*la parole*), as a temporal process, is individual. Every individual has his own way of speaking. But in a scientific analysis of language we are not concerned with these individual differences; we are studying a social fact which follows general rules—rules quite independent of the individual speaker. Without such rules language could not accomplish its principal task; it could not be employed as a means of communication between all the members of the speaking community. "Synchronical" linguistics deals with constant structural relations; "diachronical" linguistics deals with phenomena varying and developing in time.[17] The fundamental structural unity of language may be studied and tested in two ways. This unity appears both on the material and on the formal side, manifesting itself not only in the system of grammatical forms but also in its sound system. The character of a language depends on both factors. But the structural problems of phonology were a much later discovery than those of syntax or morphology. That there is an order and consistency in the forms of speech is obvious and indubitable. The classification of these forms and their reduction to definite rules became one of the first tasks of a scientific grammar. At a very early period the methods for this study were brought to a high degree of perfection. Modern linguists still allude to Panini's Sanskrit grammar, which dates from sometime between 350 and 250 B.C., as one of the greatest monuments of human intelligence. They insist that no other language to this day has been so perfectly described. The Greek grammarians made a careful analysis of the parts of speech which they found in the Greek language, and they were interested in all sorts of syntactical and stylistic matters. The material aspect of the problem, however, was unknown, and its importance remained unrecognized up to the beginning of the nineteenth century. Here we find the first attempts to deal with the phenomena of sound change in a scientific way. Modern historical linguistics began with an investigation of uniform phonetic correspondences. In 1818 R. K. Rask showed that the words of the Germanic languages bear a regular formal relation in matters of sound to the words of other Indo-European languages. In his German grammar Jakob Grimm gave a systematic exposition of the correspondences of consonants between the Germanic and other Indo-European languages. These first observations became the basis of modern linguistics and comparative grammar. But they were understood and interpreted in a merely historical sense. It was from a romantic love of the past that Jakob Grimm received his first and most profound inspiration. The same ro-

17. See Ferdinand de Saussure's lectures published posthumously under the title, Cours de linguistique générale (1915; 2d ed. Paris, 1922).

mantic spirit led Friedrich Schlegel to his discovery of the language and wisdom of India.[18] In the second half of the nineteenth century, however, the interest in linguistic studies was dictated by other intellectual impulses, and a materialistic interpretation began to predominate. The great ambition of the so-called "New Grammarians" was to prove that the methods of linguistics were on a level with those of the natural sciences. If linguistics was to be regarded as an exact science it could not be content with vague empirical rules describing particular historical occurrences. It would have to discover laws which in their logical form were comparable to the general laws of nature. The phenomena of phonetic change appeared to prove the existence of such laws. The New Grammarians denied that there was such a thing as a sporadic sound change. Every phonetic change according to them follows inviolable rules. Hence the task of linguistics is to trace back all the phenomena of human speech to this fundamental stratum: the phonetic laws which are necessary and admit to no exceptions.[19]

Modern structuralism, as developed in the works of Trubetzkoy and in the *Travaux du Cercle Linguistique de Prague*, approached the problem from a quite different angle. It did not give up hope of finding a "necessity" in the phenomena of human speech; on the contrary, it emphasized this necessity. But for structuralism the very concept of necessity had to be redefined, and understood rather in a teleological than in a merely causal sense. Language is not simply an aggregate of sounds and words; it is a system. On the other hand its systematic order cannot be described in terms of physical or historical causality. Every individual idiom has a structure of its own both in a formal and in a material sense. If we examine the phonemes of different languages we find divergent types which cannot be subsumed under a uniform and rigid scheme. In the choice of these phonemes different languages exhibit their own peculiar characteristics. Neverthe-

18. *Über die Sprache und Weisheit der Inder* (1808).

19. This program, for instance, was developed by H. Osthoff and K. Brugmann in *Morphologische Untersuchungen* (Leipzig, 1878). For details see Bloomfield, *op cit.*, chaps. i, xx, xxi.

less a strict connection can always be shown to exist among the phonemes of a given language. This connection is relative, not absolute; it is hypothetical, not apodictic. We cannot deduce it a priori from general logical rules; we have to rely on our empirical data. Yet even these data show an inner coherence. Once we have found some fundamental data we are in a position to derive from them other data which are invariably connected with them. "Il faudrait étudier," writes V. Bröndal, formulating the program of this new structuralism, "les conditions de la structure linguistique, distinguer dans les systèmes phonologiques et morphologiques ce qui est possible de ce qui est impossible, le contingent du nécessaire." [20]

If we accept this view, even the material basis of human speech, even the sound phenomena themselves, must be studied in a new way and under a different aspect. As a matter of fact we can no longer admit that there is a merely material basis. The distinction between form and matter proves artificial and inadequate. Speech is an indissoluble unity which cannot be divided into the two independent and isolated factors, form and matter. It is in just this principle that the difference lies between the new phonology and former types of phonetics. What we study in phonology are not physical but significant sounds. Linguistics is not interested in the nature of sounds but in their semantic function. The positivistic schools of the nineteenth century were convinced that phonetics and semantics required separate study according to different methods. The speech-sounds were regarded as mere physical phenomena which could be described, indeed had to be described, in terms of physics or physiology. From the general methodological point of view of the New Grammarians such a conception was not only understandable but

20. V. Bröndal, "Structure et variabilité des système morphologiques," Scientia (Août, 1935), p. 119. For a detailed account of the problems and methods of modern linguistic structuralism see the articles published in Travaux du Cercle Linguistique de Prague (1929 ff.); especially H. F. Pos, "Perspectives du structuralisme," Travaux (1929), pp. 71 ff. A general survey of the history of structuralism has been given by Roman Jakobson, "La Scuola Linguistica di Praga," La cultura (Anno XII), pp. 633 ff.

necessary. For their fundamental thesis—the thesis that phonetic laws admit of no exception—was based upon the assumption that phonetic change is independent of nonphonetic factors. Since sound change is nothing but a change in the habit of articulation—it was thought—it must affect a phoneme at every occurrence regardless of the nature of any particular linguistic form in which the phoneme happens to occur. This dualism has disappeared from recent linguistics. Phonetics is no longer a separate field but has now become part and parcel of semantics itself. For the phoneme is not a physical unit but a unit of meaning. It has been defined as a "minimum-unit of distinctive sound-feature." Among the gross acoustic features of any utterance there are certain features which are significant; for these are used to express differences of meaning whereas others are nondistinctive. Every language has its system of phonemes, of distinctive sounds. In Chinese the change in the pitch of a sound is one of the most important means of changing the meaning of words, whereas in other languages such a change is without significance.[21] From the indefinite multitude of possible physical sounds every language selects a limited number of sounds as its phonemes. But the selection is not made at random, for the phonemes make up a coherent whole. They can be reduced to general types, to certain phonetic patterns.[22] These phonetic patterns seem to be among the most persistent and characteristic features of language. Sapir emphasizes the fact that every language has a strong tendency to keep its phonetic pattern intact: "We shall ascribe the major concordances and divergences in linguistic form—phonetic pattern and morphology—to the autonomous drift of language, not to the complicating effect of single, diffused features that cluster now this way, now that. Language is probably the most self-contained, the most massively

21. Among the languages of the Indo-European family Swedish is, so far as I know, the only one in which the pitch of a tone or the accent has a definite semantic function. In some Swedish words the meaning may be completely changed by the acuteness or graveness of the sound.

22. For details see Bloomfield, op. cit., especially chaps. v. and vi.

resistant of all social phenomena. It is easier to kill it off than to disintegrate its individual form." [23]

It is, however, very difficult to answer the question as to what this "individual form" of a language really means. When confronted with this question we are always on the horns of a dilemma. We have two extremes to avoid, two radical solutions, which are both in a sense inadequate. If the thesis that every language has its individual form were to imply that it is needless to look for any common features in human speech, we should have to admit that the mere thought of a philosophy of language is a castle in the air. But what is open to objection from an empirical point of view is not so much the existence as the clear statement of these common features. In Greek philosophy the very term "Logos" always suggested and supported the idea of a fundamental identity between the act of speech and the act of thought. Grammar and logic were conceived as two different branches of knowledge with the same subject matter. Even modern logicians whose systems have greatly deviated from the classical Aristotelian logic have still been of the same opinion. John Stuart Mill, the founder of an "inductive logic," asserted that grammar is the most elementary part of logic because it is the beginning of the analysis of the thinking process. According to Mill the principles and rules of grammar are the means by which the forms of language are made to correspond with the universal forms of thought. But Mill was not content with this statement. He even assumed that a particular part-of-speech system—a system which had been deduced from Latin and Greek grammar

23. Sapir, *Language*, p. 220. For the difference between "phonetics" and "phonology" see Trubetzkoy, "La phonologie actuelle," in *Journal de psychologie* (Paris, 1933), Vol. XXX. According to Trubetzkoy it is the task of phonetics to study the material factors of the sounds of human speech, the vibrations of the air, corresponding to different sounds or sound-producing movements of the speaker. Phonology, instead of studying the physical sounds, studies the "phonemes," that is to say, the constitutive elements of linguistic meaning. From the viewpoint of phonology the sound is only "the material symbol of the phoneme." The phoneme itself is "immaterial" since meaning is not describable in terms of physics or physiology.

—had a general and objective validity. The distinctions between the various parts of speech, between the cases of nouns, the modes and tenses of verbs, and the functions of participles, were believed by Mill to be distinctions in thought and not merely in words. "The structure of every sentence," he declares, "is a lesson in logic." [24] The advancement of linguistic research made this position more and more untenable. For it came generally to be recognized that the system of the parts of speech is not of a fixed and uniform character but varies from one language to another. It was observed, moreover, that there are many features even of those languages which are derived from the Latin which cannot be adequately expressed in the usual terms and categories of Latin grammar. Students of French often stressed the fact that French grammar would have assumed a quite different shape if it had not been written by the disciples of Aristotle. They maintained that the application of the distinctions of Latin grammar to English or French had resulted in many grave errors and had proved to be a serious obstacle to the unprejudiced description of linguistic phenomena.[25] Many grammatical distinctions which we think fundamental and necessary lose their value or at least become very uncertain as soon as we examine languages other than those of the Indo-European family. That there must exist a definite and unique system of the parts of speech, which is to be regarded as a necessary constituent of rational speech and thought, has turned out to be an illusion.[26]

All this does not necessarily prove that we must give up the old concept of a *grammaire générale et raisonnée*, a general grammar based on rational principles. But we must redefine this concept and we must formulate it in a new sense. To stretch all languages upon the Procrustean bed of a single system of the parts of speech would be a vain attempt. Many modern linguists have gone so far as to warn us against the

24. The following paragraph is based on my article, "The Influence of Language upon the Development of Scientific Thought," *Journal of Philosophy*, XXXIX, No. 12 (June, 1942), 309-327.

25. See F. Brunot, *La pensée et la langue* (Paris, 1922).

26. For more details see Bloomfield, *op. cit.*, pp. 6 ff., and Sapir, *op. cit.*, pp. 124 ff.

very term "general grammar," thinking that it represents rather an idol than a scientific ideal.[27] Such an uncompromisingly radical attitude has not, however, been shared by all students of the field. Serious efforts have been made to maintain and defend the conception of a philosophical grammar. Otto Jespersen wrote a book especially devoted to the philosophy of grammar in which he tried to prove that, beside or above or behind the syntactic categories which depend on the structure of each language as it is actually found, there are some categories which are independent of the more or less accidental facts of existing languages. They are universal in that they are applicable to all languages. Jespersen proposed calling these categories "notional," and he considered it the grammarian's task in each case to investigate the relation between the notional and the syntactic categories. The same view has been expressed by other scholars, as, for instance, Hjelmstev and Bröndal.[28] According to Sapir every language contains certain necessary and indispensable categories side by side with others that are of a more accidental character.[29] The idea of a general or philosophical grammar is, therefore, by no means invalidated by the progress of linguistic research, although we can no longer hope to realize such a grammar by the simple means that were employed in former attempts. Human speech has to fulfil not only a universal logical task but also a social task which depends on the specific social conditions of the speaking community. Hence we cannot expect a real identity, a one-to-one correspondence between grammatical and logical forms. An empirical and descriptive analysis of grammatical forms sets itself a different task and leads to other results than that structural analysis which, for instance, is given in Carnap's work on the *Logical Syntax of Language*.

3   In order to find a clue of Ariadne to guide us through the complicated and baffling labyrinth of human speech we

27. See, for instance, Vendryès, *Le langage* (Paris, 1922), p. 193.
28. See Hjelmstev, *Principes de grammaire générale* (Copenhagen, 1928), Bröndal, *Ordklassarne*. (Résumé: *Les parties du discours, partes orationis*, Copenhagen, 1928.)
29. Sapir, *op. cit.*, pp. 124 ff.

may proceed in a twofold manner. We may attempt to find a logical and systematic or a chronological and genetic order. In the second case we try to trace the individual idioms and the various linguistic types back to a former comparatively simple and amorphous stage. Attempts of this sort were often made by linguists of the nineteenth century when the opinion became current that human speech, before it could attain its present form, had had to pass through a state in which there were no definite syntactical or morphological forms. Languages at first consisted of simple elements, of monosyllabic roots. Romanticism favored this view. A. W. Schlegel propounded a theory according to which language developed from a former unorganized amorphous state. From this state it passed in a fixed order to other, more advanced stages—to an isolating, an agglutinating, a flexional stage. The flexional languages are according to Schlegel the last step in this evolution; they are the really organic languages. A thorough descriptive analysis has in most cases destroyed the evidence on which these theories were based. In the case of Chinese, which was usually cited as an example of a language consisting of monosyllabic roots, it could be made to appear probable that its present isolating stage was preceded by a former flexional stage.[30] We know of no language devoid of formal or structural elements, although the expression of formal relations, such as the difference between subject and object, between attribute and predicate, varies widely from language to language. Without form language has the appearance of being not merely a highly questionable historical construct but a contradiction in terms. The languages of the most uncivilized nations are by no means formless; on the contrary they exhibit in most cases a very complicated structure. A. Meillet, a modern linguist who possessed a most comprehensive knowledge of the languages of the world, declared that no known idiom gives us the slightest idea of what primitive language may have been. All forms of human speech are perfect in so far as they succeed in expressing human feelings and thoughts in a clear and appropriate manner. The so-called primitive languages are

30. See B. Karlgren, "Le Proto-Chinois, langue flexionelle," *Journal asiatique* (1902).

as much in congruity with the conditions of primitive civilization and with the general tendency of the primitive mind as our own languages are with the ends of our refined and sophisticated culture. In the languages of the Bantu family, for instance, every substantive belongs to a definite class, and every such class is characterized by its special prefix. These prefixes do not appear only in the nouns themselves but have to be repeated, in accordance with a very complicated system of concords and congruences, in all other parts of the sentence which refer to the noun.[31]

The variety of individual idioms and the heterogeneity of linguistic types appear in a quite different light depending on whether they are looked at from a philosophical or from a scientific viewpoint. The linguist rejoices in this variety; he plunges into the ocean of human speech without hoping to sound its real depth. In all ages philosophy has moved in the opposite direction. Leibniz insisted that without a *Characteristica generalis* we shall never find a *Scientia generalis*. Modern symbolic logic follows the same tendency. But even if this task were accomplished, a philosophy of human culture would still have to face the same problem. In an analysis of human culture we must accept the facts in their concrete shape, in all their diversity and divergence. The philosophy of language is here confronted with the same dilemma as appears in the study of every symbolic form. The highest, indeed the only, task of all these forms is to unite men. But none of them can bring about this unity without at the same time dividing and separating men. Thus what was intended to secure the harmony of culture becomes the source of the deepest discords and dissensions. This is the great antinomy, the dialectic of the religious life.[32] The same dialectic appears in human speech. Without speech there would be no community of men. Yet there is no more serious obstacle to such community than the diversity of speech. Myth and religion refuse to regard this diversity as a necessary and unavoidable fact. They attribute it rather to a fault or guilt of man than to his original

31. For further details see C. Meinhof, *Grundzüge einer vergleichenden Grammatik der Bantu-Sprachen* (Berlin, 1906).
32. See above, Chap. 7, p. 99.

constitution and the nature of things. In many mythologies we find striking analogies to the Biblical tale of the Tower of Babel. Even in modern times, man has always retained a deep longing for that Golden Age in which mankind was still in possession of a uniform language. He looks back at his primeval state as at a lost paradise. Nor did the old dream of a *lingua Adamica*—of the "real" language of the first ancestors of man, a language which did not consist merely of conventional signs but which expressed rather the very nature and essence of things—vanish completely even in the realm of philosophy. The problem of this *lingua Adamica* continued to be seriously discussed by the philosophical thinkers and mystics of the seventeenth century.[33]

Yet the true unity of language, if there is such a unity, cannot be a substantial one; it must rather be defined as a functional unity. Such a unity does not presuppose a material or formal identity. Two different languages may represent opposite extremes both with respect to their phonetic systems and to their parts-of-speech systems. This does not prevent them from accomplishing the same task in the life of the speaking community. The important thing here is not the variety of means but their fitness for and congruity with the end. We may think that this common end is attained more perfectly in one linguistic type than in another. Even Humboldt, who, generally speaking, was loath to pass judgment on the value of particular idioms, still regarded the flexional languages as a sort of paragon and model of excellence. To him the flexional form was *die einzig gesetzmässige Form,* the only form which is entirely consistent and follows strict rules.[34] Modern linguists have warned us against such judgments. They tell us that we have no common and unique standard for estimating the value of linguistic types. In comparing types it may appear that the one has definite advantages over the other, but a closer analysis usually convinces us that what we term the defects of a certain type may be compensated and

33. See, for instance, Leibniz, *Nouveaux essais sur l'entendement humain,* Bk. III, chap. ii.

34. Humboldt, *op. cit.,* VII, Pt. II, 162.

counterbalanced by other merits. If we wish to understand language, declares Sapir, we must disabuse our minds of preferred values and accustom ourselves to look upon English and Hottentot with the same cool yet interested detachment.[35]

If it were the task of human speech to copy or imitate the given or ready-made order of things we could scarcely maintain any such detachment. We could not avoid the conclusion that, after all, one of two different copies must be the better; that the one must be nearer to, the other farther from, the original. Yet if we ascribe to speech a productive and constructive rather than a merely reproductive function, we shall judge quite differently. In this case it is not the "work" of language but its "energy" which is of paramount importance. In order to measure this energy one must study the linguistic process itself instead of simply analyzing its outcome, its product, and final results.

Psychologists are unanimous in emphasizing that without insight into the true nature of human speech our knowledge of the development of the human mind would remain perfunctory and inadequate. There is, however, still considerable uncertainty as to the methods of a psychology of speech. Whether we study the phenomena in a psychological or phonetic laboratory or rely on merely introspective methods we invariably derive the same impression that these phenomena are so evanescent and fluctuating that they defy all efforts at stabilization. In what, then, consists that fundamental difference between the mental attitude which we may ascribe to a speechless creature—a human being before the acquisition of speech or an animal—and that other frame of mind which characterizes an adult who has fully mastered his mother tongue?

Curiously enough it is easier to answer this question on the basis of abnormal instances of speech development. Our consideration of the cases of Helen Keller and Laura Bridgman[36] illustrated the fact that with the first understanding of the

35. Sapir, op. cit., p. 130.
36. See above, Chap. 3, pp. 53–59.

symbolism of speech a real revolution takes place in the life of the child. From this point on his whole personal and intellectual life assumes an entirely new shape. Roughly speaking, this change may be described by saying that the child passes from a more subjective state to an objective state, from a merely emotional attitude to a theoretical attitude. The same change may be noted in the life of every normal child, though in a much less spectacular way. The child himself has a clear sense of the significance of the new instrument for his mental development. He is not satisfied with being taught in a purely receptive manner but takes an active share in the process of speech which is at the same time a process of progressive objectification. The teachers of Helen Keller and Laura Bridgman have told us with what eagerness and impatience both children, once they had understood the use of names, continued to ask for the particular names of all the objects in their environment.[37] This, too, is a general feature in the normal development of speech. "By the beginning of the twenty-third month," says D. R. Major, "the child had developed a mania for going about naming things, as if to tell others their names, or to call our attention to the things he was examining. He would look at, point toward, or put his hand on an article, speak its name, then look at his companions." [38] Such an attitude would not be understandable were it not for the fact that the name, in the mental growth of the child, has a function of the first importance to perform. If a child when learning to talk had simply to learn a certain vocabulary, if he only had to impress on his mind and memory a great mass of artificial and arbitrary sounds, this would be a purely mechanical process. It would be very laborious and tiresome, and would require too great conscious effort for the child to make without a certain reluctance since what he is expected to do would be entirely disconnected from actual biological needs. The "hunger for names" which at a certain age appears in every normal child and which has been described by all stu-

37. See above, Chap. 3, pp. 54–55.
38. David R. Major, *First Steps in Mental Growth* (New York, Macmillan, 1906), pp. 321 f.

dents of child psychology [39] proves the contrary. It reminds us that we are here confronted with a quite different problem. By learning to name things a child does not simply add a list of artificial signs to his previous knowledge of ready-made empirical objects. He learns rather to form the concepts of those objects, to come to terms with the objective world. Henceforth the child stands on firmer ground. His vague, uncertain, fluctuating perceptions and his dim feelings begin to assume a new shape. They may be said to crystallize around the name as a fixed center, a focus of thought. Without the help of the name every new advance made in the process of objectification would always run the risk of being lost again in the next moment. The first names of which a child makes conscious use may be compared to a stick by the aid of which a blind man gropes his way. And language, taken as a whole, becomes the gateway to a new world. All progress here opens a new perspective and widens and enriches our concrete experience. Eagerness and enthusiasm to talk do not originate in a mere desire for learning or using names; they mark the desire for the detection and conquest of an objective world.[40]

We can still when learning a foreign language subject ourselves to an experience similar to that of the child. Here it is not sufficient to acquire a new vocabulary or to acquaint ourselves with a system of abstract grammatical rules. All this is necessary but it is only the first and less important step. If we do not learn to think in the new language all our efforts remain fruitless. In most cases we find it extremely difficult to fulfil this requirement. Linguists and psychologists have often raised the question as to how it is possible for a child by his own efforts to accomplish a task that no adult can ever perform in the same way or as well. We can perhaps answer this puzzling question by looking back at our former analysis. In a later and more advanced state of our conscious life we can never repeat the process which led to our first entrance into

39. See, for instance, Clara and William Stern, Die Kindersprache (Leipzig, 1907), pp. 175 ff.

40. For a more detailed discussion of this problem see Cassirer, "Le langage et la construction du monde des objets," Journal de psychologie, XXXe Année (1933), pp. 18–44.

172

the world of human speech. In the freshness, in the agility and elasticity of early childhood this process had a quite different meaning. Paradoxically enough the real difficulty consists much less in the learning of the new language than in the forgetting of a former one. We are no longer in the mental condition of the child who for the first time approaches a conception of the objective world. To the adult the objective world already has a definite shape as a result of speech activity, which has in a sense molded all our other activities. Our perceptions, intuitions, and concepts have coalesced with the terms and speech forms of our mother tongue. Great efforts are required to release the bond between words and things. And yet, when we set about to learn a new language, we have to make such efforts and to separate the two elements. Overcoming this difficulty always marks a new important step in the learning of a language. When penetrating into the "spirit" of a foreign tongue we invariably have the impression of approaching a new world, a world which has an intellectual structure of its own. It is like a voyage of discovery in an alien land, and the greatest gain from such a voyage lies in our having learned to look upon our mother tongue in a new light. "Wer fremde Sprachen nicht kennt, weiss nichts von seiner eigenen," said Goethe.[41] So long as we know no foreign languages we are in a sense ignorant of our own, for we fail to see its specific structure and its distinctive features. A comparison of different languages shows us that there are no exact synonyms. Corresponding terms from two languages seldom refer to the same objects or actions. They cover different fields which interpenetrate and give us many-colored views and varied perspectives of our experience.

This becomes especially clear if we consider the methods of classification employed in different languages, particularly in those of divergent linguistic types. Classification is one of the fundamental features of human speech. The very act of denomination depends on a process of classification. To give a name to an object or action is to subsume it under a certain class concept. If this subsumption were once and for all pre-

41. Goethe, *Sprüche in Prosa*, "Werke," XLII, Pt. II, 118.

scribed by the nature of things, it would be unique and uniform. Yet the names which occur in human speech cannot be interpreted in any such invariable manner. They are not designed to refer to substantial things, independent entities which exist by themselves. They are determined rather by human interests and human purposes. But these interests are not fixed and invariable. Nor are the classifications to be found in human speech made at random; they are based on certain constant and recurring elements in our sense experience. Without such recurrences there would be no foothold, no point of support, for our linguistic concepts. But the combination or separation of perceptual data depends upon the free choice of a frame of reference. There is no rigid and preestablished scheme according to which our divisions and subdivisions might once for all be made. Even in languages closely akin and agreeing in their general structure we do not find identical names. As Humboldt pointed out, the Greek and Latin terms for the moon, although they refer to the same object, do not express the same intention or concept. The Greek term (mēn) denotes the function of the moon to "measure" time: the Latin term (luna, luc-na) denotes the moon's lucidity or brightness. Thus we have obviously isolated and focused attention on two very different features of the object. But the act itself, the process of concentration and condensation, is the same. The name of an object lays no claim upon its nature; it is not intended to be *physei on*, to give us the truth of a thing. The function of a name is always limited to emphasizing a particular aspect of a thing, and it is precisely this restriction and limitation upon which the value of the name depends. It is not the function of a name to refer exhaustively to a concrete situation, but merely to single out and dwell upon a certain aspect. The isolation of this aspect is not a negative but a positive act. For in the act of denomination we select, out of the multiplicity and diffusion of our sense data, certain fixed centers of perception. These centers are not the same as in logical or scientific thought. The terms of ordinary speech are not to be measured by the same standards as those in which we express scientific concepts. As compared with scientific terminology the words of common speech always exhibit a certain vagueness; almost without exception they are so indistinct and ill-defined as not to stand the test of logical analysis. But notwithstanding this unavoidable and inherent defect our everyday terms and names are the milestones on the road which leads to scientific concepts; it is in these terms that we receive our first objective or theoretical view of the world. Such a view is not simply "given"; it is the result of a constructive intellectual effort which without the constant assistance of language could not attain its end.

This end is not, however, to be reached at any one time. The ascent to higher levels of abstraction, to more general and comprehensive names and ideas, is a difficult and laborious task. The analysis of language provides us with a wealth of materials for studying the character of the mental processes which finally lead to the accomplishment of this task. Human speech evolves from a first comparatively concrete state to a more abstract state. Our first names are concrete ones. They attach themselves to the apprehension of particular facts or actions. All the shades or nuances that we find in our concrete experience are described minutely and circumstantially, but they are not subsumed under a common genus. Hammer-Purgstall has written a paper in which he enumerates the various names for the camel in Arabic. There are no less than five to six thousand terms used in describing a camel; yet none of these gives us a general biological concept. All express concrete details concerning the shape, the size, the color, the age, and the gait of the animal.[42] These divisions are still very far from any scientific or systematic classification, but serve quite different purposes. In many languages of aboriginal American tribes we find an astounding variety of terms for a particular action, for instance for walking or striking. Such terms bear to each other rather a relation of juxtaposition than of subordination. A blow with the fist cannot be described with the same term as a blow with the palm, and a blow with a weapon requires another name than one with a

42. See Hammer-Purgstall, Academy of Vienna, Philosophical-historical class, Vols. VI and VII (1855 f.).

whip or rod.[43] In his description of the Bakairi language—an idiom spoken by an Indian tribe in Central Brazil—Karl von den Steinen relates that each species of parrot and palm tree has its individual name, whereas there exists no name to express the genus "parrot" or "palm." "The Bakairi," he asserts, "attach themselves so much to the numerous particular notions that they take no interest in the common characteristics. They are choked in the abundance of the material and cannot manage it economically. They have only small coin but in that they must be said to be excessively rich rather than poor." [44] As a matter of fact there exists no uniform measure for the wealth or poverty of a given idiom. Every classification is directed and dictated by special needs, and it is clear that these needs vary according to the different conditions of man's social and cultural life. In primitive civilization the interest in the concrete and particular aspects of things necessarily prevails. Human speech always conforms to and is commensurate with certain forms of human life. An interest in mere "universals" is neither possible nor necessary in an Indian tribe. It is enough, and it is more important, to distinguish objects by certain visible and palpable characteristics. In many languages a round thing cannot be treated in the same way as a square or oblong thing, for they belong to different genders which are distinguished by special linguistic means, such as the use of prefixes. In languages of the Bantu family we find no less than twenty gender classes of nouns. In languages of aboriginal American tribes, as for instance in Algonquian, some objects belong to an animate gender, others to an inanimate gender. Even here it is easy to understand that and why this distinction, from the viewpoint of the primitive mind, must appear to be of particular interest and of vital importance. It is indeed a much more characteristic and striking difference than that which is expressed in our abstract logical class names. The same slow passage from concrete to abstract names can also be studied in the denomination of

43. For further details see *Philosophie der symbolischen Formen*, I, 257 ff.

44. K. von den Steinen, *Unter den Naturvölkern Zentral-Brasiliens*, p. 81.

the qualities of things. In many languages we find an abundance of color names. Each individual shade of a given color has its special name, whereas our general terms—blue, green, red, and so on—are missing. Color names vary according to the nature of the objects: one word for gray may, for example, be used in speaking of wool or geese, another of horses, another of cattle, and still another when speaking of the hair of men and certain other animals.[45] The same holds good for the category of number: different numerals are required for referring to different classes of objects.[46] The ascent to universal concepts and categories appears, therefore, to be very slow in the development of human speech; but each new advance in this direction leads to a more comprehensive survey, to a better orientation and organization of our perceptual world.

9   Art

1   Beauty appears to be one of the most clearly known of human phenomena. Unobscured by any aura of secrecy and mystery, its character and nature stand in no need of subtle and complicated metaphysical theories for their explanation. Beauty is part and parcel of human experience; it is palpable and unmistakable. Nevertheless, in this history of philosophical thought the phenomenon of beauty has always proved to be one of the greatest paradoxes. Up to the time of Kant a philosophy of beauty always meant an attempt to reduce our aesthetic experience to an alien principle and to subject art to an alien jurisdiction. Kant in his *Critique of Judgment* was the first to give a clear and convincing proof of the autonomy of art. All former systems had looked for a principle of art within the sphere either of theoretical knowledge or of the moral life. If art was regarded as the offspring of theoretical activity it became necessary to analyze the logical rules to which this particular activity conforms. But in this case logic

45. See the examples given in Jespersen, *Language*, p. 429.
46. For more details see *Philosophie der symbolischen Formen*, I, 188 ff.

itself was no longer a homogeneous whole. It had to be divided into separate and comparatively independent parts. The logic of the imagination had to be distinguished from the logic of rational and scientific thought. In his *Aesthetica* (1750) Alexander Baumgarten had made the first comprehensive systematic attempt to construct a logic of the imagination. But even this attempt, which in a sense proved to be decisive and invaluable, could not secure for art a really autonomous value. For the logic of the imagination could never command the same dignity as the logic of the pure intellect. If there was a theory of art, then it could only be a *gnoseologia inferior*, an analysis of the "lower," sensuous part of human knowledge. Art could, on the other hand, be described as an emblem of moral truth. It was conceived as an allegory, a figurative expression which under its sensuous form concealed an ethical sense. But in both cases, in its moral as well as in its theoretical interpretation, art possessed no independent value of its own. In the hierarchy of human knowledge and of human life art was only a preparatory stage, a subordinate and subservient means pointing to some higher end.

The philosophy of art exhibits the same conflict between two antagonistic tendencies that we encounter in the philosophy of language. This is of course no mere historical coincidence. It goes back to one and the same basic division in the interpretation of reality. Language and art are constantly oscillating between two opposite poles, an objective and a subjective pole. No theory of language or art could forget or suppress either one of these poles, though the stress may be laid now on the one and now on the other.

In the first case language and art are subsumed under a common heading, the category of imitation; and their principal function is mimetic. Language originates in an imitation of sounds, art is an imitation of outward things. Imitation is a fundamental instinct, an irreducible fact of human nature. "Imitation," says Aristotle, "is natural to man from childhood, one of his advantages over the lower animals being this, that he is the most imitative creature in the world, and learns at first by imitation." And imitation is also an inexhaustible source of delight, as is proved by the fact that, though the objects themselves may be painful to see, we delight never-theless in viewing the most realistic representations of them in art—the forms, for example, of the lowest animals and of dead bodies. Aristotle describes this delight rather as a theoretical than as a specifically aesthetic experience. "To be learning something," he declares, "is the greatest of pleasures not only to the philosopher but also to the rest of mankind, however small their capacity for it; the reason of the delight in seeing the picture is that one is at the same time learning—gathering the meaning of things, e.g., that the man there is so-and-so." [1] At first sight this principle seems only to apply to the representative arts. It could, however, easily be trans-ferred to all the other forms. Music itself became a picture of things. Even flute playing or dancing are, after all, nothing but imitations; for the flute player or the dancer represents by his rhythms men's characters as well as what they do and suffer.[2] And the whole history of poetics was influenced by the device of Horace, "ut pictura poesis," and by the saying of Simonides, "painting is mute poetry and poetry a speaking picture." Poetry is differentiated from painting by the mode and means, but not by the general function of imitation.

But it should be observed that the most radical theories of imitation were not intended to restrict the work of art to a merely mechanical reproduction of reality. All of them had to make allowance to a certain extent for the creativeness of the artist. It was not easy to reconcile these two demands. If imitation is the true aim of art, it is clear that the spontaneity, the productive power of the artist is a disturbing rather than a constructive factor. Instead of describing things in their true nature it falsifies the aspect of things. This disturbance intro-duced by the subjectivity of the artist could not be denied by the classical theories of imitation. But it could be confined within its proper limits and subjected to general rules. Thus the principle ars simia naturae could not be maintained in a strict and uncompromising sense. For not even nature itself is infallible, nor does it always attain its end. In such a case art

1. Aristotle, Poetics, 4. 1448^{b} 5–17. In Aristotle on the Art of Poetry, ed. by Ingram Bywater (Oxford, 1909), pp. 8–11.
2. Idem, 1. 1447^{a} 26. Ed. Bywater, pp. 2–5.

must come to the aid of nature and actually correct or perfect it.

> But Nature mars—wherein she doth resemble
> The craftsman who about his labour goes
> And keeps the knack, although his fingers tremble.[3]

If "all beauty is truth," all truth is not necessarily beauty. In order to reach the highest beauty it is just as essential to deviate from nature as to reproduce nature. To determine the measure, the right proportion, of this deviation, became one of the principal tasks of a theory of art. Aristotle had asserted that for the purposes of poetry a convincing impossibility is preferable to an unconvincing possibility. To the objection of a critic that Zeuxis had painted men such as could never exist in reality, the right answer is that it is *better* they should be like that, for the artist *ought* to improve on his model.[4]

The neoclassicists—from the Italians of the sixteenth century to the work of Abbé Batteux, *Les beaux arts reduits à un même principe* (1747)—took their point of departure from the same principle. Art does not reproduce nature in a general and indiscriminate sense; it reproduces *"la belle nature."* But if imitation is the real purpose of art the very concept of any such "beautiful nature" is highly questionable. For how can we improve on our model without difiguring it? How can we transcend the reality of things without trespassing against the laws of truth? From the point of view of this theory poetry and art in general never can be anything but an agreeable falsity.

The general theory of imitation seemed to hold its ground and to defy all attacks up to the first half of the eighteenth century. But even in the treatise of Batteux, who was perhaps the last resolute champion of this theory,[5] we feel a certain

3. Dante, *Paradiso*, XIII, v. 76. English trans. by Melville Best Anderson, *The Divine Comedy* (World Book Co., 1921), p. 357.

4. Aristotle, *op. cit.*, 25. 1461[b]. Ed. Bywater, pp. 86–87.

5. To be sure, even in the nineteenth century the general theory of imitation still played an important role. It is, for instance, maintained and defended in Taine's *Philosophie de l'art*.

uneasiness with regard to its universal validity. The stumbling block for this theory had always been the phenomenon of lyrical poetry. The arguments by which Batteux attempted to include lyrical poetry under the general scheme of imitative art are weak and inconclusive. And indeed all these superficial arguments were suddenly swept away by the appearance of a new force. Even in the field of aesthetics the name of Rousseau marks a decisive turning point in the general history of ideas. Rousseau rejected the whole classical and neoclassical tradition of the theory of art. To him art is not a description or reproduction of the empirical world but an overflow of emotions and passions. Rousseau's *Nouvelle Héloise* proved to be a new revolutionary power. The mimetic principle that had prevailed for many centuries had, henceforward, to give way to a new conception and a new ideal—to the ideal of "characteristic art." From this point we can trace the triumph of a new principle throughout the whole of European literature. In Germany Herder and Goethe followed the example of Rousseau. Thus the whole theory of beauty had to assume a new shape. Beauty in the traditional sense of the term is by no means the only aim of art; it is in fact but a secondary and derivative feature. "Do not let a misconception come between us"; Goethe admonishes his reader in his paper "Von deutscher Baukunst"; "do not let the effeminate doctrine of the modern beauty-monger make you too tender to enjoy significant roughness, lest in the end your enfeebled feeling should be able to endure nothing but unmeaning smoothness. They try to make you believe that the fine arts arose from our supposed inclination to beautify the world around us. That is not true. . . .

"Art is formative long before it is beautiful, and yet it is then true and great art, very often truer and greater than beautiful art itself. For man has in him a formative nature, which displays itself in activity as soon as his existence is secure; . . . And so the savage remodels with bizarre traits, horrible forms and coarse colours, his 'cocos,' his feathers, and his own body. And though this imagery consists of the most capricious forms, yet without proportions of shape, its parts will agree together, for a single feeling has created them into a characteristic whole.

"Now this characteristic art is the only true art. When it acts on what lies round it from inward, single, individual, original, independent feeling, careless and even ignorant of all that is alien to it, then, whether born of rude savagery or of cultivated sensibility, it is whole and living." [6]

With Rousseau and Goethe there began a new period of aesthetic theory. Characteristic art has gained a definitive victory over imitative art. But in order to understand this characteristic art in its true sense we must avoid a one-sided interpretation. It is not enough to lay the stress upon the emotional side of the work of art. It is true that all characteristic or expressive art is "the spontaneous overflow of powerful feelings." But if we were to accept this Wordsworthian definition without reserve, we should only be led to a change of sign, not to a decisive change of meaning. In this case art would remain reproductive; but, instead of being a reproduction of things, of physical objects, it would become a reproduction of our inner life, of our affections and emotions. Using once more our analogy with the philosophy of language, we might say that in this case we had only exchanged an onomatopoetic theory of art for an interjectional theory. But this is not the sense in which the term "characteristic art" was understood by Goethe. The passage cited above was written in 1773, in Goethe's youthful "Sturm und Drang" period. Yet in no period of his life could he ever neglect the objective pole of his poetry. Art is indeed expressive, but it cannot be expressive without being formative. And this formative process is carried out in a certain sensuous medium. "As soon as he is free from care and fear," writes Goethe, "the demigod, creative in repose, gropes round him for matter into which to breathe his spirit." In many modern aesthetic theories—especially that of Croce and his disciples and followers—this material factor is forgotten or minimized. Croce is interested only in the fact of expression, not in the mode. The mode he

6. Goethe, "Von deutscher Baukunst," "Werke," XXXVII, 148 f. English trans. by Bernard Bosanquet in *Three Lectures on Aesthetic* (London, Macmillan, 1923), pp. 114 ff.

takes to be irrelevant both for the character and for the value of the work of art. The only thing which matters is the intuition of the artist, not the embodiment of this intuition in a particular material. The material has a technical but not an aesthetical importance. Croce's philosophy is a philosophy of the spirit emphasizing the purely spiritual character of the work of art. But in his theory the whole spiritual energy is contained and expended in the formation of the intuition alone. When this process is completed the artistic creation has been achieved. What follows is only an external reproduction which is necessary for the communication of the intuition but meaningless with respect to its essence. But for a great painter, a great musician, or a great poet, the colors, the lines, rhythms, and words are not merely a part of his technical apparatus; they are necessary moments of the productive process itself.

This is just as true of the specifically expressive arts as of the representative arts. Even in lyrical poetry emotion is not the only and decisive feature. It is of course true that the great lyrical poets are capable of the deepest emotions and that an artist who is not endowed with powerful feelings will never produce anything except shallow and frivolous art. But from this fact we cannot conclude that the function of lyrical poetry and of art in general can be adequately described as the artist's ability "to make a clean breast of his feelings." "What the artist is trying to do," says R. G. Collingwood, "is to express a given emotion. To express it, and to express it well, are the same thing. . . . Every utterance and every gesture that each one of us makes is a work of art." [7] But here again the whole constructive process which is a prerequisite both of the production and of the contemplation of the work of art is entirely overlooked. Every gesture is no more a work of art than every interjection is an act of speech. Both the gesture and the interjection are deficient in one essential and indispensable feature. They are involuntary and instinctive reactions; they possess no real spontaneity. The moment of purposiveness is necessary for linguistic and artistic expression. In every act of speech and in every artistic creation we find a

7. R. G. Collingwood, *The Principles of Art* (Oxford, Clarendon Press, 1938), pp. 279, 282, 285.

definite teleological structure. An actor in a drama really "acts" his part. Each individual utterance is a part of a coherent structural whole. The accent and rhythm of his words, the modulation of his voice, the expressions of his face, and the postures of his body all tend to the same end—to the embodiment of human character. All this is not simply "expression"; it is also representation and interpretation. Not even a lyric poem is wholly devoid of this general tendency of art. The lyric poet is not just a man who indulges in displays of feeling. To be swayed by emotion alone is sentimentality, not art. An artist who is absorbed not in the contemplation and creation of forms but rather in his own pleasure or in his enjoyment of "the joy of grief" becomes a sentimentalist. Hence we can hardly ascribe to lyric art a more subjective character than to all the other forms of art. For it contains the same sort of embodiment, and the same process of objectification. "Poetry," wrote Mallarmé, "is not written with ideas, it is written with words." It is written with images, sounds, and rhythms which, just as in the case of dramatic poetry and dramatic representation, coalesce into an indivisible whole. In every great lyrical poem we find this concrete and indivisible unity.

Like all the other symbolic forms art is not the mere reproduction of a ready-made, given reality. It is one of the ways leading to an objective view of things and of human life. It is not an imitation but a discovery of reality. We do not, however, discover nature through art in the same sense in which the scientist uses the term "nature." Language and science are the two main processes by which we ascertain and determine our concepts of the external world. We must classify our sense perceptions and bring them under general notions and general rules in order to give them an objective meaning. Such classification is the result of a persistent effort toward simplification. The work of art in like manner implies such an act of condensation and concentration. When Aristotle wanted to describe the real difference between poetry and history he insisted upon this process. What a drama gives us, he asserts, is a single action (*mia praxis*) which is a complete whole in itself, with all the organic unity of a living creature; whereas the historian has to deal not with one action but with one period and all that happened therein to one or more persons, however disconnected the several events may have been.[8]

In this respect beauty as well as truth may be described in terms of the same classical formula: they are "a unity in the manifold." But in the two cases there is a difference of stress. Language and science are abbreviations of reality; art is an intensification of reality. Language and science depend upon one and the same process of abstraction; art may be described as a continuous process of concretion. In our scientific description of a given object we begin with a great number of observations which at first sight are only a loose conglomerate of detached facts. But the farther we proceed the more these individual phenomena tend to assume a definite shape and become a systematic whole. What science is searching for is some central features of a given object from which all its particular qualities may be derived. If a chemist knows the atomic number of a certain element he possesses a clue to a full insight into its structure and constitution. From this number he may deduce all the characteristic properties of the element. But art does not admit of this sort of conceptual simplification and deductive generalization. It does not inquire into the qualities or causes of things; it gives us the intuition of the form of things. But this too is by no means a mere repetition of something we had before. It is a true and genuine discovery. The artist is just as much a discoverer of the forms of nature as the scientist is a discoverer of facts or natural laws. The great artists of all times have been cognizant of this special task and special gift of art. Leonardo da Vinci spoke of the purpose of painting and sculpture in the words "saper vedere." According to him the painter and sculptor are the great teachers in the realm of the visible world. For the awareness of pure forms of things is by no means an instinctive gift, a gift of nature. We may have met with an object of our ordinary sense experience a thousand times without ever having "seen" its form. We are still at a loss if asked to describe not its physical qualities or effects but its pure

8. Aristotle, op. cit., 23. 1459[a] 17–29. Ed. Bywater, pp. 70–73.

visual shape and structure. It is art that fills this gap. Here
we live in the realm of pure forms rather than in that of the
analysis and scrutiny of sense objects or the study of their
effects.

From a merely theoretical point of view we may subscribe
to the words of Kant that mathematics is the "pride of human
reason." But for this triumph of scientific reason we have to
pay a very high price. Science means abstraction, and abstraction is always an impoverishment of reality. The forms of
things as they are described in scientific concepts tend more
and more to become mere formulae. These formulae are of a
surprising simplicity. A single formula, like the Newtonian
law of gravitation, seems to comprise and explain the whole
structure of our material universe. It would seem as though
reality were not only accessible to our scientific abstractions
but exhaustible by them. But as soon as we approach the field
of art this proves to be an illusion. For the aspects of things
are innumerable, and they vary from one moment to another.
Any attempt to comprehend them within a simple formula
would be in vain. Heraclitus' saying that the sun is new every
day is true for the sun of the artist if not for the sun of the
scientist. When the scientist describes an object he characterizes it by a set of numbers, by its physical and chemical con-
stants. Art has not only a different aim but a different object.
If we say of two artists that they paint "the same" landscape
we describe our aesthetic experience very inadequately. From
the point of view of art such a pretended sameness is quite
illusory. We cannot speak of one and the same thing as the
subject matter of both painters. For the artist does not portray
or copy a certain empirical object—a landscape with its hills
and mountains, its brooks and rivers. What he gives us is the
individual and momentary physiognomy of the landscape. He
wishes to express the atmosphere of things, the play of light
and shadow. A landscape is not "the same" in early twilight,
in midday heat, or on a rainy or sunny day. Our aesthetic
perception exhibits a much greater variety and belongs to a
much more complex order than our ordinary sense perception.
In sense perception we are content with apprehending the
common and constant features of the objects of our surround-

ings. Aesthetic experience is incomparably richer. It is pregnant with infinite possibilities which remain unrealized in ordinary sense experience. In the work of the artist these possibilities become actualities; they are brought into the open and take on a definite shape. The revelation of this inexhaustibility of the aspects of things is one of the great privileges and one of the deepest charms of art.

The painter Ludwig Richter relates in his memoirs how once when he was in Tivoli as a young man he and three friends set out to paint the same landscape. They were all firmly resolved not to deviate from nature; they wished to reproduce what they had seen as accurately as possible. Nevertheless the result was four totally different pictures, as different from one another as the personalities of the artists. From this experience the narrator concluded that there is no such thing as objective vision, and that form and color are always apprehended according to individual temperament.[9] Not even the most determined champions of a strict and uncompromising naturalism could overlook or deny this factor. Émile Zola defines the work of art as *"un coin de la nature vu à travers un tempérament."* What is referred to here as temperament is not merely singularity or idiosyncrasy. When absorbed in the intuition of a great work of art we do not feel a separation between the subjective and the objective worlds. We do not live in our plain commonplace reality of physical things, nor do we live wholly within an individual sphere. Beyond these two spheres we detect a new realm, the realm of plastic, musical, poetical forms; and these forms have a real universality. Kant distinguishes sharply between what he calls *"aesthetic* universality*"* and the "objective validity" which belongs to our logical and scientific judgments.[10] In our aesthetic judgments, he contends, we are not concerned with

9. I take this account from Heinrich Wölfflin's *Principles of Art History.*

10. In Kant's terminology the former is called *Gemeingültigkeit* whereas the latter is called *Allgemeingültigkeit*—a distinction which is difficult to render in corresponding English terms. For a systematic interpretation of the two terms see H. W. Cassirer, A Commentary on Kant's *"Critique of Judgment"* (London, 1938), pp. 190 ff.

the object as such but with the pure contemplation of the object. Aesthetic universality means that the predicate of beauty is not restricted to a special individual but extends over the whole field of judging subjects. If the work of art were nothing but the freak and frenzy of an individual artist it would not possess this universal communicability. The imagination of the artist does not arbitrarily invent the forms of things. It shows us these forms in their true shape, making them visible and recognizable. The artist chooses a certain aspect of reality, but this process of selection is at the same time a process of objectification. Once we have entered into his perspective we are forced to look on the world with his eyes. It would seem as if we had never before seen the world in this peculiar light. Yet we are convinced that this light is not merely a momentary flash. By virtue of the work of art it has become durable and permanent. Once reality has been disclosed to us in this particular way, we continue to see it in this shape.

A sharp distinction between the objective and the subjective, the representative and the expressive arts is thus difficult to maintain. The Parthenon frieze or a Mass by Bach, Michelangelo's "Sistine Chapel" or a poem of Leopardi, a sonata of Beethoven or a novel of Dostoievski are neither merely representative nor merely expressive. They are symbolic in a new and deeper sense. The works of the great lyrical poets—of Goethe or Hölderlin, of Wordsworth or Shelley—do not give us *disjecti membra poetae*, scattered and incoherent fragments of the poet's life. They are not simply a momentary outburst of passionate feeling; they reveal a deep unity and continuity. The great tragic and comic writers on the other hand—Euripides and Shakespeare, Cervantes and Molière—do not entertain us with detached scenes from the spectacle of life. Taken in themselves these scenes are but fugitive shadows. But suddenly we begin to see behind these shadows and to envisage a new reality. Through his characters and actions the comic and the tragic poet reveals his view of human life as a whole, of its greatness and weakness, its sublimity and its absurdity. "Art," wrote Goethe, "does not undertake to emulate nature in its breadth and depth. It sticks to the surface of natural phenomena; but it has its own depth, its own power; it crystallizes the highest moments of these superficial phenomena by recognizing in them the character of lawfulness, the perfection of harmonious proportion, the summit of beauty, the dignity of significance, the height of passion." [11] This fixation of the "highest moments of phenomena" is neither an imitation of physical things nor a mere overflow of powerful feelings. It is an interpretation of reality—not by concepts but by intuitions; not through the medium of thought but through that of sensuous forms.

From Plato to Tolstoi art has been accused of exciting our emotions and thus of disturbing the order and harmony of our moral life. Poetical imagination, according to Plato, waters our experience of lust and anger, of desire and pain, and makes them grow when they ought to starve with drought. [12] Tolstoi sees in art a source of infection. "Not only is infection," he says, "a sign of art, but the degree of infectiousness is also the sole measure of excellence in art." But the flaw in this theory is obvious. Tolstoi suppresses a fundamental moment of art, the moment of form. The aesthetic experience—the experience of contemplation—is a different state of mind from the coolness of our theoretical and the sobriety of our moral judgment. It is filled with the liveliest energies of passion, but passion itself is here transformed both in its nature and in its meaning. Wordsworth defines poetry as "emotion recollected in tranquillity." But the tranquillity we feel in great poetry is not that of recollection. The emotions aroused by the poet do not belong to a remote past. They are "here"— alive and immediate. We are aware of their full strength, but this strength tends in a new direction. It is rather seen than immediately felt. Our passions are no longer dark and impenetrable powers; they become, as it were, transparent. Shakespeare never gives us an aesthetic theory. He does not speculate about the nature of art. Yet in the only passage in which he speaks of the character and function of dramatic art the whole stress is laid upon this point. "The purpose of play-

11. Goethe, Notes to a translation of Diderot's "Essai sur la peinture," "Werke," XLV, 260.

12. Plato, Republic, 606D (Jowett trans.).

ing," as Hamlet explains, "both at the first and now, was and is, to hold, as 'twere, the mirror up to nature; to show virtue her own feature, scorn her own image, and the very age and body of the time his form and pressure." But the image of a passion is not the passion itself. The poet who represents a passion does not infect us with this passion. At a Shakespeare play we are not infected with the ambition of Macbeth, with the cruelty of Richard III, or with the jealousy of Othello. We are not at the mercy of these emotions; we look through them; we seem to penetrate into their very nature and essence. In this respect Shakespeare's theory of dramatic art, if he had such a theory, is in complete agreement with the conception of the fine arts of the great painters and sculptors of the Renaissance. He would have subscribed to the words of Leonardo da Vinci that "*saper vedere*" is the highest gift of the artist. The great painters show us the forms of outward things; the great dramatists show us the forms of our inner life. Dramatic art discloses a new breadth and depth of life. It conveys an awareness of human things and human destinies, of human greatness and misery, in comparison to which our ordinary existence appears poor and trivial. All of us feel, vaguely and dimly, the infinite potentialities of life, which silently await the moment when they are to be called forth from dormancy into the clear and intense light of consciousness. It is not the degree of infection but the degree of intensification and illumination which is the measure of the excellence of art.

If we accept this view of art we can come to a better understanding of a problem first encountered in the Aristotelian theory of catharsis. We need not enter here into all the difficulties of the Aristotelian term or into the innumerable efforts of the commentators to clear up these difficulties.[13] What seems to be clear and what is now generally admitted is that the cathartic process described by Aristotle does not mean a purification or a change in the character and quality of the passions themselves but a change in the human soul. By tragic

13. For details see Jakob Bernays, *Zwei Abhandlungen über die Aristotelische Theorie des Dramas* (Berlin, 1880) and Ingram Bywater, *Aristotle on the Art of Poetry* (Oxford, 1909), pp. 152 ff.

poetry the soul acquires a new attitude toward its emotions. The soul experiences the emotions of pity and fear, but instead of being disturbed and disquieted by them it is brought to a state of rest and peace. At first sight this would seem to be a contradiction. For what Aristotle looks upon as the effect of tragedy is a synthesis of two moments which in real life, in our practical existence, exclude each other. The highest intensification of our emotional life is thought of as at the same time giving us a sense of repose. We live through all our passions feeling their full range and highest tension. But what we leave behind when passing the threshold of art is the hard pressure, the compulsion of our emotions. The tragic poet is not the slave but the master of his emotions; and he is able to transfer this mastery to the spectators. In his work we are not swayed and carried away by our emotions. Aesthetic freedom is not the absence of passions, not Stoic apathy, but just the contrary. It means that our emotional life acquires its greatest strength, and that in this very strength it changes its form. For here we no longer live in the immediate reality of things but in a world of pure sensuous forms. In this world all our feelings undergo a sort of transubstantiation with respect to their essence and their character. The passions themselves are relieved of their material burden. We feel their form and their life but not their encumbrance. The calmness of the work of art is, paradoxically, a dynamic, not a static calmness. Art gives us the motions of the human soul in all their depth and variety. But the form, the measure and rhythm, of these motions is not comparable to any single state of emotion. What we feel in art is not a simple or single emotional quality. It is the dynamic process of life itself—the continuous oscillation between opposite poles, between joy and grief, hope and fear, exultation and despair. To give aesthetic form to our passions is to transform them into a free and active state. In the work of the artist the power of passion itself has been made a formative power.

It may be objected that all this applies to the artist but not to ourselves, the spectators and auditors. But such an objection would imply a misunderstanding of the artistic process. Like the process of speech the artistic process is a dialogical and dialectic one. Not even the spectator is left to a merely passive role. We cannot understand a work of art without, to a certain degree, repeating and reconstructing the creative process by which it has come into being. By the nature of this creative process the passions themselves are turned into actions. If in real life we had to endure all those emotions through which we live in Sophocles' *Oedipus* or in Shakespeare's *King Lear* we should scarcely survive the shock and strain. But art turns all these pains and outrages, these cruelties and atrocities, into a means of self-liberation, thus giving us an inner freedom which cannot be attained in any other way.

The attempt to characterize a work of art by some particular emotional feature must, therefore, inevitably fail to do it justice. If what art tries to express is no special state but the very dynamic process of our inner life, then any such qualification could hardly be more than perfunctory and superficial. Art must always give us motion rather than mere emotion. Even the distinction between tragic and comic art is much more a conventional than a necessary one. It relates to the content and motives but not to the form and essence of art. Plato had long since denied the existence of these artificial and traditional boundaries. At the end of the *Symposium* he describes Socrates as engaged in a conversation with Agathon, the tragic poet, and Aristophanes, the comic poet. Socrates compels the two poets to admit that the true tragedian is the true artist in comedy, and vice versa.[14] A commentary on this passage is given in the *Philebus*. In comedy as well as in tragedy, Plato maintains in this dialogue, we always experience a mixed feeling of pleasure and pain. In this the poet follows the rules of nature itself since he portrays "the whole comedy and tragedy of life." [15] In every great poem—in Shakespeare's plays, in Dante's *Commedia*, in Goethe's *Faust*—we must indeed pass through the whole gamut of human emotions. If we were unable to grasp the most delicate nuances of the different shades of feeling, unable to follow the continuous variations in rhythm and tone, if unmoved by sudden dynamic

14. Plato, *Symposium*, 223 (Jowett trans.).
15. *Philebus*, 48 ff. (Jowett trans.).

changes, we could not understand and feel the poem. We may speak of the individual temperament of the artist, but the work of art, as such, has no special temperament. We cannot subsume it under any traditional psychological class concept. To speak of Mozart's music as cheerful or serene, of Beethoven's as grave, somber, or sublime would betray an unpenetrating taste. Here too the distinction between tragedy and comedy becomes irrelevant. The question whether Mozart's *Don Giovanni* is a tragedy or an *opera buffa* is scarcely worth answering. Beethoven's composition based on Schiller's "Hymn to Joy" expresses the highest degree of exultation. But when listening to it we do not for a moment forget the tragic accents of the Ninth Symphony. All these contrasts must be present and they must be felt in their full strength. In our aesthetic experience they coalesce into one indivisible whole. What we hear is the whole scale of human emotions from the lowest to the highest note; it is the motion and vibration of our whole being. The greatest comedians themselves can by no means give us an easy beauty. Their work is often filled with great bitterness. Aristophanes is one of the sharpest and sternest critics of human nature; Molière is nowhere greater than in his *Misanthrope* or *Tartuffe*. Nevertheless the bitterness of the great comic writers is not the acerbity of the satirist or the severity of the moralist. It does not lead to a moral verdict upon human life. Comic art possesses in the highest degree that faculty shared by all art, sympathetic vision. By virtue of this faculty it can accept human life with all its defects and foibles, its follies and vices. Great comic art has always been a sort of *encomium moriae*, a praise of folly. In comic perspective all things begin to take on a new face. We are perhaps never nearer to our human world than in the works of a great comic writer—in Cervantes' *Don Quixote*, Sterne's *Tristram Shandy*, or in Dickens' *Pickwick Papers*. We become observant of the minutest details; we see this world in all its narrowness, its pettiness, and silliness. We live in this restricted world, but we are no longer imprisoned by it. Such is the peculiar character of the comic catharsis. Things and events begin to lose their material weight; scorn is dissolved into laughter and laughter is liberation.

That beauty is not an immediate property of things, that it necessarily involves a relation to the human mind, is a point which seems to be admitted by almost all aesthetic theories. In his essay "Of the Standard of Taste" Hume declares: "Beauty is no quality in things themselves: it exists merely in the mind which contemplates them." But this statement is ambiguous. If we understand mind in Hume's own sense, and think of self as nothing but a bundle of impressions, it would be very difficult to find in such a bundle that predicate which we call beauty. Beauty cannot be defined by its mere *percipi*, as "being perceived"; it must be defined in terms of an activity of the mind, of the function of perceiving and by a characteristic direction of this function. It does not consist of passive percepts; it is a mode, a process of perceptualization. But this process is not merely subjective in character; on the contrary, it is one of the conditions of our intuition of an objective world. The artistic eye is not a passive eye that receives and registers the impression of things. It is a constructive eye, and it is only by constructive acts that we can discover the beauty of natural things. The sense of beauty is the susceptibility to the dynamic life of forms, and this life cannot be apprehended except by a corresponding dynamic process in ourselves.

To be sure, in the various aesthetic theories this polarity, which as we have seen is an inherent condition of beauty, has led to diametrically opposed interpretations. According to Albrecht Dürer the real gift of the artist is to "elicit" beauty from nature. "Denn wahrhaftig steckt die Kunst in der Natur, wer sie heraus kann reissen, der hat sie." [16] On the other hand we find spiritualistic theories which deny any connection between the beauty of art and the so-called beauty of nature. The beauty of nature is understood as merely a metaphor. Croce thinks it sheer rhetoric to speak of a beautiful river or tree. Nature to him is stupid when compared with art; she is mute save when man makes her speak. The contradiction between these conceptions may perhaps be resolved by dis-

16. "For art standeth firmly fixed in Nature—and who can rend her from thence, he only possesseth her." See William M. Conway, *Literary Remains of Albrecht Dürer* (1889), p. 182.

tinguishing sharply between organic beauty and aesthetic beauty. There are many natural beauties with no specific aesthetic character. The organic beauty of a landscape is not the same as that aesthetic beauty which we feel in the works of the great landscape painters. Even we, the spectators, are fully aware of this difference. I may walk through a landscape and feel its charms. I may enjoy the mildness of the air, the freshness of the meadows, the variety and cheerfulness of the coloring, and the fragrant odor of the flowers. But I may then experience a sudden change in my frame of mind. Thereupon I see the landscape with an artist's eye—I begin to form a picture of it. I have now entered a new realm—the realm not of living things but of "living forms." No longer in the immediate reality of things, I live now in the rhythm of spatial forms, in the harmony and contrast of colors, in the balance of light and shadow. In such absorption in the dynamic aspect of form consists the aesthetic experience.

2   All the controversies between the various aesthetic schools may in a sense be reduced to one point. What all these schools have to admit is that art is an independent "universe of discourse." Even the most radical defenders of a strict realism who wished to limit art to a mimetic function alone have had to make allowance for the specific power of the artistic imagination. But the various schools differed widely in their evaluation of this power. The classical and neoclassical theories did not encourage the free play of imagination. From their point of view the imagination of the artist is a great but rather questionable gift. Boileau himself did not deny that, psychologically speaking, the gift of imagination is indispensable for every true poet. But if the poet indulges in the mere play of this natural impulse and instinctive power, he will never achieve perfection. The poet's imagination must be guided and controlled by reason and subjected to its rules. Even when deviating from the natural the poet must respect the laws of reason, and these laws restrict him to the field of the probable. French classicism defined this field in purely objective terms. The dramatic

unities of space and time became physical facts measurable by a linear standard or by a clock.

An entirely different conception of the character and function of poetic imagination was introduced by the romantic theory of art. This theory is not the work of the so-called "romantic school" in Germany. It had been developed much earlier and had begun to play a decisive role in both French and English literature during the eighteenth century. One of the best and most concise expressions of this theory is to be found in Edward Young's *Conjectures on Original Composition* (1759). "The pen of an original writer," says Young, "like Armida's wand out of a barren waste calls a blooming spring." From this time on the classical views of the probable were supplanted more and more by their opposite. The marvelous and miraculous are now believed to be the only subjects that admit of true poetical portraiture. In eighteenth-century aesthetics we can trace step by step the rise of this new ideal. The Swiss critics Bodmer and Breitinger appeal to Milton in justification of the "wonderful in poetry." [17] The wonderful gradually outweighs and eclipses the probable as a literary subject. The new theory seemed to be embodied in the works of the greatest poets. Shakespeare himself had illustrated it in his description of the poet's imagination:

> The lunatic, the lover, and the poet
> Are of imagination all compact:
> One sees more devils than vast hell can hold,
> That is, the madman; the lover, all as frantic,
> Sees Helen's beauty in a brow of Egypt:
> The poet's eye, in a fine frenzy rolling,
> Doth glance from heaven to earth, from earth to heaven;
> And, as imagination bodies forth
> The forms of things unknown, the poet's pen
> Turns them to shapes, and gives to airy nothing
> A local habitation and a name.[18]

Yet the romantic conception of poetry found no solid sup-

17. Cf. Bodmer and Breitinger, *Diskurse der Maler* (1721–23).
18. *Midsummer Night's Dream*, Act V, sc. 1.

port in Shakespeare. If we stood in need of proof that the world of the artist is not a merely "fantastic" universe, we could find no better, no more classical, witness than Shakespeare. The light in which he sees nature and human life is no mere "fancy light in fancy caught." But there is still another form of imagination with which poetry seems to be indissolubly connected. When Vico made his first systematic attempt to create a "logic of the imagination" he turned back to the world of myth. He speaks of three different ages: the age of gods, the age of heroes, and the age of man. It is in the two former ages, he declared, that we have to look for the true origin of poetry. Mankind could not begin with abstract thought or with a rational language. It had to pass through the era of the symbolic language of myth and poetry. The first nations did not think in concepts but in poetic images; they spoke in fables and wrote in hieroglyphs. The poet and the maker of myth seem, indeed, to live in the same world. They are endowed with the same fundamental power, the power of personification. They cannot contemplate any object without giving to it an inner life and a personal shape. The modern poet often looks back at the mystical, the "divine" or "heroic" ages, as at a lost paradise. In his poem "The Gods of Greece" Schiller expressed this feeling. He wished to recall the times of the Greek poets, for whom myth was not an empty allegory but a living power. The poet yearns for this golden age of poetry in which all things were still full of gods, in which every hill was the dwelling place of an oread, every tree the home of a dryad.

But this complaint of the modern poet appears to be unfounded. For it is one of the greatest privileges of art that it can never lose this "divine age." Here the source of imaginative creation never dries up, for it is indestructible and inexhaustible. In every age and in every great artist the operation of the imagination reappears in new forms and in new force. In the lyrical poets, first and foremost, we feel this continuous rebirth and regeneration. They cannot touch a thing without imbuing it with their own inner life. Wordsworth has described this gift as the inherent power of his poetry:

To every natural form, rock, fruits or flower,
Even the loose stones that cover the highway,
I gave a moral life: I saw them feel,
Or linked them to some feeling: the great mass
Lay imbedded in a quickening soul, and all
That I beheld respired with inward meaning.[19]

But with these powers of invention and of universal anima-
tion we are only in the anteroom of art. The artist must not
only feel the "inward meaning" of things and their moral life,
he must externalize his feelings. The highest and most characteristic power of artistic imagination appears in this latter
act. Externalization means visible or tangible embodiment
not simply in a particular material medium—in clay, bronze,
or marble—but in sensuous forms, in rhythms, in color pattern, in lines and design, in plastic shapes. It is the structure,
the balance and order, of these forms which affects us in the
work of art. Every art has its own characteristic idiom, which
is unmistakable and unexchangeable. The idioms of the various arts may be interconnected, as, for instance, when a lyric
is set to music or a poem is illustrated; but they are not trans-
latable into each other. Each idiom has a special task to fulfil
in the "architectonic" of art. "The problems of form arising
from this architectonic structure," states Adolf Hildebrand,
"though they are not given us immediately and self-evidently
by Nature, are yet the true problems of art. Material acquired
through a direct study of Nature is, by the architectonic
process, transformed into an artistic unity. When we speak of
the imitative aspect of art, we are referring to material which
has not yet been developed in this manner. Through architectonic development, then, sculpture and painting emerge from
the sphere of mere naturalism into the realm of true art." [20]
Even in poetry we find this architectonic development. Without it poetical imitation or invention would lose its force. The

19. *Prelude*, III, 127–132.
20. Adolf Hildebrand, *Das Problem der Form in der bildenden
Kunst*. English trans. by Max Meyer and R. M. Ogden, *The Problem
of Form in Painting and Sculpture* (New York, G. E. Stechert Co.,
1907), p. 12.

horrors of Dante's *Inferno* would remain unalleviated horrors, the raptures of his *Paradiso* would be visionary dreams were they not molded into a new shape by the magic of Dante's diction and verse.

In his theory of tragedy Aristotle stressed the invention of the tragic plot. Of all the necessary ingredients of tragedy—spectacle, characters, fable, diction, melody, and thought—he thought the combination of the incidents of the story (*hê tôn pragmatôn systasis*) the most important. For tragedy is essentially an imitation not of persons but of action and life. In a play the persons do not act in order to portray the characters; the characters are represented for the sake of the action. A tragedy is impossible without action, but there may be tragedy without character.[21] French classicism adopted and emphasized this Aristotelian theory. Corneille in the prefaces to his plays everywhere insists upon this point. He speaks with pride of his tragedy *Heraclius* because here the plot was so complicated that it needed a special intellectual effort to understand and unravel it. It is clear, however, that this sort of intellectual activity and intellectual pleasure is no necessary element of the artistic process. To enjoy the plots of Shakespeare—to follow with the keenest interest "the combination of the incidents of the story" in *Othello*, *Macbeth*, or *Lear*—does not necessarily mean that one understands and feels the tragic art of Shakespeare. Without Shakespeare's language, without the power of his dramatic diction, all this would remain unimpressive. The context of a poem cannot be separated from its form—from the verse, the melody, the rhythm. These formal elements are not merely external or technical means to reproduce a given intuition; they are part and parcel of the artistic intuition itself.

In romantic thought the theory of poetic imagination had reached its climax. Imagination is no longer that special human activity which builds up the human world of art. It now has universal metaphysical value. Poetic imagination is the only clue to reality. Fichte's idealism is based upon his conception of "productive imagination." Schelling declared in

21. Aristotle, op. cit., 6. 1450ᵃ 7–25. Ed. Bywater, pp. 18–19.

his *System of Transcendental Idealism* that art is the consummation of philosophy. In nature, in morality, in history we are still living in the propylaeum of philosophical wisdom; in art we enter into the sanctuary itself. Romantic writers in both verse and prose expressed themselves in the same vein. The distinction between poetry and philosophy was felt to be shallow and superficial. According to Friedrich Schlegel the highest task of a modern poet is to strive after a new form of poetry which he describes as "transcendental poetry." No other poetic genre can give us the essence of the poetic spirit, the "poetry of poetry." [22] To poeticize philosophy and to philosophize poetry—such was the highest aim of all the romantic thinkers. The true poem is not the work of the individual artist; it is the universe itself, the one work of art which is forever perfecting itself. Hence all the deepest mysteries of all the arts and sciences appertain to poetry.[23] "Poetry," said Novalis, "is what is absolutely and genuinely real. That is the kernel of my philosophy. The more poetic, the more true." [24]

By this conception poetry and art seemed to be elevated to a rank and dignity they had never before possessed. They became a *novum organum* for discovering the wealth and depth of the universe. Nevertheless this exuberant and ecstatic praise of poetic imagination had its strict limitations. In order to achieve their metaphysical aim the romanticist had to make a serious sacrifice. The infinite had been declared to be the true, indeed the only, subject of art. The beautiful was conceived as a symbolic representation of the infinite. He only can be an artist, according to Friedrich Schlegel, who has a religion of his own, an original conception of the infinite.[25] But in this event what becomes of our finite world, the world of sense experience? Clearly this world as such has no claim to beauty. Over against the true universe, the universe of the poet

22. Cf. Schlegel, "Athenäumsfragmente," 238, in *Prosaische Jugendschriften*, ed. by J. Minor (2d ed. Vienna, 1906), II, 242.
23. Schlegel, "Gespräch über die Poesie" (1800), op. cit., II, 364.
24. Novalis, ed. J. Minor, III, 11. Cf. O. Walzel, German Romanticism, English trans. by Alma E. Lussky (New York, 1932), p. 28.
25. *Ideen*, 13, in *Prosaische Jugendschriften*, II, 290.

and artist, we find our common and prosaic world deficient in all poetic beauty. A dualism of this kind is an essential feature in all romantic theories of art. When Goethe began to publish *Wilhelm Meister's Lehrjahre* the first romantic critics hailed the work with extravagant expressions of enthusiasm. Novalis saw in Goethe "the incarnation of the poetic spirit on earth." But as the work continued, as the romantic figure of Mignon and the harpist were overshadowed by more realistic characters and more prosaic events, Novalis grew deeply disappointed. He not only revoked his first judgment; he went so far as to call Goethe a traitor to the cause of poetry. *Wilhelm Meister* came to be looked upon as a satire, a *"Candide* against poetry." When poetry loses sight of the wonderful, it loses its significance and justification. Poetry cannot thrive in our trivial and commonplace world. The miraculous, the marvelous, and the mysterious are the only subjects that admit of a truly poetic treatment.

This conception of poetry is, however, rather a qualification and limitation than a genuine account of the creative process of art. Curiously enough the great realists of the nineteenth century had in this respect a keener insight into the art process than their romantic adversaries. They maintained a radical and uncompromising naturalism. But it was precisely this naturalism which led them to a more profound conception of artistic form. Denying the "pure forms" of the idealistic schools they concentrated upon the material aspect of things. By virtue of this sheer concentration they were able to overcome the conventional dualism between the poetic and the prosaic spheres. The nature of a work of art, according to the realists, does not depend on the greatness or smallness of its subject matter. No subject whatever is impermeable to the formative energy of art. One of the greatest triumphs of art is to make us see commonplace things in their real shape and in their true light. Balzac plunged into the most trifling features of the "human comedy," Flaubert made profound analyses of the meanest characters. In some of Émile Zola's novels we discover minute descriptions of the structure of a locomotive, of a department store, or of a coal mine. No technical detail, however insignificant, was omitted from these accounts.

Nevertheless, running through the works of all these realists great imaginative power is observable, which is by no means inferior to that of the romantic writers. The fact that this power could not be openly acknowledged was a serious drawback to the naturalistic theories of art. In their attempts to refute the romantic conceptions of a transcendental poetry they reverted to the old definition of art as an imitation of nature. In so doing they missed the principal point, since they failed to recognize the symbolic character of art. If such a characterization of art were admitted, there seemed to be no escape from the metaphysical theories of romanticism. Art is, indeed, symbolism, but the symbolism of art must be understood in an immanent, not in a transcendent sense. Beauty is "The Infinite finitely presented" according to Schelling. The real subject of art is not, however, the metaphysical Infinite of Schelling, nor is it the Absolute of Hegel. It is to be sought in certain fundamental structural elements of our sense experience itself—in lines, design, in architectural, musical forms. These elements are, so to speak, omnipresent. Free of all mystery, they are patent and unconcealed; they are visible, audible, tangible. In this sense Goethe did not hesitate to say that art does not pretend to show the metaphysical depth of things, it merely sticks to the surface of natural phenomena. But this surface is not immediately given. We do not know it before we discover it in the works of the great artists. This discovery, however, is not confined to a special field. To the extent that human language can express everything, the lowest and the highest things, art can embrace and pervade the whole sphere of human experience. Nothing in the physical or moral world, no natural thing and no human action, is by its nature and essence excluded from the realm of art, because nothing resists its formative and creative process. "Quicquid essentia dignum est," says Bacon in his *Novum Organum,* "id etiam scientia dignum est." [26] This dictum holds for art as well as for science.

26. Bacon, *Novum Organum,* Liber I, Aphor. CXX.

3   The psychological theories of art have a clear and palpable advantage over all the metaphysical theories. They are not obliged to give a general theory of beauty. They limit themselves to a narrower compass, for they are concerned only with the fact of beauty and with a descriptive analysis of this fact. The first task of psychological analysis is to determine the class of phenomena to which our experience of beauty belongs. This problem entails no difficulty. No one could ever deny that the work of art gives us the highest pleasure, perhaps the most durable and intense pleasure of which human nature is capable. As soon as we choose this psychological approach the secret of art seems, therefore, to be solved. There is nothing less mysterious than pleasure and pain. To call into question these best-known phenomena—phenomena not merely of human life but of life in general—would be absurd. Here if anywhere we find a *dos moi pou stô*, a fixed and immovable place to stand. If we succeed in connecting our aesthetic experience with this point there can no longer be any uncertainty as to the character of beauty and art.

The utter simplicity of this solution appears to recommend it. On the other hand all the theories of aesthetic hedonism have the defects of their qualities. They begin with the statement of a simple, undeniable, obvious fact; but after the first few steps they fall short of their purpose and come to a sudden standstill. Pleasure is an immediate datum of our experience. But when taken as a psychological principle its meaning becomes vague and ambiguous in the extreme. The term extends over such a large field as to cover the most diverse and heterogeneous phenomena. It is always tempting to introduce a general term broad enough to include the most disparate references. Yet if we yield to this temptation we are in danger of losing sight of significant and important differences. The systems of ethical and aesthetic hedonism have always been prone to obliterate these specific differences. Kant stresses this point in a characteristic remark in the *Critique of Practical Reason*. If the determination of our will, Kant argues, rests upon the feeling of agreeableness or disagreeableness which we expect from any cause, then it is all the same to us by what sort of ideas we are to be affected. The only thing that concerns us in making our choice is how great, how long continued, how easily obtained, and how often repeated this agreeableness is.

"Just as to the man who wants money to spend, it is all the same whether the gold was dug out of the mountain or washed out of the sand, provided it is everywhere accepted at the same value; so the man who cares only for the enjoyment of life does not ask whether the ideas are of the understanding or of the senses, but only *how much* and *how great* pleasure they will give us for the longest time." [27] If pleasure is the common denominator it is only the degree, not the kind, which really matters—all pleasures whatever are on the same level and may be traced back to a common psychological and biological origin.

In contemporary thought the theory of aesthetic hedonism has found its clearest expression in the philosophy of Santayana. According to Santayana beauty is pleasure regarded as a quality of things; it is "pleasure objectified." But this is begging the question. For how can pleasure—the most subjective state of our mind—ever be objectified? Science, says Santayana, "is the response to the demand for information, and in it we ask for the whole truth and nothing but the truth. Art is the response to the demand for entertainment, . . . and truth enters into it only as it subserves these ends." [28] But if this were the end of art we should be bound to say that art, in its highest achievements, fails to attain its real end. The "demand for entertainment" may be satisfied by much better and cheaper means. To think that the great artists worked for this purpose, that Michelangelo constructed Saint Peter's Cathedral, that Dante or Milton wrote their poems, for the sake of entertainment, is impossible. They would undoubtedly have subscribed to Aristotle's dictum that "to exert oneself and work for the sake of amusement seems silly and utterly

27. *Critique of Practical Reason*, trans. by T. K. Abbott (6th ed., New York, Longmans, Green & Co., 1927), p. 110.
28. *The Sense of Beauty* (New York, Charles Scribner's Sons, 1896), p. 22.

childish." [29] If art is enjoyment it is not the enjoyment of things but the enjoyment of forms. Delight in forms is quite different from delight in things or sense impressions. Forms cannot simply be impressed on our minds; we must produce them in order to feel their beauty. It is a common flaw of all the ancient and modern systems of aesthetic hedonism that they offer us a psychological theory of aesthetic pleasure which completely fails to account for the fundamental fact of aesthetic creativeness. In aesthetic life we experience a radical transformation. Pleasure itself is no longer a mere affection; it becomes a function. For the artist's eye is not simply an eye that reacts to or reproduces sense impressions. Its activity is not confined to receiving or registering the impressions of outward things or to combining these impressions in new and arbitrary ways. A great painter or musician is not characterized by his sensitiveness to color or sounds but by his power to elicit from his static material a dynamic life of forms. Only in this sense, then, can the pleasure we find in art be objectified. To define beauty as "pleasure objectified" contains, therefore, the whole problem in a nutshell. Objectification is always a constructive process. The physical world—the world of constant things and qualities—is no mere bundle of sense data, nor is the world of art a bundle of feelings and emotions. The first depends upon acts of theoretical objectification, objectification by concepts and scientific constructs; the second upon formative acts of a different type, acts of contemplation.

Other modern theories protesting against all attempts to identify art and pleasure lie open to the same objection as the theories of aesthetic hedonism. They try to find the explanation of the work of art by connecting it with other well-known phenomena. These phenomena are, however, on an entirely different level; they are passive, not active states of mind. Between the two classes we may find some analogies but we cannot trace them back to one and the same metaphysical or psychological origin. It is the struggle against the rationalist and intellectualist theories of art which is a common feature and a fundamental motive of these theories. French classicism

29. Aristotle, *Nicomachean Ethics*, 1776[b] 33.

had in a sense turned the work of art into an arithmetical problem which was to be solved by a sort of rule of three. The reaction against this conception was necessary and beneficial. But the first romantic critics—especially the German romanticists—went immediately to the opposite extreme. They declared the abstract intellectualism of the enlightenment to be a travesty upon art. We cannot understand the work of art by subjecting it to logical rules. A textbook on poetics cannot teach us how to write a good poem. For art arises from other and deeper sources. In order to discover these sources we must first forget our common standards, we must plunge into the mysteries of our unconscious life. The artist is a sort of somnambulist who must pursue his way without the interference or control of any conscious activity. To awake him would be to destroy his power. "It is the beginning of all poetry," said Friedrich Schlegel, "to abolish the law and method of the rationally proceeding reason and to plunge us once more into the ravishing confusion of fantasy, the original chaos of human nature." [30] Art is a waking dream to which we voluntarily surrender ourselves. This same romantic conception has left its mark upon contemporary metaphysical systems. Bergson gave a theory of beauty which was intended as the last and most conclusive proof of his general metaphysical principles. According to him there is no better illustration of the fundamental dualism, of the incompatibility, of intuition with reason than the work of art. What we call rational or scientific truth is superficial and conventional. Art is the escape from this shallow and narrow conventional world. It leads us back to the very sources of reality. If reality is "creative evolution" it is in the creativeness of art that we must seek the evidence for and the fundamental manifestation of the creativeness of life. At first sight this would appear to be a truly dynamic or energetic philosophy of beauty. But the intuition of Bergson is not a really active principle. It is a mode of receptivity, not of spontaneity. Aesthetic intuition, too, is everywhere described by Bergson as a passive capability, not as an active

30. For a fuller documentation and for a criticism of these early romantic theories of art see Irving Babbitt, *The New Laokoon*, chap. iv.

form. ". . . the object of art," writes Bergson, "is to put to sleep the active or rather resistant powers of our personality, and thus to bring us into a state of perfect responsiveness, in which we realize the idea that is suggested to us and sympathize with the feeling that is expressed. In the processes of art we shall find, in a weakened form, a refined and in some measure spiritualized version of the processes commonly used to induce the state of hypnosis. . . . The feeling of the beautiful is no specific feeling . . . every feeling experienced by us will assume an aesthetic character, provided that it has been *suggested*, and not *caused*. . . . There are thus distinct phases in the progress of an aesthetic feeling, as in the state of hypnosis . . ." [31] Our experience of beauty is not, however, of such a hypnotic character. By hypnosis we may prompt a man to certain actions or we may force upon him some sentiment. But beauty, in its genuine and specific sense, cannot be impressed upon our minds in this way. In order to feel it one must coöperate with the artist. One must not only sympathize with the artist's feelings but also enter into his creative activity. If the artist should succeed in putting to sleep the active powers of our personality he would paralyze our sense of beauty. The apprehension of beauty, the awareness of the dynamism of forms, cannot be communicated in this way. For beauty depends both on feelings of a specific kind and on an act of judgment and contemplation.

One of the great contributions of Shaftesbury to the theory of art was his insistence on this point. In his "Moralists" he gives an impressive account of the experience of beauty—an experience which he regarded as a specific privilege of human nature. "Nor will you deny beauty," writes Shaftesbury, "to the wild field, or to these flowers which grow around us, on this verdant couch. And yet, as lovely as are these forms of nature, the shining grass or silvered moss, the flowry thyme, wild rose, or honey-suckle; 'tis not their beauty allures the neighboring herds, delights the brouzing fawn, or kid and spreads the joy we see amidst the feeding flocks: 'Tis not the

31. Bergson, *Essai sur les données immédiates de la conscience*. English trans. by R. L. Pogson, *Time and Free Will* (London, Macmillan, 1912), pp. 14 ff.

Form rejoices; but that which is beneath the form: 'tis savouriness attracts, hunger impels; . . . for never can the *Form* be of real force where it is uncontemplated, unjudged of, unexamined, and stands only as the accidental note or token of what appeases provoked sense. . . . If brutes therefore . . . be incapable of knowing and enjoying beauty, as being brutes, and having sense only . . . for their own share; it follows, that neither can man by the same *sense* . . . conceive or enjoy *beauty:* but all the *beauty* . . . he enjoys, is in a nobler way, and by the help of what is noblest, his mind and reason." [32] Shaftesbury's praise of mind and reason was very far from the intellectualism of the enlightenment. His rhapsody on the beauty and infinite creative power of nature was an entirely new feature of eighteenth-century intellectual history. In this respect he was one of the first champions of romanticism. But Shaftesbury's romanticism was of a Platonic type. His theory of aesthetic form was a Platonic conception by virtue of which he was led to react and protest against the sensationalism of the English empiricists. [33]

The objection raised against the metaphysics of Bergson holds also for the psychological theory of Nietzsche. In one of his first writings, *The Birth of Tragedy from the Spirit of Music*, Nietzsche challenged the conceptions of the great classicists of the eighteenth century. It is not, he argues, the ideal of Winckelmann that we find in Greek art. In Aeschylus, in Sophocles or Euripides we seek in vain for "noble simplicity and quiet grandeur." The greatness of Greek tragedy consists in the depth and extreme tension of violent emotions. Greek tragedy was the offspring of a Dionysiac cult; its power was an orgiastic power. But orgy alone could not produce Greek drama. The force of Dionysus was counterbalanced by the force of Apollo. This fundamental polarity is the essence of every great work of art. Great art of all times has arisen from

32. Shaftesbury, "The Moralists," sec. 2, Pt. III. See *Characteristics* (1714), II, 424 f.

33. For a detailed discussion of Shaftesbury's place in the philosophy of the eighteenth century, see Cassirer, *Die platonische Renaissance in England und die Schule von Cambridge* (Leipzig, 1932), chap. vi.

the interpenetration of two opposing forces—from an orgiastic impulse and a visionary state. It is the same contrast as exists between the dream state and the state of intoxication. Both these states release all manner of artistic powers from within us, but each unfetters powers of a different kind. Dream gives us the power of vision, of association, of poetry; intoxication gives us the power of grand attitudes, of passion, of song and dance.[34] Even in this theory of its psychological origin one of the essential features of art has disappeared. For artistic inspiration is not intoxication, artistic imagination is not dream or hallucination. Every great work of art is characterized by a deep structural unity. We cannot account for this unity by reducing it to two different states which, like the dream state and the state of intoxication, are entirely diffused and disorganized. We cannot integrate a structural whole out of amorphous elements.

Of a different type are those theories which hope to elucidate the nature of art by reducing it to the function of play. To these theories one cannot object that they overlook or underrate the free activity of man. Play is an active function; it is not confined within the boundaries of the empirically given. On the other hand the pleasure we find in play is completely disinterested. None of the specific qualities and conditions of the work of art seems, therefore, to be missing in play activity. Most of the exponents of the play theory of art have, indeed, assured us that they were quite unable to find any difference between the two functions.[35] They have declared that there is not a single characteristic of art which does not apply to games of illusion, and no characteristic of such games which could not also be found in art. But all the arguments that may be alleged for this thesis are purely negative. Psychologically speaking, play and art bear a close resemblance to each other. They are nonutilitarian and unrelated to any practical end. In play as in art we leave behind us our immediate practical needs in order to give our world a

34. Cf. Nietzsche, The Will to Power. English trans. by A. M. Ludovici (London, 1910), p. 240.
35. See, for instance Konrad Lange, Das Wesen der Kunst (Berlin 1901). 2 vols.

new shape. But this analogy is not sufficient to prove a real identity. Artistic imagination always remains sharply distinguished from that sort of imagination which characterizes our play activity. In play we have to do with simulated images which may become so vivid and impressive as to be taken for realities. To define art as a mere sum of such simulated images would indicate a very meager conception of its character and task. What we call *"aesthetic semblance"* is not the same phenomenon that we experience in games of illusion. Play gives us illusive images; art gives us a new kind of truth—a truth not of empirical things but of pure forms.

In our aesthetic analysis above we distinguished between three different kinds of imagination: the power of invention, the power of personification, and the power to produce pure sensuous forms. In the play of a child we find the two former powers, but not the third. The child plays with *things*, the artist plays with *forms*, with lines and designs, rhythms and melodies. In a playing child we admire the facility and quickness of transformation. The greatest tasks are performed with the scantiest means. Any piece of wood may be turned into a living being. Nevertheless, this transformation signifies only a metamorphosis of the objects themselves; it does not mean a metamorphosis of objects into forms. In play we merely rearrange and redistribute the materials given to sense perception. Art is constructive and creative in another and a deeper sense. A child at play does not live in the same world of rigid empirical facts as the adult. The child's world has a much greater mobility and transmutability. Yet the playing child, nevertheless, does no more than exchange the actual things of his environment for other possible things. No such exchange as this characterizes genuine artistic activity. Here the requirement is much more severe. For the artist dissolves the hard stuff of things in the crucible of his imagination, and the result of this process is the discovery of a new world of poetical, musical, or plastic forms. To be sure, a great many ostensible works of art are very far from satisfying this requirement. It is the task of the aesthetic judgment or of artistic taste to distinguish between a genuine work of art and those other spurious products which are indeed playthings, or at most "the response to the demand for entertainment."

A closer analysis of the psychological origin and psychological effects of play and art leads to the same conclusion. Play gives us diversion and recreation but it also serves a different purpose. Play has a general biological relevance in so far as it anticipates future activities. It has often been pointed out that the play of a child has a propaedeutic value. The boy playing war and the little girl dressing her doll are both accomplishing a sort of preparation and education for other more serious tasks. The function of fine art cannot be accounted for in this manner. Here is neither diversion nor preparation. Some modern aestheticians have found it necessary to distinguish sharply between two types of beauty. One is the beauty of "great" art; the other is described as "easy" beauty.[36] But, strictly speaking, the beauty of a work of art is never "easy." The enjoyment of art does not originate in a softening or relaxing process but in intensification of all our energies. The diversion which we find in play is the very opposite of that attitude which is a necessary prerequisite of aesthetic contemplation and aesthetic judgment. Art demands the fullest concentration. As soon as we fail to concentrate and give way to a mere play of pleasurable feelings and associations, we have lost sight of the work of art as such.

The play theory of art has developed in two entirely different directions. In the history of aesthetics Schiller, Darwin, and Spencer are usually regarded as the outstanding representatives of this theory. Yet it is difficult to find a point of contact between the views of Schiller and modern biological theories of art. In their fundamental tendency these views are not only divergent but in a sense incompatible. The very term "play" is understood and explained in Schiller's accounts in a sense quite different from that of all the subsequent theories. Schiller's is a transcendental and idealistic theory; Darwin's and Spencer's theories are biological and naturalistic. Darwin and Spencer regard play and beauty as general natural

36. See Bernard Bosanquet, *Three Lectures on Aesthetics*, and S. Alexander, *Beauty and Other Forms of Value*.

phenomena, while Schiller connects them with the world of freedom. And, according to his Kantian dualism, freedom does not signify the same thing as nature; on the contrary, it represents the opposite pole. Both freedom and beauty belong to the intelligible, not to the phenomenal world. In all the naturalistic variants of the play theory of art the play of animals was studied side by side with that of men. Schiller could not admit any such view. For him play is not a general organic activity but a specifically human one. "Man only plays when in the full meaning of the word he is a man, and *he is only completely a man when he plays.*" [37] To speak of an analogy, let alone an identity, between human and animal play or, in the human sphere, between the play of art and the so-called games of illusion, is quite alien to the theory of Schiller. To him this analogy would have appeared to be a basic misconception.

If the historical background of Schiller's theory is taken into consideration his viewpoint is easily understandable. He did not hesitate to connect the "ideal" world of art with the play of a child because in his mind the world of the child had undergone a process of idealization and sublimation. For Schiller spoke as a pupil and admirer of Rousseau, and he saw the life of the child in the new light in which the French philosopher had placed him. "There is deep meaning in the play of a child," Schiller asserted. Yet even though we admit this thesis it must be said that the "meaning" of play is different from that of beauty. Schiller himself defines beauty as "living form." To him the awareness of living forms is the first and indispensable step which leads to the experience of freedom. Aesthetic contemplation or reflection, according to Schiller, is the first liberal attitude of man toward the universe. "Whereas desire seizes at once its object, reflection removes it to a distance and renders it inalienably her own by saving it from the greed of passion." [38] It is precisely this "liberal," this conscious and reflective attitude which is lack-

37. Schiller, *Briefe über die ästhetische Erziehung des Menschen* (1795), Letter XV. English trans., *Essays Aesthetical and Philosophical* (London, George Bell & Sons, 1916), p. 71.
38. Schiller, *op. cit.*, Letter XXV. English trans., p. 102.

ing in a child's play, and which marks the boundary line between play and art.

On the other hand this "removal to a distance" which is here described as one of the necessary and most characteristic features of the work of art has always proved to be a stumbling block for aesthetic theory. If this be true, it was objected, art is no longer something really human, for it has lost all connection with human life. The defenders of the principle *l'art pour l'art* did not, however, fear this objection; on the contrary they openly defied it. They held it to be the highest merit and privilege of art that it burns all bridges linking it with commonplace reality. Art must remain a mystery inaccessible to the *profanum vulgus*. "A poem," said Stéphane Mallarmé, "must be an enigma for the vulgar, chamber-music for the initiated." [39] Ortega y Gasset has written a book in which he foretells and defends the "dehumanization" of art. In this process he thinks that the point will at last be reached at which the human element will almost vanish from art.[40] Other critics have supported a diametrically opposed thesis. "When we look at a picture or read a poem or listen to music," I. A. Richards insists, "we are not doing something quite unlike what we were doing on our way to the Gallery or when we dressed in the morning. The fashion in which the experience is caused in us is different, and as a rule the experience is more complex and, if we are successful, more unified. But our activity is not of a fundamentally different kind." [41] But this theoretical antagonism is no real antinomy. If beauty according to Schiller's definition is "living form" it unites in its nature and essence the two elements which here stand opposed. To be sure, it is not the same thing to live in the realm of forms as to live in that of things, of the empirical objects of our surroundings. The forms of art, on the other hand, are not empty forms. They perform a definite task in the construction and organization of human experience. To live

39. Quoted from Katherine Gilbert, *Studies in Recent Aesthetic* (Chapel Hill, 1927), p. 18.
40. Ortega y Gasset, *La dezhumanización del' arte* (Madrid, 1925).
41. I. A. Richards, *Principles of Literary Criticism* (New York, Harcourt, Brace, 1925), pp. 16–17.

in the realm of forms does not signify an evasion of the issues of life; it represents, on the contrary, the realization of one of the highest energies of life itself. We cannot speak of art as "extrahuman" or "superhuman" without overlooking one of its fundamental features, its constructive power in the framing of our human universe.

All aesthetic theories which attempt to account for art in terms of analogies taken from disordered and disintegrated spheres of human experience—from hypnosis, dream, or intoxication—miss the main point. A great lyrical poet has the power to give definite shape to our most obscure feelings. This is possible only because his work, though dealing with a subject which is apparently irrational and ineffable, possesses a clear organization and articulation. Not even in the most extravagant creations of art do we ever find the "ravishing confusions of fantasy," the "original chaos of human nature." This definition of art, given by the romantic writers,[42] is a contradiction in terms. Every work of art has an intuitive structure, and that means a character of rationality. Every single element must be felt as part of a comprehensive whole. If in a lyrical poem we change one of the words, an accent or a rhythm, we are in danger of destroying the specific tone and charm of the poem. Art is not fettered to the rationality of things or events. It may infringe all those laws of probability which classical aestheticians declared to be the constitutional laws of art. It may give us the most bizarre and grotesque vision, and yet retain a rationality of its own—the rationality of form. We may in this way interpret a saying of Goethe's which at first sight looks paradoxical, "Art: a second nature; mysterious too, but more understandable, for it originates in the understanding." [43]

Science gives us order in thoughts; morality gives us order in actions; art gives us order in the apprehension of visible, tangible, and audible appearances. Aesthetic theory was very

42. See above, p. 161.

43. "Kunst: eine andere Natur, auch geheimnisvoll, aber verständlicher; denn sie entspringt aus dem Verstande." See Maximen und Reflexionen, ed. Max Hecker, in "Schriften der Goethe-Gesellschaft," XXI (1907), 229.

slow indeed to recognize and fully realize these fundamental differences. But if instead of seeking a metaphysical theory of beauty we simply analyze our immediate experience of the work of art we can hardly miss the mark. Art may be defined as a symbolic language. But this leaves us only with the common genus, not the specific difference. In modern aesthetics the interest in the common genus seems to prevail to such a degree as almost to eclipse and obliterate the specific difference. Croce insists that there is not only a close relation but a complete identity between language and art. To his way of thinking it is quite arbitrary to distinguish between the two activities. Whoever studies general linguistics, according to Croce, studies aesthetic problems—and vice versa. There is, however, an unmistakable difference between the symbols of art and the linguistic terms of ordinary speech or writing. These two activities agree neither in character nor purpose; they do not employ the same means, nor do they tend toward the same ends. Neither language nor art gives us mere imitation of things or actions; both are representations. But a representation in the medium of sensuous forms differs widely from a verbal or conceptual representation. The description of a landscape by a painter or poet and that by a geographer or geologist have scarcely anything in common. Both the mode of description and the motive are different in the work of a scientist and in the work of an artist. A geographer may depict a landscape in a plastic manner, and he may even paint it in rich and vivid colors. But what he wishes to convey is not the vision of the landscape but its empirical concept. To this end he has to compare its form with other forms; he has to find out, by observation and induction, its characteristic features. The geologist goes a step farther in this empirical delineation. He does not content himself with a record of physical facts, for he wishes to divulge the origin of these facts. He distinguishes the strata by which the soil has been built up, noting chronological differences; and he goes back to the general causal laws according to which the earth has reached its present shape. For the artist all these empirical relations, all these comparisons with other facts, and all this research into causal relations do not exist. Our ordinary empirical concepts may be, roughly speaking, divided into two classes according as they have to do with practical or theoretical interests. The one class is concerned with the use of things and with the question "What is that for?" The other is concerned with the causes of things and with the question "Whence?" But upon entering the realm of art we have to forget all such questions. Behind the existence, the nature, the empirical properties of things, we suddenly discover their forms. These forms are no static elements. What they show is a mobile order, which reveals to us a new horizon of nature. Even the greatest admirers of art have often spoken of it as if it were a mere accessory, an embellishment or ornament, of life. But this is to underrate its real significance and its real role in human culture. A mere duplicate of reality would always be of a very questionable value. Only by conceiving art as a special direction, a new orientation, of our thoughts, our imagination, and our feelings, can we comprehend its true meaning and function. The plastic arts make us see the sensible world in all its richness and multifariousness. What would we know of the innumerable nuances in the aspect of things were it not for the works of the great painters and sculptors? Poetry is, similarly, the revelation of our personal life. The infinite potentialities of which we had but a dim and obscure presentiment are brought to light by the lyric poet, by the novelist, and by the dramatist. Such art is in no sense mere counterfeit or facsimile, but a genuine manifestation of our inner life.

So long as we live in the world of sense impressions alone we merely touch the surface of reality. Awareness of the depth of things always requires an effort on the part of our active and constructive energies. But since these energies do not move in the same direction, and do not tend toward the same end, they cannot give us the same aspect of reality. There is a conceptual depth as well as a purely visual depth. The first is discovered by science; the second is revealed in art. The first aids us in understanding the reasons of things; the second in seeing their forms. In science we try to trace phenomena back to their first causes, and to general laws and principles.

In art we are absorbed in their immediate appearance, and we enjoy this appearance to the fullest extent in all its richness and variety. Here we are not concerned with the uniformity of laws but with the multiformity and diversity of intuitions. Even art may be described as knowledge, but art is knowledge of a peculiar and specific kind. We may well subscribe to the observation of Shaftesbury that "all beauty is truth." But the truth of beauty does not consist in a theoretical description or explanation of things; it consists rather in the "sympathetic vision" of things.[44] The two views of truth are in contrast with one another, but not in conflict or contradiction. Since art and science move in entirely different planes they cannot contradict or thwart one another. The conceptual interpretation of science does not preclude the intuitive interpretation of art. Each has its own perspective and, so to speak, its own angle of refraction. The psychology of sense perception has taught us that without the use of both eyes, without a binocular vision, there would be no awareness of the third dimension of space. The depth of human experience in the same sense depends on the fact that we are able to vary our modes of seeing, that we can alternate our views of reality. *Rerum videre formas* is a no less important and indispensable task than *rerum cognoscere causas*. In ordinary experience we connect phenomena according to the category of causality or finality. According as we are interested in the theoretical reasons or the practical effects of things, we think of them as causes or as means. Thus we habitually lose sight of their immediate appearance until we can no longer see them face to face. Art, on the other hand, teaches us to visualize, not merely to conceptualize or utilize, things. Art gives us a richer, more vivid and colorful image of reality, and a more profound insight into its formal structure. It is characteristic of the

44. See De Witt H. Parker, *The Principles of Aesthetics*, p. 39: "Scientific truth is the fidelity of a description to the external objects of experience; artistic truth is sympathetic vision—the organization into clearness of experience itself." The difference between scientific and aesthetic experience has recently been illustrated in a very instructive article by Prof. F. S. C. Northrup in the review *Furioso*, I, No. 4, 71 ff.

nature of man that he is not limited to one specific and single approach to reality but can choose his point of view and so pass from one aspect of things to another.

10 History

After all the various and divergent definitions of the nature of man which had been given in the history of philosophy, modern philosophers were often led to the conclusion that the very question is in a sense misleading and contradictory. In our modern world, says Ortega y Gasset, we are experiencing a breakdown of the classical, the Greek theory of being and, accordingly, of the classical theory of man.

"Nature is a thing, a great thing, that is composed of many lesser things. Now, whatever be the differences between things, they all have one basic feature in common, which consists simply in the fact that things *are*, they have their being. And this signifies not only that they exist, that they are, in front of us, but also that they possess a given, fixed structure or consistency. . . . An alternative expression is the word 'nature.' And the task of natural science is to penetrate beneath changing appearances to that permanent nature or texture. . . . To-day we know that all the marvels of the natural sciences, inexhaustible though they be in principle, must always come to a full stop before the strange reality of human life. Why? If all things have given up a large part of their secret to physical science, why does this alone hold out so stoutly? The explanation must go deep, down to the roots. Perchance it is no less than this: that man is not a thing, that it is false to talk of human nature, that man has no nature. . . . Human life . . . is not a thing, has not a nature, and in consequence we must make up our minds to think of it in terms and categories and concepts that will be *radically* different from such as shed light on the phenomena of matter . . ." Till now our logic has been a logic of being, based upon the fundamental concepts of Eleatic thought. But with these concepts we can never hope to understand the distinctive character of man. Eleaticism was the radical intellectualization of human life. It is time to break out of this magic circle. "In order to speak of man's being we must first elaborate a non-Eleatic concept of being, as others have elaborated a non-Euclidean geometry. The time has come for the seed sown by Heraclitus to bring forth its mighty harvest." Having learned to immunize ourselves against intellectualism we are now conscious of a liberation from naturalism. *"Man has no nature, what he has is . . . history."* [1]

The conflict between being and becoming, which in Plato's *Theaetetus* is described as the fundamental theme of Greek philosophical thought, is, however, not resolved if we pass from the world of nature to the world of history. Since Kant's *Critique of Pure Reason* we conceive the dualism between being and becoming as a logical rather than a metaphysical dualism. We no longer speak of a world of absolute change as opposed to another world of absolute rest. We do not regard substance and change as different realms of being but as categories—as conditions and presuppositions of our empirical knowledge. These categories are universal principles; they are not confined to special objects of knowledge. We must therefore expect to find them in all forms of human experience. As a matter of fact even the world of history cannot be understood and interpreted in terms of mere change. This world too includes a substantial element, an element of being—not, however, to be defined in the same sense as in the physical world. Without this element we could scarcely speak, as does Ortega y Gasset, of history as a system. A system always presupposes, if not an identical nature, at least an identical structure. As a matter of fact this structural identity—an identity of form, not of matter—has always been emphasized by the great historians. They have told us that man has a history *because* he has a nature. Such was the judgment of the historians of the Renaissance, for instance, of Machiavelli, and many modern historians have upheld this view. Beneath the temporal flux and behind the polymorphism of human life they have hoped to discover the constant features of

1. Ortega y Gasset, "History as a System," in *Philosophy and History, Essays Presented to Ernst Cassirer*, pp. 293, 294, 300, 305, 313.

human nature. In his *Thoughts on World History* Jakob Burckhardt defined the task of the historian as an attempt to ascertain the constant, recurrent, typical elements, because such elements as these can evoke a resonant echo in our intellect and feelings.[2]

What we call "historical consciousness" is a very late product of human civilization. It is not to be found before the time of the great Greek historians. And even the Greek thinkers were still unable to offer a philosophical analysis of the specific form of historical thought. Such an analysis did not appear until the eighteenth century. The concept of history first reaches maturity in the work of Vico and Herder. When man first became cognizant of the problem of time, when he was no longer confined within the narrow circle of his immediate desires and needs, when he began to inquire into the origin of things, he could find only a mythical, not a historical origin. In order to understand the world—the physical world as well as the social world—he had to project it upon the mythical past. In myth we find the first attempts to ascertain a chronological order of things and events, to give a cosmology and a genealogy of gods and men. But this cosmology and genealogy do not signify a historical distinction in the proper sense. The past, present, and future are still tied up together; they form an undifferentiated unity and an indiscriminate whole. Mythical time has no definite structure; it is still an "eternal time." From the point of view of the mythical consciousness the past has never passed away; it is always here and now. When man begins to unravel the complex web of the mythical imagination he feels himself transported into a new world; he begins to form a new concept of truth.

We can follow the individual stages of this process when studying the development of Greek historical thought from Herodotus to Thucydides. Thucydides is the first thinker to see and describe the history of his own times and to look back at the past with a clear and critical mind. And he is aware of

2. Jakob Burckhardt, *Weltgeschichtliche Betrachtungen*, ed. by Jakob Oeri (Berlin and Stuttgart, 1905), p. 4. English ed. by James Hastings Nichols, *Force and Freedom; Reflections on History* (New York, Pantheon Books, 1943), p. 82.

the fact that this is a new and decisive step. He is convinced that the clear discrimination between mythical and historical thought, between legend and truth, is the characteristic feature which will make his work an "everlasting possession." [3] Other great historians have felt similarly. In an autobiographical sketch Ranke tells how he first became aware of his mission as a historian. As a youth he was very much attracted by the romantic-historical writings of Walter Scott. He read them with a lively sympathy, but he also took offense at some points. He was shocked when he found that the description of the conflict between Louis XI and Charles the Bold was in flagrant contradiction with the historical facts. "I studied Commines and the contemporary reports which are attached to the editions of this author and became convinced that a Louis XI and a Charles the Bold, as they are described in Scott's *Quentin Durward*, had never existed. In this comparison I found that the historical evidence was more beautiful and, at any rate, more interesting than all romantic fiction. I turned away from it and resolved to avoid all invention and fabrication in my works and stick to the facts." [4]

To define historical truth as "concordance with the facts"— *adaequatio res et intellectus*—is however no satisfactory solution of the problem. It begs the question instead of solving it. That history has to begin with facts and that, in a sense, these facts are not only the beginning but the end, the alpha and omega of our historical knowledge, is undeniable. But what is a historical fact? All factual truth implies theoretical truth.[5] When we speak of facts we do not simply refer to our immediate sense data. We are thinking of empirical, that is to say objective, facts. This objectivity is not given; it always implies an act and a complicated process of judgment. If we wish to know the difference between scientific facts—between the facts of physics, of biology, of history—we must, therefore, always begin with an analysis of judgments. We must study

3. *ktêma es aei*, Thucydides, *De bello Peloponnesiaco*, I, 22.

4. Ranke, "Aufsätze zur eigenen Lebensgeschichte" (November, 1885), in "Sämmtliche Werke," ed. A. Dove, LIII, 61.

5. "Das Höchste wäre: zu begreifen, dass alles Faktische schon Theorie ist." Goethe, *Maximen und Reflexionen*, p. 125.

the modes of knowledge by which these facts are accessible.

What makes the difference between a physical fact and a historical fact? Both are regarded as parts of one empirical reality; to both we ascribe objective truth. But if we wish to ascertain the nature of this truth, we proceed in different ways. A physical fact is determined by observation and experiment. This process of objectification attains its end if we succeed in describing the given phenomena in mathematical language, in the language of numbers. A phenomenon which cannot be so described, which is not reducible to a process of measurement, is not a part of our physical world. Defining the task of physics Max Planck says that the physicist has to measure all measurable things and to render all unmeasurable things measurable. Not all physical things or processes are immediately measurable; in many, if not most, cases we are dependent on indirect methods of verification and measurement. But the physical facts are always related by causal laws to other phenomena which are directly observable or measurable. If a physicist is in doubt about the results of an experiment he can repeat and correct it. He finds his objects present at every moment, ready to answer his questions. But with the historian the case is different. His facts belong to the past, and the past is gone forever. We cannot reconstruct it; we cannot waken it to a new life in a mere physical, objective sense. All we can do is to "remember" it—give it a new ideal existence. Ideal reconstruction, not empirical observation, is the first step in historical knowledge. What we call a scientific fact is always the answer to a scientific question which we have formulated beforehand. But to what can the historian direct this question? He cannot confront the events themselves, and he cannot enter into the forms of a former life. He has only an indirect approach to his subject matter. He must consult his sources. But these sources are not physical things in the usual sense of this term. They all imply a new and specific moment. The historian, like the physicist, lives in a material world. Yet what he finds at the very beginning of his research is not a world of physical objects but a symbolic universe—a world of symbols. He must, first of all, learn to read these symbols. Any historical fact, however simple it may appear, can only be determined and understood by such a previous analysis of symbols. Not things or events but documents or monuments are the first and immediate objects of our historical knowledge. Only through the mediation and intervention of these symbolic data can we grasp the real historical data—the events and the men of the past.

Before entering into a general discussion of the problem I should like to clarify this point by reference to a specific concrete example. About thirty-five years ago an old Egyptian papyrus was found in Egypt under the débris of a house. It contained several inscriptions which seemed to be the notes of a lawyer or public notary concerning his business—drafts of testaments, legal contracts, and so on. Up to this point the papyrus belonged simply to the material world; it had no historical importance, and, so to speak, no historical existence. But a second text was then discovered under the first which after a closer examination could be recognized as the remnants of four hitherto unknown comedies of Menander. At this moment the nature and significance of the codex changed completely. Here was no longer a mere "piece of matter"; this papyrus had become a historical document of the highest value and interest. It bore witness to an important stage in the development of Greek literature. Yet this significance was not immediately obvious. The codex had to be submitted to all sorts of critical tests, to careful linguistic, philological, literary, and aesthetic analysis. After this complicated process it was no longer a mere thing; it was charged with meaning. It had become a symbol, and this symbol gave us new insight into Greek culture—into Greek life and Greek poetry.[6]

All this seems obvious and unmistakable. But, curiously enough, precisely this fundamental characteristic of historical knowledge has been entirely overlooked in most of our modern discussions of historical method and historical truth. Most writers looked for the difference between history and science in the *logic*, not in the *object* of history. They took the greatest pains to construct a new logic of history. But all these attempts

6. For details of this discovery see Gustave Lefebre, *Fragments d'un manuscrit de Ménandre, découverts et publiés* (LeCaire, Impression de l'Institut Français d'Archéologie, 1907).

were doomed to failure. For logic is, after all, a very simple and uniform thing. It is one because truth is one. In his quest of truth the historian is bound to the same formal rules as the scientist. In his modes of reasoning and arguing, in his inductive inferences, in his investigation of causes, he obeys the same general laws of thought as a physicist or biologist. So far as these fundamental theoretical activities of the human mind are concerned we can make no discrimination between the different fields of knowledge. As regards this problem we must subscribe to the words of Descartes: "The sciences taken all together are identical with human wisdom, which always remains one and the same, however applied to different subjects, and suffers no more differentiation proceeding from them than the light of the sun experiences from the variety of the things which it illumines." [7]

No matter how heterogeneous the objects of human knowledge may be, the forms of knowledge always show an inner unity and a logical homogeneity. Historical and scientific thought are distinguishable not by their logical form but by their objectives and subject matter. If we wanted to describe this distinction it would not be enough to say that the scientist has to do with present objects whereas the historian has to do with past objects. Such a distinction would be misleading. The scientist may very well, like the historian, inquire into the remote origin of things. Such an attempt, for instance, was made by Kant. In 1755 Kant developed an astronomical theory which also became a universal history of the material world. He applied the new method of physics, the Newtonian method, to the solution of a historical problem. In so doing he developed the nebular hypothesis by which he tried to describe the evolution of the present cosmic order from a former undifferentiated and unorganized state of matter. This was a problem of natural history, but it was not history in the specific sense of the term. History does not aim to disclose a former state of the physical world but rather a former stage

7. Descartes, *Regulae ad directionem ingenii*, I, "Oeuvres," ed. Charles Adam and Paul Tannery (Paris, 1897), X, 360. English trans. by Elizabeth S. Haldane and G. R. T. Ross, "The Philosophical Works of Descartes" (Cambridge University Press, 1911), I, 1.

of human life and human culture. For the solution of this problem it can make use of scientific methods, but it cannot restrict itself only to the data available by these methods. No object whatever is exempt from the laws of nature. Historical objects have no separate and self-contained reality; they are embodied in physical objects. But in spite of this embodiment they belong, so to speak, to a higher dimension. What we call the historic sense does not change the shape of things, nor does it detect in them a new quality. But it does give to things and events a new depth. When the scientist wishes to go back into the past he employs no concepts or categories but those of his observations of the present. He connects the present with the past by following backward the chain of causes and effects. He studies in the present the material traces left by the past. This is, for instance, the method of geology or paleontology. History too has to begin with these traces, for without them it could not take a single step. But this is only a first and preliminary task. To this actual, empirical reconstruction history adds a symbolic reconstruction. The historian must learn to read and interpret his documents and monuments not only as dead remnants of the past but as living messages from it, messages addressing us in a language of their own. The symbolic content of these messages is, however, not immediately observable. It is the work of the linguist, the philologist, and the historian to make them speak and to make us understand their language. Not in the logical structure of historical thought but in this special task, in this special mandate, consists the fundamental distinction between the works of the historian and the geologist or paleontologist. If the historian fails to decipher the symbolic language of his monuments history remains to him a sealed book. In a certain sense the historian is much more of a linguist than a scientist. But he not only studies the spoken and written languages of mankind; he tries to penetrate into the sense of all the various symbolic idioms. He finds his texts not merely in books, in annals or memoirs. He has to read hieroglyphs or cuneiform inscriptions, look at colors on a canvas, at statues in marble or bronze, at cathedrals or temples, at coins or gems. But he does not consider all these things simply with the mind of an antiquary who wishes to collect and preserve the treasures of olden times. What the historian is in search of is rather the materialization of the spirit of a former age. He detects the same spirit in laws and statutes, in charters and bills of right, in social institutions and political constitutions, in religious rites and ceremonies. To the true historian such material is not petrified fact but living form. History is the attempt to fuse together all these *disjecta membra*, the scattered limbs of the past and to synthesize them and mold them into new shape.

Among the modern founders of a philosophy of history Herder had the clearest insight into this side of the historical process. His works give us not merely a recollection but a resurrection of the past. Herder was no historian in the proper sense. He has left us no great historical work. And even his philosophical achievement is not to be compared with the work of Hegel. Nevertheless, he was the pioneer of a new ideal of historical truth. Without him the work of Ranke or Hegel would not have been possible. For he possessed the great personal power of revivifying the past, of imparting an eloquence to all the fragments and remnants of man's moral, religious, and cultural life. It was this feature of Herder's work which aroused the enthusiasm of Goethe. As he wrote in one of his letters, he did not find in Herder's historical descriptions the mere "husk and shell of human beings." What excited his profound admiration was Herder's "manner of sweeping—not simply sifting gold out of the rubbish, but regenerating the rubbish itself to a living plant." [8]

It is this "palingenesis," this rebirth of the past, which marks and distinguishes the great historian. Friedrich Schlegel called the historian *einen rückwärts gekehrten Propheten*, a retrospective prophet.[9] There is also a prophecy of the past, a revelation of its hidden life. History cannot predict the events to come; it can only interpret the past. But human life is an

8. "Deine Art zu fegen—und nicht etwa aus dem Kehricht Gold zu sieben, sondern den Kehricht zur lebendigen Pflanze umzupalingenesieren, legt mich immer auf die Knie meines Herzens." Goethe an Herder, May 1775, *Briefe* (Weimar ed.), II, 262.

9. "Athenäumsfragmente," 80, *op. cit.*, II, 215.

organism in which all elements imply and explain each other. Consequently a new understanding of the past gives us at the same time a new prospect of the future, which in turn becomes an impulse to intellectual and social life. For this double view of the world in prospect and in retrospect the historian must select his point of departure. He cannot find it except in his own time. He cannot go beyond the conditions of his present experience. Historical knowledge is the answer to definite questions, an answer which must be given by the past; but the questions themselves are put and dictated by the present—by our present intellectual interests and our present moral and social needs.

This connection between present and past is undeniable; but we may draw from it very different conclusions concerning the certainty and value of historical knowledge. In contemporary philosophy Croce is the champion of the most radical "historicism." To him history is not merely a special province but the whole of reality. His thesis that all history is contemporary history leads, therefore, to a complete identification of philosophy and history. Above and beyond the human realm of history there is no other realm of being, no other subject matter for philosophical thought.[10] The opposite inference was drawn by Nietzsche. He, too, insisted that "we can only explain the past by what is highest in the present." But this assertion served him only as a starting point for a violent attack on the value of history. In his "Thoughts out of Season," with which he began his work as a philosopher and as a critic of modern culture, Nietzsche challenged the so-called "historic sense" of our times. He tried to prove that this historic sense, far from being a merit and privilege of our cultural life, is its intrinsic danger. It is a malady from which we suffer. History has no meaning except as the servant of life and action. If the servant usurps the power, if he sets us as the master, he obstructs the energies of life. By excess of history our life has become maimed and degenerate. It hinders the mighty impulse to new deeds and paralyzes the doer.

10. For this problem see Guido Calogero, "On the So-Called Identity of History and Philosophy," in *Philosophy and History, Essays Presented to Ernst Cassirer*, pp. 35-52.

For most of us can only do if we forget. The unrestricted historic sense pushed to its logical extreme uproots the future.[11] But this judgment depends on Nietzsche's artificial discrimination between the life of action and the life of thought. When Nietzsche made this attack he was still an adherent and pupil of Schopenhauer's. He conceived life as the manifestation of a blind will. Blindness came to be the very condition for Nietzsche of the truly active life; thought and consciousness were opposed to vitality. If we reject this presupposition Nietzsche's consequences become untenable. To be sure our consciousness of the past should not enfeeble or cripple our active powers. If employed in the right way it gives us a freer survey of the present and strengthens our responsibility with regard to the future. Man cannot mold the form of the future without being aware of his present conditions and of the limitations of his past. As Leibniz used to say: *on recède pour mieux sauter*, one draws back to leap higher. Heraclitus coined for the physical world the maxim *hodos anô katô miê*, the way up and the way down are one and the same.[12] We can in a sense apply the same statement to the historical world. Even our historical consciousness is a "unity of opposites": it connects the opposite poles of time and gives us thereby our feeling for the continuity of human culture.

This unity and continuity become especially clear in the field of our intellectual culture, in the history of mathematics or science or philosophy. Nobody could ever attempt to write a history of mathematics or philosophy without having a clear insight into the systematic problems of the two sciences. The facts of the philosophical past, the doctrines and systems of the great thinkers, are meaningless without an interpretation. And this process of interpretation never comes to a complete standstill. As soon as we have reached a new center and a new line of vision in our own thoughts we must revise our judgments. No example is perhaps more characteristic and instructive in this respect than the change in our portrait of

11. Nietzsche, *Vom Nutzen und Nachteil der Historie für das Leben*, in "Unzeit gemässe Betrachtungen" (1874), Pt. III. English trans. ed. by Oscar Levy, Vol. II.
12. Fragment 60, in Diels, *Die Fragmente der Vorsokratiker*, I, 164.

Socrates. We have the Socrates of Xenophon and Plato; we have a Stoic, a sceptic, a mystic, a rationalistic, and a romantic Socrates. They are entirely dissimilar. Nevertheless they are not untrue; each of them gives us a new aspect, a characteristic perspective of the historical Socrates and his intellectual and moral physiognomy. Plato saw in Socrates the great dialectician and the great ethical teacher; Montaigne saw in him the antidogmatic philosopher who confessed his ignorance; Friedrich Schlegel and the romantic thinkers laid the emphasis upon Socratic irony. And in the case of Plato himself we can trace the same development. We have a mystic Plato, the Plato of neo-Platonism; a Christian Plato, the Plato of Augustine and Marsilio Ficino; a rationalistic Plato, the Plato of Moses Mendelssohn; and a few decades ago we were offered a Kantian Plato. We may smile at all these different interpretations. Yet they have not only a negative but also a positive side. They have all in their measure contributed to an understanding and to a systematic valuation of Plato's work. Each has insisted on a certain aspect which is contained in this work, but which could only be made manifest by a complicated process of thought. When speaking of Plato in his *Critique of Pure Reason* Kant indicated this fact. ". . . it is by no means unusual," he said, "upon comparing the thoughts which an author has expressed in regard to his subject, . . . to find that we understand him better than he has understood himself. As he has not sufficiently determined his concept, he has sometimes spoken, or even thought, in opposition to his own intention." [13] The history of philosophy shows us very clearly that the full determination of a concept is very rarely the work of that thinker who first introduced that concept. For a philosophical concept is, generally speaking, rather a problem than the solution of a problem—and the full significance of this problem cannot be understood so long as it is still in its first implicit state. It must become explicit in order to be comprehended in its true meaning, and this transition from an implicit to an explicit state is the work of the future.

13. Kant, *Critique of Pure Reason* (2d ed.), p. 370. Trans. by Norman Kemp Smith (London, Macmillan, 1929), p. 310.

It may be objected that this continuous process of interpretation and reinterpretation is indeed necessary in the history of ideas, but that the necessity no longer holds when we come to "real" history—to the history of man and human actions. Here it would seem as though we had to do with hard, obvious, palpable facts, facts which have simply to be related in order to be known. But not even political history forms an exception to the general methodological rule. What holds for the interpretation of a great thinker and his philosophical works holds also for judgments concerning a great political character. Friedrich Gundolf has written a whole book not about Caesar but about the history of Caesar's fame and the varying interpretations of his character and political mission from antiquity down to our own time.[14] Even in our social and political life many fundamental tendencies prove their full force and significance only at a relatively late stage. A political ideal and a social program, long since conceived in an implicit sense, become explicit through a later development. ". . . many ideas of the germinal American," writes S. E. Morison in his history of the United States, "can be traced back to the mother country. In England these ideas persisted through the centuries despite a certain twisting and thwarting at the hands of Tudor monarchs and Whig aristocrats; in America they found opportunity for free development. Thus we . . . find stout old English prejudices embalmed in the American Bills of Rights, and institutions long obsolete in England . . . lasting with little change in the American States until the middle of the nineteenth century. It was an unconscious mission of the United States to make explicit what had long been implicit in the British Constitution, and to prove the value of principles that had largely been forgotten in the England of George III." [15] In political history it is by no means the bare facts which interest us. We wish to understand not only the actions but the actors. Our judgment of the course of political events depends upon our conception of the men who were

14. Friedrich Gundolf, *Caesar, Geschichte seines Ruhm* (Berlin, 1924).

15. S. E. Morison, *The Oxford History of the United States* (Oxford, Clarendon Press, 1927), I, 39 f.

engaged in them. As soon as we see these individual men in a new light we have to alter our ideas of the events. Yet even so a true historical vision is not to be attained without a constant process of revision. Ferrero's *Greatness and Decline of Rome* differs on many important points from Mommsen's description of the same period. This disagreement is to a large extent due to the fact that the two authors have an entirely different conception of Cicero. In order to form a just judgment of Cicero it is not sufficient, however, simply to know all the events of his consulate, the part he played in the disclosure of the Catiline conspiracy or in the civil wars between Pompey and Caesar. All these matters remain dubious and ambiguous so long as I do not know the man, so long as I do not understand his personality and character. To this end some symbolic interpretation is required. I must not only study his orations or his philosophical writings; I must read his letters to his daughter Tullia and his intimate friends; I must have a feeling for the charms and defects of his personal style. Only by taking all this circumstantial evidence together can I arrive at a true picture of Cicero and his role in the political life of Rome. Unless the historian remains a mere annalist, unless he contents himself with a chronological narration of events, he must always perform this very difficult task; he must detect the unity behind innumerable and often contradictory utterances of a historical character.

To illustrate this point I wish to quote another characteristic example taken from the work of Ferrero. One of the most important events in Roman history—an event which decided the future destiny of Rome and, consequently, the future of the world—was the Battle of Actium. The usual version is that Antony lost this battle because Cleopatra, who was frightened and despaired of the issue, turned her vessel about and fled. Antony decided to follow her, abandoning his soldiers and friends for the sake of Cleopatra. If this traditional version is correct, then we must subscribe to Pascal's saying; we must admit that, had Cleopatra's nose been shorter, the whole face of the earth would have been changed.[16]

16. Pascal, *Pensées*, ed. Louandre, p. 196.

But Ferrero reads the historical text in a quite different manner. He declares the love story of Antony and Cleopatra to be a legend. Antony, he tells us, did not marry Cleopatra because he was passionately in love with her. On the contrary, Antony was pursuing a great political plan. "Antony wanted Egypt and not the beautiful person of its queen; he meant by this dynastic marriage to establish the Roman protectorate in the valley of the Nile, and to be able to dispose, for the Persian campaign, of the treasures of the Kingdom of the Ptolemies. . . . With a dynastic marriage, he was able to secure for himself all the advantages of effective possession, without running the risks of annexation; so he resolved upon this artifice which . . . had probably been imagined by Caesar. . . . The romance of Antony and Cleopatra covers, at least in its beginnings, a political treaty. With the marriage, Cleopatra seeks to steady her wavering power; Antony, to place the valley of the Nile under the Roman protectorate. . . . The actual history of Antony and Cleopatra is one of the most tragic episodes of a struggle that lacerated the Roman Empire for four centuries, until it finally destroyed it, the struggle between the Orient and Occident. . . . In the light of these considerations, the conduct of Antony becomes very clear. The marriage at Antioch, by which he places Egypt under the Roman protectorate, is the decisive act of a policy that looks to transporting the centre of his government toward the Orient . . ." [17]

If we accept this interpretation of the characters of Antony and Cleopatra then individual events, even the Battle of Actium, appear in a new and different light. Antony's flight from the battle, declares Ferrero, was by no means induced by fear, nor was it an act of blind and passionate love. It was a political act carefully thought out beforehand. "With the obstinacy, the certainty and the vehemence of an ambitious woman, of a confident and self-willed queen, Cleopatra strove to persuade the triumvir . . . to fall back upon Egypt by

17. Guglielmo Ferrero, "The History and Legend of Antony and Cleopatra," in *Characters and Events of Roman History, from Caesar to Nero* (New York, G. P. Putnam's Sons, 1909), pp. 39–68.

sea. . . . At the beginning of July Antony seems to have contemplated the abandonment of the war and a return to Egypt. It was impossible, however, to proclaim his intention of leaving Italy to Octavianus, of deserting the republican cause and betraying the Roman senators, who had left Italy for his sake. Cleopatra's ingenuity therefore conceived another device; a naval battle to mask the retreat was to be fought. Part of the army should be sent on board the fleet, other troops should be despatched to guard the most important points in Greece; the fleet should sail out in order of battle and should attack if the enemy advanced; then sail would be made for Egypt." [18]

I am not setting forward here any opinion as to the correctness of this statement. What I wish to illustrate by this example is the general method of the historical interpretation of political events. In physics the facts are explained when we succeed in arranging them in a threefold serial order: in the order of space, time, cause and effect. Thereby they become fully determined; and it is just this determination which we mean when speaking of the truth or reality of physical facts. The objectivity of historical facts belongs, however, to a different and higher order. Here too we have to do with determining the place and the time of events. But when it comes to the investigation of their causes we have a new problem to face. If we knew all the facts in their chronological order we should have a general scheme and a skeleton of history; but we should not have its real life. Yet an understanding of human life is the general theme and the ultimate aim of historical knowledge. In history we regard all the works of man, and all his deeds, as precipitates of his life; and we wish to reconstitute them into this original state, we wish to understand and feel the life from which they are derived.

In this respect historical thought is not the reproduction, but the reverse, of the actual historical process. In our historical documents and monuments we find a past life which has

18. Ferrero, *Grandezza e decadenza di Roma* (Milan, 1907), III, 502–539. English trans. by H. J. Chaytor, *Greatness and Decline of Rome* (New York, G. P. Putnam's Sons, 1908), IV, 95 ff.

assumed a certain form. Man cannot live his life without constant efforts to express it. The modes of this expression are variable and innumerable. But they are all so many testimonies of one and the same fundamental tendency. Plato's theory of love defines love as a desire for immortality. In love man strives to break the chain of his individual and ephemeral existence. This fundamental instinct may be satisfied in two ways. "Those who are pregnant in the body only betake themselves to women and beget children—this is the character of their love; their offspring, as they hope, will preserve their memory and give them blessedness and immortality. . . . But souls which are pregnant conceive that which is proper for the soul to conceive or contain." [19]

Hence a culture may be described as the product and offspring of this Platonic love. Even in the most primitive stage of human civilization, even in mythical thought, we find this passionate protest against the fact of death.[20] In the higher cultural strata—in religion, art, history, philosophy—this protest assumes a new shape. Man begins to detect in himself a new power by which he dares to challenge the power of time. He emerges from the mere flux of things, striving to eternize and immortalize human life. The Egyptian pyramids seem to be built for eternity. The great artists think and speak of their works as *monumenta aere perennius*. They feel sure they have raised a monument which shall not be destroyed by the countless years and the flight of ages. But this claim is bound to a special condition. In order to endure, the works of man must be constantly renewed and restored. A physical thing remains in its present state of existence through its physical inertia. It retains its same nature so long as it is not altered or destroyed by external forces. But human works are vulnerable from a quite different angle. They are subject to change and decay not only in a material but also in a mental sense. Even if their existence continues they are in constant danger of losing their meaning. Their reality is symbolic, not physical; and such reality never ceases to require interpreta-

19. Plato, *Symposium*, 208–209; Jowett trans., I, 579 f.
20. See above, p. 113–114.

tion and reinterpretation. And this is where the great task of history begins. The thought of the historian bears quite a different relation to its object from that of the physicist or naturalist. Material objects maintain their existence independently of the work of the scientist, but historical objects have true being only so long as they are remembered—and the act of remembrance must be unbroken and continuous. The historian must not only observe his objects like the naturalist; he must preserve them. His hope of keeping them in their physical existence can be frustrated at any moment. By the fire which destroyed the library of Alexandria innumerable and invaluable documents were lost forever. But even the surviving monuments would gradually fade away if they were not constantly kept alive by the art of the historian. In order to possess the world of culture we must incessantly reconquer it by historical recollection. But recollection does not mean merely the act of reproduction. It is a new intellectual synthesis—a constructive act. In this reconstruction the human mind moves in the opposite direction from that of the original process. All works of culture originate in an act of solidification and stabilization. Man could not communicate his thoughts and feelings, and he could not, accordingly, live in a social world, if he had not the special gift of objectifying his thoughts, of giving them a solid and permanent shape. Behind these fixed and static shapes, these petrified works of human culture, history detects the original dynamic impulses. It is the gift of the great historians to reduce all mere facts to their *fieri*, all products to processes, all static things or institutions to their creative energies. The political historians give us a life full of passions and emotions, violent struggles of political parties, of conflicts and wars between different nations.

But not all this is necessary to give to a historical work its dynamic character and accent. When Mommsen wrote his *Roman History* he spoke as a great political historian and in a new and modern tone. "I wanted to bring down the ancients," he said in a letter, "from the fantastic pedestal on which they appear into the real world. That is why the consul had to become the burgomaster. Perhaps I have overdone it; but my intention was sound enough." [21] Mommsen's later works appear to be conceived and written in an entirely different style. Nevertheless they do not lose their dramatic character. It may appear paradoxical to attribute such a character to works which deal with the most arid subjects, as, for instance, the history of coinage or of Roman public law. But it is all done in the same spirit. Mommsen's *Römisches Staatsrecht* is not a mere codification of constitutional laws. These laws are filled with life; we feel behind them the great powers which were necessary to build up such a system. We feel the great intellectual and moral forces which alone could produce this organism of Roman law; the gift of the Roman spirit for ordering, organizing, and commanding. Here too Mommsen's intention was to show us the Roman world in the mirror of Roman law. "As long as jurisprudence ignored the State and the people," he said, "and history and philology ignored law, both knocked in vain at the door of the Roman world."

If we understand the task of history in this way many of the problems which in the last decades have been discussed so eagerly and have found such diverse and divergent answers can be disentangled without difficulty. Modern philosophers have often attempted to construct a special logic of history. Natural science, they have told us, is based upon a logic of universals, history upon a logic of individuals. Windelband declared the judgment of natural science to be nomothetic, those of history to be idiographic.[22] The former give us general laws; the latter describe particular facts. This distinction became the basis of Rickert's whole theory of historical knowledge. "Empirical reality becomes nature, if we consider it with regard to the universal; it becomes history, if we consider it with regard to the particular." [23]

21. Mommsen in a letter to Henzen; quoted after G. P. Gooch, *History and Historians in the Nineteenth Century* (London, Longmans, Green & Co., 1913; new ed. 1935), p. 457.

22. Windelband, "Geschichte und Naturwissenschaft," in *Präludien* (5th ed. Tübingen, 1915), Vol. II.

23. Rickert, *Die Grenzen der naturwissenschaftlichen Begriffsbildung* (Tübingen, 1902), p. 255.

But it is not possible to separate the two moments of universality and particularity in this abstract and artificial way. A judgment is always the synthetic unity of both moments; it contains an element of universality and of particularity. These elements are not mutually opposed; they imply and interpenetrate one another. "Universality" is not a term which designates a certain field of thought; it is an expression of the very character, of the function of thought. Thought is always universal. On the other hand the description of particular facts, of a "here" and "now," is by no means a privilege of history. The uniqueness of historical events has often been thought to be the character distinguishing history from science. Yet this criterion is not sufficient. A geologist who gives us a description of the various states of the earth in different geological periods gives us a report on concrete and unique events. These events cannot be repeated; they will not occur in the same order a second time. In this respect the description of the geologist does not differ from that of a historian who, for instance, like Gregorovius tells us the story of the city of Rome in the Middle Ages. But the historian does not merely give us a series of events in a definite chronological order. For him these events are only the husk beneath which he looks for a human and cultural life—a life of actions and passions, of questions and answers, of tensions and solutions. The historian cannot invent a new language and a new logic for all this. He cannot think or speak without using general terms. But he infuses into his concepts and words his own inner feelings, and thus gives them a new sound and a new color—the color of a personal life.

The fundamental dilemma of historical thought begins at precisely this point. Undoubtedly it is the richness and variety, the depth and intensity, of his personal experience which is the distinctive mark of the great historian. Otherwise his work would remain lifeless and colorless. But how can we hope in this way to attain the ultimate objective of historical knowledge, how can we find out the truth of things and events? Is not a personal truth a contradiction in terms? Ranke once expressed the wish to extinguish his own self in order to make himself the pure mirror of things, in order to see the events in the way in which they actually occurred. It is clear, however, that this paradoxical statement was intended as a problem, not as a solution. If the historian succeeded in effacing his personal life he would not thereby achieve a higher objectivity. He would on the contrary deprive himself of the very instrument of all historical thought. If I put out the light of my own personal experience I cannot see and I cannot judge of the experience of others. Without a rich personal experience in the field of art no one can write a history of art; no one but a systematic thinker can give us a history of philosophy. The seeming antithesis between the objectivity of historical truth and the subjectivity of the historian must be solved in a different way.

Perhaps the best solution is to be found not in Ranke's words but in his works. Here we find the true explanation of what historical objectivity really means and what it does not mean. When Ranke published his first writings his ideal of historical truth was by no means generally understood by his contemporaries. His work was subjected to violent attacks. A well-known historian, Heinrich von Leo, reproached Ranke for his "timid avoidance of personal views"; he contemptuously described Ranke's writings as porcelain painting, the delight of ladies and amateurs. Nowadays such a judgment would appear not only utterly unjust but absurd and grotesque. Nevertheless it was repeated by later critics, especially by the historians of the Prussian School. Heinrich von Treitschke complained of Ranke's bloodless objectivity, "which does not say which side the narrator's heart is on." [24] Sometimes Ranke's adversaries in mocking tones compared his attitude and personal style to the attitude of the sphinxes in the second part of Goethe's *Faust*:

> Sitzen vor den Pyramiden,
> Zu der Völker Hochgericht;

24. For this criticism of Ranke's work see G. P. Gooch, op. cit., chaps. vi, viii.

Überschwemmung, Krieg und Frieden—
Und verziehen kein Gesicht.[25]

Such sarcasm is, however, very superficial. No one can study
Ranke's writings without being aware of the depth of his personal life and of his religious feeling. This feeling pervades all
of his historical work. But Ranke's religious interest was broad
enough to cover the whole field of religious life. Before ven-
turing upon his description of the Reformation he had
finished his great work on the *History of the Popes*. It was
precisely the peculiar character of his religious sense which
forbade him to treat religious questions in the manner of a
zealot or in that of a mere apologist. He conceived history
as a perpetual conflict between great political and religious
ideas. To see this conflict in its true light he had to study all
the parties and all the actors in this historical play. Ranke's
sympathy, the sympathy of the true historian, is of a specific
type. It does not imply friendship or partisanship. It embraces
friends and opponents. This form of sympathy may best be
compared to that of the great poets. Euripides does not sympathize with Medea; Shakespeare does not sympathize with
Lady Macbeth or Richard III. Nevertheless they make us understand these characters; they enter into their passions and
motives. The saying *tout comprendre est tout pardonner*
holds neither for the works of the great artists nor for those of
the great historians. Their sympathy implies no moral judgment, no approbation or disapproval of single acts. Of course
the historian is entirely at liberty to judge, but before he
judges he wishes to understand and interpret.

Schiller coined the dictum *Die Weltgeschichte ist das
Weltgericht*, a saying re-echoed by Hegel and made one of
the keystones of his philosophy of history. "The lots and
deeds of the particular states and of the particular minds,"
said Hegel, "are the phenomenal dialectic of the finitude of

25. *Faust*, Pt. II, "Classische Walpurgisnacht." G. M. Priest trans-
lates as follows (New York, Knopf, 1941):
"At the pyramids our station
We look on the doom of races,
War and peace and inundation,
With eternal changeless faces."

these minds out of which arises the universal mind, the unlimited mind of the world. This mind wields its right—and
its right is the highest—in them; in universal history, the
judgment of the world. The history of the world is the judgment of the world, because it contains, in its self-dependent
universality, all special forms—the family, civil society, and
nation, reduced to ideality, i. e., to subordinate but organic
members of itself. It is the task of the spirit to produce all
these special forms." [26] Even Ranke, however opposed to
Hegel's fundamental views, could have subscribed to this one.
But he conceived the mission of the historian in a less pre-
sumptuous way. He thought that in the great trial of the
history of the world the historian had to prepare, not to
pronounce, the judgment. This is very far from moral indifference; it is, on the contrary, a feeling of the highest moral
responsibility. According to Ranke the historian is neither the
prosecutor nor the counsel for the defendant. If he speaks as
a judge, he speaks as the *juge d'instruction*. He has to collect
all the documents in the case in order to submit them to the
highest court of law, to the history of the world. If he fails in
this task, if by party favoritism or hatred he suppresses or
falsifies a single piece of testimony, then he neglects his
supreme duty.

This ethical conception of his task, of the dignity and responsibility of the historian, is one of Ranke's principal merits
and gave to his work its great and free horizon. His universal
sympathy could embrace all ages and all nations.[27] He was
able to write the history of the Popes and the history of the
Reformation, the history of France and the history of England, his work on the Ottomans and the Spanish Monarchy,
in the same spirit of impartiality and without national bias.
To him the Latin and Teutonic nations, the Greeks and

26. Hegel, *Rechtsphilosophie*, secs. 340 f. English trans. of the last
two sentences by J. Macbride Sterrett, *The Ethics of Hegel, Translated Selections from his "Rechtsphilosophie"* (Boston, Ginn & Co.,
1893), p. 207.
27. In an excellent appraisal of Ranke's personality and work Alfred
Dove mentions his *"Universalität des Mitempfindens."* See Dove,
Ausgewählte Schriftchen (1898), pp. 112 ff.

Romans, the Middle Ages and the modern national states signified one coherent organism. Every new work permitted him to enlarge his historical horizon and to offer a freer and broader prospect.

Many of Ranke's adversaries who did not possess this free and detached spirit tried to make a virtue of necessity. They asserted that it was impossible to write a work of political history without political passions and without national partiality. Treitschke, a representative of the Prussian School, even refused to study the material of non-Prussian archives. He feared lest he should be disturbed by such a study in his favorable judgment of Prussian politics.[28] Such an attitude may be understandable and excusable in a political pamphleteer or propagandist. But in a historian it symbolizes the breakdown and bankruptcy of historical knowledge. We may compare this attitude to the frame of mind of those adversaries of Galileo who consistently refused to look through the telescope and convince themselves of the truth of Galileo's astronomical discoveries because they did not wish to be disturbed in their implicit faith in the Aristotelian system. To such a conception of history we may oppose the words of Jakob Burckhardt, "Beyond the blind praise of our own country, another and more onerous duty is incumbent upon us as citizens, namely to educate ourselves to be comprehending human beings, for whom truth and the kinship with things of the spirit is the supreme good, and who can elicit our true duty as citizens from that knowledge, even if it were not innate in us. In the realm of thought, it is supremely just and right that all frontiers should be swept away.[29]

As Schiller says in his Aesthetic Letters there is an art of

28. See Ed. Fueter, *Geschichte der neueren Historiographie* (3d ed. Munich and Berlin, 1936), p. 543.

29. "Es gibt aber neben dem blinden Lobpreisen der Heimat eine ganz andere und schwerere Pflicht, nämlich sich auszubilden zum erkennenden Menschen, dem die Wahrheit und die Verwandtschaft mit allem Geistigen über alles geht und der aus dieser Erkenntnis auch seine Bürgerpflicht würde ermitteln können, wenn sie ihm nicht schon mit seinem Temperament eingeboren ist. Vollends im Reiche des Gedankens gehen alle Schlagbäume billig in die Höhe." Jakob Burckhardt, *op. cit.*, p. 11. English trans., p. 89.

passion, but there cannot be a "passionate art." [30] This same view of the passions applies also to history. The historian who was ignorant of the world of passions—of political ambitions, of religious fanaticism, and of economic and social conflicts—would give us a very dry abstract of historical events. But if he lays any claim to historical truth he himself cannot remain in this world. To all this material of the passions he must give theoretical form; and this form, like the form of the work of art, is no product and outgrowth of passion. History is a history of passions; but if history itself attempts to be passionate it ceases to be history. The historian must not exhibit the affections, the furies and frenzies which he describes. His sympathy is intellectual and imaginative, not emotional. The personal style which we feel in every line of a great historian is not an emotional or rhetorical style. A rhetorical style may have many merits; it may move and delight the reader. But it misses the principal point: it cannot lead us to an intuition and to a free and unbiased judgment of things and events.

If we bear in mind this character of historical knowledge, it is easy to distinguish historical objectivity from that form of objectivity which is the aim of natural science. A great scientist, Max Planck, described the whole process of scientific thought as a constant effort to eliminate all "anthropological" elements. We must forget man in order to study nature and to discover and formulate the laws of nature.[31] In the development of scientific thought the anthropomorphic element is progressively forced into the background until it entirely disappears in the ideal structure of physics. History proceeds in a quite different way. It can live and breathe only in the human world. Like language or art, history is fundamentally anthropomorphic. To efface its human aspects would be to destroy its specific character and nature. But the anthropomorphism of historical thought is no limitation of or impediment to its objective truth. History is not knowledge of external facts or events; it is a form of self-knowledge. In order to know myself

30. *Essays Aesthetical and Philosophical*, Letter XXII.

31. See Max Planck, *Die Einheit des physikalischen Weltbildes* (Leipzig, 1909). For further details see Cassirer, *Substance and Function*, English trans. by W. C. and M. C. Swabey (1923), pp. 306 ff.

I cannot endeavor to go beyond myself, to leap, as it were, over my own shadow. I must choose the opposite approach. In history man constantly returns to himself; he attempts to recollect and actualize the whole of his past experience. But the historical self is not a mere individual self. It is anthropomorphic but it is not egocentric. Stated in the form of a paradox, we may say that history strives after an "objective anthropomorphism." By making us cognizant of the polymorphism of human existence it frees us from the freaks and prejudices of a special and single moment. It is this enrichment and enlargement, not the effacement, of the self, of our knowing and feeling ego, which is the aim of historical knowledge.

This ideal of historical truth has developed very slowly. Even the Greek mind in all its richness and depth could not bring it to its full maturity. But in the progress of modern consciousness the discovery and formulation of this concept of history has become one of our most important tasks. In the seventeenth century historical knowledge is still eclipsed by another ideal of truth. History has not yet found its place in the sun. It is overshadowed by mathematics and mathematical physics. But then, with the beginning of the eighteenth century, there comes a new orientation of modern thought. The eighteenth century had often been looked upon as an unhistorical or antihistorical century. But this is a one-sided and erroneous view. Eighteenth-century thinkers are the very pioneers of historical thought. They pose new questions and devise new methods of answering these questions. Historical investigation was one of the necessary instruments of the philosophy of the Enlightenment.[32] But in the eighteenth century a pragmatic conception of history still prevails. No new critical concept appeared prior to the beginning of the nineteenth century, prior to the advent of Niebuhr and Ranke. From this time on, however, the modern concept of history is firmly established and it extends its influence over all the fields of human knowledge and human culture.

32. For further details see Cassirer, Die Philosophie der Aufklärung (Tübingen, 1932), chap. v, pp. 263–312.

It was, however, not easy to determine the *specific* character of historical truth and historical method. A great many philosophers were prone rather to deny than to explain this specific character. So long as the historian continues to maintain special personal views, so long as he blames or praises, approves or disapproves, they have said, he will never live up to his proper task. He will, consciously or unconsciously, distort the objective truth. The historian must lose his interest in things and events in order to see them in their true shape. This methodological postulate received its clearest and most impressive expression in Taine's historical works. The historian, declared Taine, has to act like a naturalist. He must free himself not only from all conventional prejudices but from all personal predilections and all moral standards. "The modern method which I follow," said Taine in the introduction to his *Philosophy of Art*, "and which now begins to penetrate into all the moral sciences consists in regarding the human works . . . as facts and products the properties of which have to be exhibited and the causes of which have to be investigated. When considered in this way science has neither to justify nor condemn. The moral sciences must proceed in the same way as botany which with equal interest studies the orange tree and the laurel, the pine and the beech. They are nothing else than a kind of applied botany which does not deal with plants but with the works of men. This is the general movement by which at present the moral sciences and the natural sciences are approximating one another, and by virtue of which the former will achieve the same certainty and the same progress as the latter." [33] If we accept this view the problem of the objectivity of history appears to be solved in the simplest way. Like the physicist or chemist the historian must study the causes of things instead of judging their worth. "No matter if the facts be physical or moral," says Taine, "they all have their causes; there is a cause for ambition, for courage, for truth, as there is for digestion, for muscular movement, for animal heat. Vice and virtue are products, like

33. Taine, *Philosophie de l'art* (15th ed. Paris, Librairie Hachette, 1917), Pt. I, chap. i, p. 13.

vitriol and sugar; and every complex phenomenon has its springs from other more simple phenomena on which it hangs. Let us then seek the simple phenomena for moral qualities, as we seek them for physical qualities." In both cases we will find the same universal and permanent causes, "present at every moment and in every case, everywhere and always acting, indestructible, and in the end infallibly supreme, since the accidents which thwart them, being limited and partial, end by yielding to the dull and incessant repetition of their force; in such a manner that the general structure of things, and the grand features of events, are their work; and religions, philosophies, poetries, industries, the framework of society and of families, are in fact only the imprints stamped by their seal." [34]

I do not intend here to enter into a discussion and criticism of this system of historical determinism.[35] A denial of historical causality would be precisely the wrong way to combat this determinism. For causality is a general category that extends over the whole field of human knowledge. It is not restricted to a particular realm, to the world of material phenomena. Freedom and causality are not to be considered as different or opposed metaphysical forces; they are simply different modes of judgment. Even Kant, the most resolute champion of freedom and of ethical idealism, never denied that all our empirical knowledge, the knowledge of men as well as that of physical things, has to recognize the principle of causality. It may be admitted, says Kant, "that if it were possible to have so profound an insight into a man's mental character as shown by internal as well as external actions, as to know all its motives, even the smallest, and likewise all the external occasions that can influence them, we could calculate a man's conduct for the future with as great certainty as a lunar or solar eclipse; and nevertheless we may maintain that

34. Taine, *Histoire de la littérature anglaise*, Intro. English trans., I, 6 f.

35. I have dealt with this question in a paper entitled "Naturalistische und humanistische Begründung der Kulturphilosophie," Göteborgs Kungl. Vetenskaps-och Vitterhets-Samhällets Handlingar (Gothenburg, 1939).

the man is free." [36] We are not here concerned with this aspect of the problem, with the metaphysical or ethical concept of freedom. We are interested only in the repercussion of this concept upon historical method. When studying Taine's principal works we are surprised to find that, practically speaking, this repercussion was very small. There would seem at first sight to be no greater and more radical difference than that between Taine's and Dilthey's respective conceptions of the historical world. The two thinkers approach the problem from two entirely different angles. Dilthey emphasizes the autonomy of history, its irreducibility to natural science, its character as a *Geisteswissenschaft*. Taine emphatically denies this view. History will never become a science so long as it pretends to go its own way. There is only one mode and one path of scientific thought. But this view is immediately corrected when Taine begins with his own investigation and description of historical phenomena. "What is your first remark," he asks, "on turning over the great, stiff leaves of a folio, the yellow sheets of a manuscript—a poem, a code of laws, a declaration of faith? This, you say, was not created alone. It is but a mould, like a fossil shell, an imprint, like one of these shapes embossed in stone by an animal which lived and perished. Under the shell there was an animal, and behind the document there was a man. Why do you study the shell, except to represent to yourself the animal? So do you study the document only in order to know the man. The shell and the animal are lifeless wrecks, valuable only as a clue to the entire and living existence. We must reach back to this existence, endeavour to re-create it. It is a mistake to study the document, as if it were isolated. This were to treat things like a simple pedant, to fall into the error of the bibliomaniac. Behind all, we have neither mythology nor languages, but only men, who arrange words and imagery . . . nothing exists except through some individual man; it is this individual with whom we must become acquainted. When we have established the parentage of dogmas, or the classification of poems, or the

36. Kant, *Critique of Practical Reason*, trans. by T. K. Abbott (6th ed. 1927), p. 193.

progress of constitutions, or the modification of idioms, we have only cleared the soil: genuine history is brought into existence only when the historian begins to unravel, across the lapse of time, the living man, toiling, impassioned, entrenched in his customs, with his voice and features, his gestures and his dress, distinct and complete as he from whom we have just parted in the street. Let us endeavour, then, to annihilate as far as possible this great interval of time, which prevents us from seeing man with our eyes, with the eyes of our head. . . . A language, a legislation, a catechism is never more than an abstract thing: the complete thing is the man who acts, the man corporeal and visible, who eats, walks, fights, labours. . . . Let us make the past present: in order to judge of a thing, it must be before us; there is no experience in respect of what is absent. Doubtless this reconstruction is always incomplete; it can produce only incomplete judgments; but to that we must resign ourselves. It is better to have an imperfect knowledge than a futile or false one; and there is no other means of acquainting ourselves approximately with the events of other days, than to see approximately the men of other days." [37]

All this is in perfect agreement with the view of history and historical method which we have tried to expound and defend in the foregoing. But if this view is correct it is impossible to "reduce" historical thought to the method of scientific thought. If we were to know all the laws of nature, if we could apply to man all our statistical, economic, sociological rules, still this would not help us to "see" man in this special aspect and in his individual form. Here we are not moving in a physical but in a symbolic universe. And for understanding and interpreting symbols we have to develop other methods than those of research into causes. The category of meaning is not to be reduced to the category of being.[38] If we seek a general heading under which we are to subsume historical knowledge we may describe it not as a branch of physics but as a branch of semantics. The rules of semantics, not the laws

37. Taine, op. cit., pp. 1 ff.
38. See above, p. 148.

of nature, are the general principles of historical thought. History is included in the field of hermeneutics, not in that of natural science. So much is admitted by Taine in practice but denied in theory. His theory recognizes but two tasks of the historian: he must collect the "facts" and he must investigate their causes. But what Taine completely overlooks is that these facts themselves are not immediately given to the historian. They are not observable like physical or chemical facts; they must be reconstructed. And for this reconstruction the historian must master a special and very complicated technique; he must learn to read his documents and to understand the monuments in order to have access to a single and simple fact. In history the interpretation of symbols precedes the collection of facts, and without this interpretation there is no approach to historical truth.

This brings us to another much-controverted problem. It is obvious that history cannot describe all the facts of the past. It deals only with the "memorable" facts, with the facts "worth" remembering. But where lies the difference between these memorable facts and all the rest which fall into oblivion? Rickert tried to prove that the historian, in order to distinguish between historical and nonhistorical facts, must be in possession of a certain system of formal values and that he must use this system as his standard in the selection of facts. But this theory is liable to grave objections.[39] It would seem much more natural and plausible to say that the true criterion does not consist in the value of facts but in their practical consequences. A fact becomes historically relevant if it is pregnant with consequences. Many eminent historians have supported this theory. "If we ask ourselves," says Eduard Meyer, "which of the events we know of are historical, we have to reply: historical is whatever is effective or has become effective. What is effective we first experience in the present in which we immediately perceive the effect, but we can also experience it with respect to the past. In both cases we have

39. For a criticism of this theory see Ernst Troeltsch, Der Historismus und seine Probleme, in "Gesammelte Schriften," Vol. III, and Cassirer, Zur Logik der Kulturwissenschaften (Gothenburg, 1942), pp. 41 ff.

before our eyes a mass of states of being, that is to say, of effects. The historical question is: whereby have these effects been produced? What we recognize as the cause of such an effect is a historical event." [40] But even this mark of distinction is not sufficient. If we study a historical work, especially a biographical work, we may find on almost every page mention of things and events which from a merely pragmatic point of view mean very little. A letter of Goethe's or a remark dropped in one of his conversations has left no trace in the history of literature. Nevertheless we may think it notable and memorable. Without any practical effect this letter or this utterance may still be reckoned among those documents out of which we try to construct our historical portrait of Goethe. All this is not important in its consequences but it may be highly characteristic. All historical facts are characteristic facts, for in history—in the history of nations as well as in that of individuals—we never look upon deeds or actions alone. In these deeds we see the expression of character. In our historical knowledge—which is a semantic knowledge—we do not apply the same standards as in our practical or physical knowledge. A thing that physically or practically is of no importance at all may still have very great semantic meaning. The letter iota in the Greek terms *homo-ousios* and *homoiousios* meant nothing in a physical sense; but, as a religious symbol, as an expression and interpretation of the dogma of the Trinity, it became the starting point of interminable discussions which stirred up the most violent emotions and shook the foundations of religious, social, and political life. Taine liked to base his historical descriptions upon what he called "*de tout petits faits significatifs.*" These facts were not significant with respect to their effects, but they were "expressive"; they were symbols by which the historian could read and interpret individual characters or the characters of a whole epoch. Macaulay tells us that, when he wrote his great historical work, he formed his conception of the temper of political and religious parties not from any single work but from

40. Eduard Meyer, *Zur Theorie und Methodik der Geschichte* (Halle a. S., 1902), pp. 36 f.

thousands of forgotten tracts, sermons, and satires. All these things had no great historical weight and may have had very little influence upon the general course of events. They are, nevertheless, valuable, indeed indispensable, to the historian because they help him understand characters and events.

In the second half of the nineteenth century there were many historians who set extravagant hopes upon the introduction of statistical methods. They prophesied that by the right use of this new and powerful weapon a new era of historical thought was going to be brought about. Were it possible to describe historical phenomena in terms of statistics, this would seem indeed to have a revolutionary effect upon human thought. In this case our whole knowledge of man would suddenly take on a new appearance. We should have attained a great objective, a mathematics of human nature. The first historical writers to expound this view were convinced that not only the study of great collective movements but also the study of morality and civilization were to a large degree dependent on statistical methods. For there is a moral statistics as well as a sociological or economic statistics. In fact no province of human life is exempt from strict numerical rules, which extend over every field of human action.

This thesis was vigorously defended by Buckle in the general introduction to his *History of Civilization in England* (1857). Statistics, declared Buckle, is the best and most conclusive refutation of the idol of a "free will." We now have the most extensive information, not only respecting the material interests of men but also respecting their moral peculiarities. We are now acquainted with the mortality rate, the marriage rate, and also with the crime rate of the most civilized peoples. These and similar facts have been collected, methodized, and are now ripe for use. That the creation of the science of history was retarded, and that history never was able to emulate physics or chemistry, is due to the fact that statistical methods were neglected. We did not realize that here too every event is linked to its antecedent by an inevitable connection, that each antecedent is connected with a preceding fact, and that thus the whole world—the moral world just as much as the physical—forms a necessary chain in which indeed each man may play his part. But he can by no means determine what that part shall be. "Rejecting, then, the metaphysical dogma of free will, . . . we are driven to the conclusion that the actions of men, being determined solely by their antecedents, must have a character of uniformity, that is to say, must, under precisely the same circumstances, always issue in precisely the same results." [41]

That statistics are indeed a great and valuable aid to the study of sociological or economic phenomena is of course undeniable. Even in the field of history the uniformity and regularity of certain human actions must be admitted. History does not deny that these actions, being the result of large and general causes at work upon the aggregate of society, produce certain consequences without regard to the volition of the individuals of whom society is composed. But when we come to the historical description of an individual act we have to face a quite different problem. By their very nature statistical methods restrict themselves to collective phenomena. Statistical rules are not designed to determine a single case; they deal only with certain "collectives." Buckle is very far from a clear insight into the character and purport of statistical methods. An adequate logical analysis of these methods came only at a later period.[42] He sometimes speaks of statistical laws in a rather queer way. He seems to regard them not as formulae which describe certain phenomena but as forces which produce these phenomena. This is, of course, not science but mythology. To him statistical laws are in a sense "causes" which enforce certain actions upon us. Suicide, he holds, seems to be an entirely free act. But if we study moral statistics we must judge quite otherwise. We shall find that "suicide is merely the product of the general condition of society, and that the individual felon only carries into effect what is a necessary consequence of preceding circumstances. In a given state of society, a certain number of persons must put an end

41. Buckle, *History of Civilization in England* (New York, 1858), pp. 14 f.

42. For the modern literature on statistics, see Keynes, *A Treatise on Probability* (London, 1921), and von Mises, *Wahrscheinlichkeit, Statistik und Wahrheit* (Vienna, 1928).

to their own life. . . . And the power of the larger law is so irresistible, that neither the love of life nor the fear of another world can avail anything towards even checking its operation." [43] I need scarcely say that this "must" contains a whole nest full of metaphysical fallacies. The historian, however, is not concerned with this side of the problem. If he speaks of an individual case—let us say of Cato's suicide—it is obvious that for the historical interpretation of this individual fact he cannot expect any help from statistical methods. His primary intention is not to fix a physical event in space and time but to disclose the "meaning" of Cato's death. The meaning of Cato's death is expressed in Lucan's verse, "*Victrix causa diis placuit sed victa Catoni.*" [44] Cato's suicide was not only a physical act, it was a symbolic act. It was the expression of a great character; it was the last protest of the Roman republican mind against a new order of things. All this is completely inaccessible to those "large and general causes" which we may think of as responsible for the great collective movements in history. We may try to reduce human actions to statistical rules. But by these rules we shall never attain the end which is acknowledged even by the historians of the naturalistic school. We shall not "see" the men of other days. What we shall see in this case will not be the real life, the drama of history; it will only be the motions and gestures of puppets in a puppet show and the strings by which these marionettes are worked.

The same objection holds against all attempts to reduce historical knowledge to the study of psychological types. At first sight it would seem evident that, if we can speak of general laws in history, these laws cannot be the laws of nature but only the laws of psychology. The regularity which we seek and wish to describe in history does not belong to our outer but to our inner experience. It is a regularity of psychic states, of thoughts and feelings. If we were to succeed in finding a general inviolable law which governed these thoughts and feel-

---

43. Buckle, *op. cit.*, p. 20.
44. "The conquering cause pleased the gods, but the conquered one pleased Cato."

ings and prescribed for them a definite order, then we might think we had found the clue to the historical world.

Among modern historians it was Karl Lamprecht who became convinced that he had discovered such a law. In the twelve volumes of his *German History* he tried to prove his general thesis by a concrete example. According to Lamprecht there is an invariable order in which the states of the human mind follow one another. And this order once for all determines the process of human culture. Lamprecht rejected the views of economic materialism. Every economic act, like every mental act, he declared, depends on psychological conditions. But what we need is not an individual but a social psychology, a psychology that explains the changes in the social mind. These changes are bound to a fixed and rigid scheme. Hence history must cease being a study of individuals; it must free itself from all sorts of hero worship. Its main problem has to do with social-psychic, as compared and contrasted with individual-psychic factors. Neither individual nor national differences can affect or alter the regular course of our social-psychic life. The history of civilization shows us, always and everywhere, the same sequence and the same uniform rhythm. From a first stage, which is described by Lamprecht as animism, we pass to an age of symbolism, typism, conventionalism, individualism, and subjectivism. This scheme is unchangeable and inexorable. If we accept this principle history is no longer a mere inductive science. We are in a position to make general deductive statements. Lamprecht abstracted his scheme from the facts of German history. But he by no means intended to restrict it to this one area. He thought his scheme was a generally applicable, a priori principle of all historical life. "We obtain from the total material," he wrote, "not only the idea of unity, historical and empirical, but also a general psychologic impression which absolutely declares and demands such a unity; all the simultaneous psychic incidents, the individual-psychic, as well as the socio-psychic, have a tendency to approach common similarity." [45] The

45. *What Is History?* trans. by E. A. Andrews (New York, Macmillan, 1905), p. 163.

universal psychic mechanism of the course of the various periods recurs everywhere, in modern Russia as well as in the history of Greece or Rome, in Asia as well as in Europe. If we peruse all the monuments of northern, middle, and southern Europe, along with those of the eastern Mediterranean and Asia Minor, it will appear that all these civilizations have advanced along parallel lines. "When this has been accomplished, we may estimate the importance to world-history of each individual community or nation. A scientific *Weltgeschichte* can then be written." [46]

Lamprecht's general scheme is quite different from Buckle's conception of the historical process. Nevertheless the two theories have a point of contact. In both of them we meet with the same ominous term, with the term "must." After a period of typism and conventionalism there must always follow a period of individualism and subjectivism. No special age and no special culture can ever evade this general course of things, which seems to be a sort of historical fatalism. If this conception were true the great drama of history would become a rather dull spectacle which we could divide, once for all, into single acts whose sequence would be invariable. But the reality of history is not a uniform sequence of events but the inner life of man. This life can be described and interpreted after it has been lived; it cannot be anticipated in an abstract general formula, and it cannot be reduced to a rigid scheme of three or five acts. But here I do not intend to discuss the context of Lamprecht's thesis but only to raise a formal, methodological question. How did Lamprecht get the empirical evidence upon which to base his constructive theory? Like all previous historians he had to begin with a study of documents and monuments. He was not interested merely in political events, in social organizations, in economic phenomena. He wished to embrace the whole range of cultural life. Many of his most important arguments are based on a careful analysis of religious life, of the works of music and literature. One of his greatest interests was the study of the history of the fine arts. In his history of Germany he speaks not only of

46. *Idem*, p. 219.

Kant and Beethoven but also of Feuerbach, Klinger, Boecklin. In his Historical Institute in Leipzig he amassed astoundingly rich materials on all these questions. But it is clear that, in order to interpret these materials, he had first to translate them into a different language. To use the words of Taine he had to find behind the "fossil shell" the animal, behind the document the man. "When you consider with your eyes the visible man, what do you look for?" asked Taine. "The man invisible. The words which enter your ears, the gestures, the motions of his head, the clothes he wears, visible acts and deeds of every kind, are expressions merely; somewhat is revealed beneath them, and that is a soul. An inner man is concealed beneath the outer man; the second does but reveal the first. . . . All these externals are but avenues converging to a centre; you enter them simply in order to reach that centre; and that centre is the genuine man. . . . This underworld is a new subject-matter, proper to the historian." [47] Hence it is precisely the study of the "naturalistic" historians, of Taine and Lamprecht, which confirms our own view, which convinces us that the world of history is a symbolic universe, not a physical universe.

After the publication of the first volumes of Lamprecht's *German History* the growing crisis in historical thought became more and more manifest and was felt in all its intensity. There arose a long and exasperated controversy about the character of historical method. Lamprecht had declared that all the traditional views were obsolete. He looked upon his own method as the only "scientific" and the only "modern" one.[48] His adversaries, on the other hand, were convinced that what he had given was a mere caricature of historical thought.[49] Both sides expressed themselves in very peremptory and uncompromising language. Reconciliation appeared impossible. The scholarly tenor of the debate was often disrupted by personal or political prejudices. But if we approach

47. Taine, *op. cit.*, I, 4.
48. Cf. Lamprecht, *Alte und neue Richtungen in der Geschichtswissenschaft* (1896).
49. For further details see Bernheim, *Lehrbuch der historischen Methode* (5th ed., München, Duncker, 1908), pp. 710 ff.

the problem with an entirely unbiased mind and from a merely logical viewpoint we find, in spite of all the differences of opinion, a certain fundamental unity. As we have indicated, even the naturalistic historians did not deny, indeed they could not deny, that historical facts do not belong to the same type as physical facts. They were cognizant of the fact that their documents and monuments were not simply physical things but had to be read as symbols. On the other hand it is clear that each of the symbols—a building, a work of art, a religious rite—has its material side. The human world is not a separate entity or a self-dependent reality. Man lives in physical surroundings which constantly influence him and set their seal upon all the forms of his life. In order to understand his creations—his "symbolic universe"—we must constantly bear in mind this influence. In his masterpiece Montesquieu attempted to describe the "spirit of the laws." But he found that this spirit is everywhere bound down to its physical conditions. The soil, the climate, the anthropological character of the various nations were declared to be among the fundamental conditions of their laws and institutions. It is obvious that these physical conditions must be studied by physical methods. Both historical space and historical time are imbedded in a larger whole. Historical time is but a small fragment of a universal cosmic time. If we wish to measure this time, if we are interested in the chronology of events, we must have physical instruments. In the concrete work of the historian we find no opposition between these two views. They are perfectly fused into one. It is only in our logical analysis that we can separate one fact from the other. In the investigation of a complicated chronological problem the historian can proceed in different ways. He may use material or formal criteria; he may try statistical methods or ideal methods of interpretation. The very intricate question of the chronology of the Platonic dialogues could, to a great extent, be solved by statistical observations concerning the style of Plato. By various independent stylistic criteria it could be ascertained that a certain group of the dialogues—the *Sophist*, the *Statesman*, *Philebus*, and *Timaeus*—belongs to the period of Plato's old age.[50] And when Adickes prepared his edition of Kant's manuscripts he could find no better criterion for bringing them into a definite chronological order than a chemical analysis of the ink with which the various notes had been written. If, instead of using these physical criteria, we start from an analysis of Plato's or Kant's thoughts and their logical connection we need concepts which obviously belong to another domain. If, for example, I find a drawing or etching I may immediately recognize it as a work of Rembrandt; I may even be able to say to which period of Rembrandt's life it belongs. The stylistic criteria by which I decide this question are of quite another order than the material criteria.[51] This dualism of methods does not impair the work of the historian, nor does it destroy the unity of historical thought. Both methods coöperate for a common end without disturbing or obstructing one another.

The question as to which of these methods has logical primacy over the other and which is the truly "scientific" method scarcely admits of a definite answer. If we accept Kant's definition that, in the proper sense of the word, we can apply the term "science" only to a body of knowledge the certainty of which is apodictic,[52] then it is clear that we cannot speak of a science of history. But the name we give to history does not matter provided that we have a clear insight into its general character. Without being an exact science history will always maintain its place and its inherent nature in the organism of human knowledge. What we seek in history is not the knowledge of an external thing but a knowledge of ourselves. A great historian like Jakob Burckhardt in his work on Constantine the Great or on the civilization of the Renaissance did not presume to have given a scientific description

50. For further details see W. Lutoslawski, *The Origin and Growth of Plato's Logic, with an Account of Plato's Style and of the Chronology of His Writings* (London and New York, 1907).

51. I have discussed the logical character of these "stylistic concepts" in *Zur Logik der Kulturwissenschaften* (Gothenburg, 1942), pp. 63 ff.

52. Kant, *Metaphysische Anfangsgründe der Naturwissenschaft*, Vorrede, "Werke" (ed. Cassirer), IV, 370.

of these epochs. Nor did he hesitate to propound the paradox
that history is the most unscientific of all the sciences.[53]
"What I construct historically," wrote Burckhardt in a letter,
"is not the result of criticism or speculation but of imagination seeking to fill the gaps in observations. To me history is
still in a large measure poetry, it is a series of the most beautiful and picturesque compositions."[54] The same view was
upheld by Mommsen. Mommsen was not only a scientific
genius; he was at the same time one of the greatest organizers
of scientific labor. He created the *Corpus inscriptionum;* he
organized the study of numismatics, and published his *History of the Coinage.* This was hardly the work of an artist.
But when Mommsen was admitted to the office of rector of
the University of Berlin and gave his inaugural address he
defined his ideal of the historical method by saying that the
historian belongs perhaps rather to the artists than to the
scholars. Although he was himself one of the most eminent
teachers of history he did not scruple, nevertheless, to assert
that history is not a thing which can be immediately acquired
by teaching and learning. "The treadle which guides a thousand threads, and the insight into the individuality of men
and nations, are gifts of genius which defy all teaching and
learning. If a professor of history thinks he is able to educate
historians in the same sense as classical scholars and mathematicians can be educated, he is under a dangerous and detrimental delusion. The historian is not made, he is born; he
cannot be educated, he has to educate himself."[55]

But even though we cannot deny that every great historical
work contains and implies an artistic element, it does not
thereby become a work of fiction. In his quest for truth the
historian is bound by the same strict rules as the scientist. He
has to utilize all the methods of empirical investigation. He

53. Jakob Burckhardt, *Weltgeschichtliche Betrachtungen,* p. 81.
English trans., *Force and Freedom,* p. 167.

54. *Baseler Jahrbücher* (1910), pp. 109 f.; quoted after Karl Joël,
Jakob Burckhardt als Geschichtsphilosoph (Basle, 1918).

55. Th. Mommsen, "Rektoratsrede" (1874), in *Reden und Aufsätze*
(Berlin, 1912).

has to collect all the available evidence and to compare and criticize all his sources. He is not permitted to forget or neglect any important fact. Nevertheless, the last and decisive act is always an act of the productive imagination. In a conversation with Eckermann Goethe complained that there were few men who have "imagination for the truth of reality" ("*eine Phantasie für die Wahrheit des Realen*"). "Most prefer strange countries and circumstances," he said, "of which they know nothing, and by which their imagination may be cultivated, oddly enough. Then there are others who cling altogether to reality, and, as they wholly want the poetic spirit, are too severe in their requisitions." [56] The great historians avoid both extremes. They are empiricists; they are careful observers and investigators of special facts; but they do not lack the "poetic spirit." It is the keen sense for the empirical reality of things combined with the free gift of imagination upon which the true historical synthesis or synopsis depends.

The equipoise of these opposing forces cannot be described in a general formula. The proportion appears to vary from one age to another and from one individual writer to another. In ancient history we find a different conception of the task of the historian from that of modern history. The speeches which Thucydides inserted in his historical work have no empirical basis. They were not spoken as Thucydides gives them. Yet they are neither pure fiction nor mere rhetorical adornment. They are history, not because they reproduce actual events but because, in the work of Thucydides, they fulfil an important historical function. They constitute in a 'very pregnant and concentrated form a characterization of men and events. Pericles' great funeral oration is perhaps the best and most impressive description of Athenian life and Athenian culture in the fifth century. The style of all these speeches bears the personal and genuine mark of Thucydides. "They are all distinctly Thucydidean in style," it has been said, "just as the various characters in a play of Euripides all use similar

56. Goethe to Eckermann, December 25, 1825, in *Conversations of Goethe with Eckermann and Sorel*, trans. by John Oxenford (London, 1874), p. 162.

diction." [57] Nevertheless they do not convey merely personal idiosyncrasies; they are representative of the epoch as a whole. In this sense they are objective, not subjective; they possess an ideal truth, if not an empirical truth. In modern times we have become much more susceptible to the demands of empirical truth, but we are perhaps frequently in danger of losing sight of the ideal truth of things and personalities. The just balance between these two moments depends upon the individual tact of the historian; it cannot be reduced to a general rule. In the modern historical consciousness the proportion has changed but the elements have remained the same. With regard to the distribution and strength of the two forces every historian has his personal equation.

And yet the ideality of history is not the same as the ideality of art. Art gives us an ideal description of human life by a sort of alchemistic process; it turns our empirical life into the dynamic of pure forms.[58] History does not proceed in this way. It does not go beyond the empirical reality of things and events but molds this reality into a new shape, giving it the ideality of recollection. Life in the light of history remains a great realistic drama, with all its tensions and conflicts, its greatness and misery, its hopes and illusions, its display of energies and passions. This drama, however, is not only felt; it is intuited. Seeing this spectacle in the mirror of history while we are still living in our empirical world of emotions and passions, we become aware of an inner sense of clarity and calmness—of the lucidity and serenity of pure contemplation. "The mind," wrote Jakob Burckhardt into his *Reflections on World History*, "must transmute into a possession the remembrance of its passage through the ages of the world. What was once joy and sorrow must now become knowledge. . . . Our study, however, is not only a right and a duty; it is also a supreme need. It is our freedom in the very awareness of universal bondage and the stream of necessities." [59]

57. See J. R. Bury, *The Ancient Greek Historians*, Harvard Lectures (New York, Macmillan, 1909), Lecture IV.

58. See above, pp. 192 ff.

59. Burckhardt, *op. cit.*, pp. 8 f. English trans., pp. 86 f.

Written and read in the right way history elevates us to this atmosphere of freedom amidst all the necessities of our physical, political, social, and economic life.

It was not my design in this chapter to deal with the problems of a philosophy of history. A philosophy of history, in the traditional sense of the term, is a speculative and constructive theory of the historical process itself. An analysis of human culture need not enter upon this speculative question. It sets up for itself a more simple and modest task. It seeks to determine the place of historical knowledge in the organism of human civilization. We cannot doubt that without history we should miss an essential link in the evolution of this organism. Art and history are the most powerful instruments of our inquiry into human nature. What would we know of man without these two sources of information? We should be dependent on the data of our personal life, which can give us only a subjective view and which at best are but the scattered fragments of the broken mirror of humanity. To be sure, if we wished to complete the picture suggested by these introspective data we could appeal to more objective methods. We could make psychological experiments or collect statistical facts. But in spite of this our picture of man would remain inert and colorless. We should only find the "average" man—the man of our daily practical and social intercourse. In the great works of history and art we begin to see, behind this mask of the conventional man, the features of the real, individual man. In order to find him we must go to the great historians or to the great poets—to tragic writers like Euripides or Shakespeare, to comic writers like Cervantes, Molière, or Laurence Sterne, or to our modern novelists like Dickens or Thackeray, Balzac or Flaubert, Gogol or Dostoievski. Poetry is not a mere imitation of nature; history is not a narration of dead facts and events. History as well as poetry is an organon of our self-knowledge, an indispensable instrument for building up our human universe.

11   Science[1]

Science is the last step in man's mental development and it may be regarded as the highest and most characteristic attainment of human culture. It is a very late and refined product that could not develop except under special conditions. Even the conception of science, in its specific sense, did not exist before the times of the great Greek thinkers—before the Pythagoreans and the Atomists, Plato and Aristotle. And this first conception seemed to be forgotten and eclipsed in the following centuries. It had to be rediscovered and re-established in the age of the Renaissance. After this rediscovery the triumph of science seemed to be complete and uncontested. There is no second power in our modern world which may be compared to that of scientific thought. It is held to be the summit and consummation of all our human activities, the last chapter in the history of mankind and the most important subject of a philosophy of man.

We may dispute concerning the results of science or its first principles, but its general function seems to be unquestionable. It is science that gives us the assurance of a constant world. To science we may apply the words spoken by Archimedes; *dos moi pou stô kai kosmon kinêsô* ("Give me a place to stand and I will move the universe"). In a changing universe scientific thought fixes the points of rest, the unmovable poles. In Greek language even the term *episteme* is etymologically derived from a root that means firmness and stability. The scientific process leads to a stable equilibrium, to a

1. This chapter does not of course claim to give an outline of a *philosophy* of science or of a phenomenology of knowledge. I have discussed the latter problem in the third volume of *Philosophie der symbolischen Formen* (1929); the former in *Substance and Function and Einstein's Theory of Relativity* (1910; English trans. by W. C. and M. C. Swabey, Chicago and London, 1923) and in *Determinismus und Indeterminismus in der modernen Physik* (Göteborgs Högskolas Årsskrift, 1936: 1). Here I have only tried to indicate briefly the general function of science and to determine its place in the system of symbolic forms.

stabilization and consolidation of the world of our perceptions and thoughts.

On the other hand science is not alone in having to perform this task. In our modern epistemology, both in the empiristic and rationalistic schools, we often meet with the conception that the first data of human experience are in an entirely chaotic state. Even Kant seems, in the first chapters of the *Critique of Pure Reason*, to start from this presupposition. Experience, he says, is no doubt the first product of our understanding. But it is not a simple fact; it is a compound of two opposite factors, of matter and form. The material factor is given in our sense perceptions; the formal factor is represented by our scientific concepts. These concepts, the concepts of pure understanding, give to the phenomena their synthetic unity. What we call the unity of an object cannot be anything but the formal unity of our consciousness in the synthesis of the manifold in our representations. Then and then only we say that we know an object if we have produced synthetic unity in the manifold of intuition.[2] For Kant, therefore, the whole question of the objectivity of human knowledge is indissolubly connected with the fact of science. His Transcendental Aesthetics is concerned with the problem of pure mathematics; his Transcendental Analytic attempts to explain the fact of a mathematical science of nature.

But a philosophy of human culture has to track down the problem to a more remote source. Man lived in an objective world long before he lived in a scientific world. Even before he had found his approach to science his experience was not a mere amorphous mass of sense expressions. It was an organized and articulated experience. It possessed a definite structure. But the concepts that give to this world its synthetic unity are not of the same type nor are they on the same level as our scientific concepts. They are mythical or linguistic concepts. If we analyze these concepts we find that they are by no means simple or "primitive." The first classifications of the phenomena which we find in language or myth are in a sense much more complicated and sophisticated than our

2. Kant, *Critique of Pure Reason* (1st German ed.), p. 105.

scientific classifications. Science begins with a quest for simplicity. *Simplex sigillum veri* seems to be one of its fundamental devices. This logical simplicity is, however, a *terminus ad quem*, not a *terminus a quo*. It is an end, not a beginning. Human culture begins with a much more complex and involved state of mind. Nearly all our sciences of nature had to pass through a mythical stage. In the history of scientific thought alchemy precedes chemistry, astrology precedes astronomy. Science could advance beyond these first steps only by introducing a new measure, a different logical standard of truth. Truth, it declares, is not to be attained so long as man confines himself within the narrow circle of his immediate experience, of observable facts. Instead of describing detached and isolated facts science strives to give us a comprehensive view. But this view cannot be attained by a mere extension, an enlargement and enrichment of our ordinary experience. It demands a new principle of order, a new form of intellectual interpretation. Language is the first attempt of man to articulate the world of his sense perceptions. This tendency is one of the fundamental features of human speech. Some linguists have even thought it necessary to assume a special classifying instinct in man in order to account for the fact and the structure of human speech. "Man," says Otto Jespersen, "is a classifying animal: in one sense it may be said that the whole process of speaking is nothing but distributing phenomena, of which no two are alike in every respect, into different classes on the strength of perceived similarities and dissimilarities. In the name-giving process we witness the same ineradicable and very useful tendency to see likenesses and to express similarity in the phenomena through similarity in name." [3]

But what science seeks in phenomena is much more than similarity; it is order. The first classifications that we find in human speech have no strictly theoretical aim. The names of the objects fulfil their task if they enable us to communicate our thoughts and to coördinate our practical activities. They have a teleological function, which slowly develops into a more

3. Jespersen, *Language*, pp. 388 f.

objective, a "representative" function.[4] Every apparent similarity between different phenomena is enough to designate them by a common name. In some languages a butterfly is described as a bird or a whale is described as a fish. When science began its first classifications it had to correct and to overcome these superficial similarities. Scientific terms are not made at random; they follow a definite principle of classification. The creation of a coherent systematic terminology is by no means a mere accessory feature of science; it is one of its inherent and indispensable elements. When Linnaeus created his *Philosophia botanica* he had to confront the objection that what was given here was only an artificial, not a natural system. But all systems of classification are artificial. Nature as such only contains individual and diversified phenomena. If we subsume these phenomena under class concepts and general laws we do not describe facts of nature. Every system is a work of art—a result of conscious creative activity. Even the later so-called "natural" biological systems that were opposed to the system of Linnaeus had to use new conceptual elements. They were based on a general theory of evolution. But evolution itself is not a mere fact of natural history; it is a scientific hypothesis, a regulative maxim for our observation and classification of natural phenomena. Darwin's theory opened a new and wider horizon, it gave a more complete and more coherent survey of the phenomena of organic life. This was by no means a refutation of Linnaeus' system which was always regarded by its author as a preliminary step. He was quite aware that in a certain sense he had only created a new botanical terminology, but he was convinced that this terminology had both a verbal and a real value. "*Nomina si nescis,*" he said, "*perit et cognitio rerum.*"

In this regard there seems to be no break of continuity between language and science. Our linguistic and our first scientific names may be looked upon as the result and offspring of the same classifying instinct. What is unconsciously done in language is consciously intended and methodically

4. With regard to this problem see *Philosophie der symbolischen Formen*, I, 255 ff.

performed in the scientific process. In its first stages science still had to accept the names of things in the sense in which they were used in ordinary speech. It could use them for describing the fundamental elements or qualities of things. In the first Greek systems of natural philosophy, in Aristotle, we find that these common names still have great influence on scientific thought.[5] But in Greek thought this power is no longer the only one or the prevalent one. In the times of Pythagoras and the first Pythagoreans Greek philosophy had discovered a new language, the language of numbers. This discovery marked the natal hour of our modern conception of science.

That there is a regularity, a certain uniformity, in natural events—in the movements of the planets, in the rise of the sun or the moon, in the change of the seasons—is one of the first great experiences of mankind. Even in mythical thought this experience had found its full acknowledgment and its characteristic expression. Here we meet with the first traces of the idea of a general order of nature.[6] And long before the times of Pythagoras this order had been described not only in mythical terms but also in mathematical symbols. Mythical and mathematical language interpenetrate each other in a very curious way in the first systems of Babylonian astrology which we can trace back to as early a period as about 3800 B.C. The distinction between the different star groups and the twelvefold division of the zodiac were introduced by the Babylonian astronomers. All these results would not have been attained without a new theoretical basis. But a much bolder generalization was necessary to create the first philosophy of number. The Pythagorean thinkers were the first to conceive number as an all-embracing, a really universal element. Its use is no longer confined within the limits of a special field of investigation. It extends over the whole realm of being. When Pythagoras made his first great discovery, when he found the dependence of the pitch of sound on the

5. Cf. Cassirer, "The Influence of Language upon the Development of Scientific Thought," *Journal of Philosophy*, XXXIX, No. 12 (June, 1942), 309–327.

6. See *Philosophie der symbolischen Formen*, II, 141 ff.

length of the vibrating chords, it was not the fact itself but the interpretation of the fact which became decisive for the future orientation of philosophical and mathematical thought. Pythagoras could not think of this discovery as an isolated phenomenon. One of the most profound mysteries, the mystery of beauty, seemed to be disclosed here. To the Greek mind beauty always had an entirely objective meaning. Beauty is truth; it is a fundamental character of reality. If the beauty which we feel in the harmony of sounds is reducible to a simple numerical ratio it is number that reveals to us the fundamental structure of the cosmic order. "Number," says one of the Pythagorean texts, "is the guide and master of human thought. Without its power everything would remain obscure and confused." [7] We would not live in a world of truth, but in a world of deception and illusion. In number, and in number alone, we find an *intelligible* universe.

That this universe is a new universe of discourse—that the world of number is a symbolic world—was a conception entirely alien to the mind of the Pythagorean thinkers. Here as in all other cases there could be no sharp distinction between symbol and object. The symbol not only explained the object; it definitely took the place of the object. Things were not only related to or expressible by numbers; they *were* numbers. We no longer maintain this Pythagorean thesis of the substantial reality of number; we do not regard it as the very core of reality. But what we have to acknowledge is that number is one of the fundamental functions of human knowledge, a necessary step in the great process of objectification. This process begins in language, but in science it assumes an entirely new shape. For the symbolism of number is of quite a different logical type from the symbolism of speech. In language we find the first efforts of classification, but these are still uncoördinated. They cannot lead to a true systematization. For the symbols of language themselves have no definite systematic order. Every single linguistic term has a special "area of meaning." It is, as Gardiner says, "a beam of light,

7. See Philolaos, Fragments 4, 11, in Diels, *Die Fragmente der Vorsokratiker*, I, 408, 411.

illumining first this portion and then that portion of the field within which the thing, or rather the complex concatenation of things signified by a sentence lies." [8] But all these different beams of light do not have a common focus. They are dispersed and isolated. In the "synthesis of the manifold" every new word makes a new start.

This state of affairs is completely changed as soon as we enter into the realm of number. We cannot speak of single or isolated numbers. The essence of number is always relative, not absolute. A single number is only a single place in a general systematic order. It has no being of its own, no self-contained reality. Its meaning is defined by the position it occupies in the whole numerical system. The series of the natural numbers is an infinite series. But this infinity sets no limits to our theoretical knowledge. It does not mean any indeterminateness, an *Apeiron* in the Platonic sense; it means just the contrary. In the progress of numbers we do not meet with an external limitation, with a "last term." But what we find here is limitation by virtue of an intrinsic logical principle. All the terms are bound together by a common bond. They originate in one and the same generative relation, that relation which connects a number n with its immediate successor $(n+1)$. From this very simple relation we can derive all the properties of the integer numbers. This distinctive mark and the greatest logical privilege of this system is its complete transparency. In our modern theories—in the theories of Frege and Russell, of Peano and Dedekind—number has lost all its ontological secrets. We conceive it as a new and powerful symbolism which, for all scientific purposes, is infinitely superior to the symbolism of speech. For what we find here are no longer detached words but terms that proceed according to one and the same fundamental plan and that, therefore, show us a clear and definite structural law.

Nevertheless, the Pythagorean discovery meant only a first step in the development of natural science. The whole Pythagorean theory of number was suddenly called in question by a new fact. When the Pythagoreans detected that in a right-

8. Gardiner, *The Theory of Speech and Language*, p. 51.

268

angled triangle the line that subtends the right angle has no common measure with the two other sides they had to face an entirely new problem. In the whole history of Greek thought, especially in the dialogues of Plato, we feel the deep repercussion of this dilemma. It designates a genuine crisis in Greek mathematics. No ancient thinker could solve the problem in our modern way, by the introduction of the so-called "irrational numbers." From the point of view of Greek logic and mathematics irrational numbers were a contradiction in terms. They were an *arrhêton*, a thing not to be thought of and not to be spoken of.[9] Since number had been defined as an integer or as a ratio between integers, an incommensurable length was a length which did not admit of any numerical expression, which defied and set at nought all the logical powers of number. What the Pythagoreans had sought and what they had found in number was the perfect harmony of all kinds of beings and all forms of knowledge, of perception, intuition, and thought. From now on arithmetic, geometry, physics, music, astronomy seemed to form a unique and coherent whole. All things in heaven and on earth became "a harmony and a number." [10] The discovery of incommensurable lengths, however, was the breakdown of this thesis. Henceforth there was no real harmony between arithmetic and geometry, between the realm of discrete numbers and the realm of continuous quantities.

It took the efforts of many centuries of mathematical and philosophical thought to restore this harmony. A logical theory of the mathematical continuum is one of the latest achievements of mathematical thought.[11] And without such a theory all the creation of new numbers—of the fractions, the irrational numbers, and so on—always seemed to be a very questionable and precarious enterprise. If the human mind by its own power could arbitrarily create a new sphere of things we should have to change all our concepts of objective

9. Cf. Heinrich Scholz and H. Hasse, Die Grundlagen Krise der griechischen Mathematik (Charlottenburg, 1928).

10. Cf. Aristotle, Metaphysics, I, 5, 985b.

11. See Hermann Weyl, Das Kontinuum. Kritische Untersuchungen über die Grundlagen der Analysis (Leipzig, 1918).

truth. But here too the dilemma loses its force as soon as we take into account the symbolic character of number. In this case it becomes evident that in the introduction of new classes of numbers we do not create new objects but new symbols. The natural numbers are in this respect on the same level as the fractional or irrational numbers. They too are not descriptions or images of concrete things, of physical objects. Rather they express very simple relations. The enlargement of the natural realm of numbers, its extension over a larger field, only means the introduction of new symbols which are apt to describe relations of a higher order. The new numbers are symbols not of simple relations but of "relations of relations," of "relations of relations of relations," and so on. All this is not in contradiction to the character of the integers; it elucidates and confirms this character. In order to fill the gap between the integers, which are discrete quantities, and the world of physical events contained in the continuum of space and time mathematical thought was bound to find a new instrument. If number had been a "thing," a *substantia quae in se est et per se concipitur*, the problem would have been insoluble. But since it was a symbolic language, it was only necessary to develop the vocabulary, the morphology, and syntax of this language in a consistent way. What was required here was not a change in the nature and essence of number but only a change of meaning. A philosophy of mathematics had to prove that such a change does not lead to an ambiguity or a contradiction—that quantities not capable of being exactly expressed by integral numbers or the ratios between integral numbers became entirely understandable and expressible by the introduction of new symbols.

That all geometrical questions admit of such a transformation was one of the first great discoveries of modern philosophy. Descartes' analytical geometry gave the first convincing proof of this relation between extension and number. Henceforth the language of geometry ceased being a special idiom. It became a part of a much more comprehensive language, of a *mathesis universalis*. But for Descartes it was not yet possible to master the physical world, the world of matter and motion, in the same way. His attempts to develop a mathematical physics failed. The material of our physical world is composed of sense data, and the stubborn and refractory facts represented by these sense data seemed to resist all the efforts of Descartes' logical and rational thought. His physics remained a network of arbitrary assumptions. But if Descartes as a physicist could err in his means, he did not err in his fundamental philosophical aim. Henceforth this aim was clearly understood and firmly established. In all its single branches physics tended to one and the same point; it attempted to bring the whole world of natural phenomena under the control of number.

In this general methodological ideal we find no antagonism between classical and modern physics. Quantum mechanics is in a sense the true renaissance, the renovation and confirmation of the classical Pythagorean ideal. But here too it was necessary to introduce a much more abstract symbolic language. When Democritus described the structure of his atoms he had recourse to analogies taken from the world of our sense experience. He gave a picture, an image of the atom, which resembles the common objects of our macrocosm. The atoms were distinguished from each other by their shape, their size, and the arrangement of their parts. Their connection was explained by material links; the single atoms were supplied with hooks and eyes, with balls and sockets to rend them attachable. All this imagery, this figurative illustration has vanished in our modern theories of the atom. In Bohr's model of the atom there is none of this picturesque language. Science no longer speaks the language of common sense-experience; it speaks the Pythagorean language. The pure symbolism of number supersedes and obliterates the symbolism of common speech. Not only the macrocosm but also the microcosm—the world of interatomic phenomena—could now be described in this language; and this proved to be the opening for an entirely new systematic interpretation. "After the discovery of spectral-analysis," wrote Arnold Sommerfeld in the preface to his book, *Atomic Structure and Spectral Lines*,[12] "no one

12. (German ed. 1919) English trans. by Henry L. Brose (New York, Dutton, 1923).

trained in physics could doubt that the problem of the atom would be solved when physicists had learned to understand the language of spectra. So manifold was the enormous amount of material that had been accumulated in sixty years of spectroscopic research that it seemed at first beyond the possibility of disentanglement. . . . What we are nowadays hearing of the language of spectra is a true 'music of the spheres' within the atom, chords of integral relationships, an order and harmony that becomes ever more perfect in spite of the manifold variety. . . . All integral laws of spectral lines and of atomic theory spring originally from the quantum theory. It is the mysterious *organon* on which Nature plays her music of the spectra, and according to the rhythm of which she regulates the structure of the atom and nuclei."

The history of chemistry is one of the best and most striking examples of this slow transformation of scientific language. Much later than physics chemistry entered "on the highway of science." It was by no means the lack of new empirical evidence that for many centuries obstructed the progress of chemical thought and kept chemistry within the bounds of prescientific concepts. If we study the history of alchemy we find that the alchemists possessed an astounding talent for observation. They amassed a great bulk of valuable facts, a raw material without which chemistry could scarcely have been developed.[13] But the form in which this raw material was presented was quite inadequate. When the alchemist began to describe his observations he had no instrument at his disposal but a half-mythical language, full of obscure and ill-defined terms. He spoke in metaphors and allegories, not in scientific concepts. This obscure language left its mark upon his whole conception of nature. Nature became a realm of obscure qualities understandable only to the initiated, to the adepts. A new stream of chemical thought begins in the period of the Renaissance. In the schools of "iatrochemistry" biological and medical thought becomes prevalent. But a true

13. For the history of alchemy see E. O. von Lippmann, *Entstehung und Ausbreitung der Alchimie* (Berlin, Springer, 1919), and Lynn Thorndike, *A History of Magic and Experimental Science* (New York, 1923–41). 6 vols.

scientific approach to the problems of chemistry was not attained until the seventeenth century. Robert Boyle's *Chymista scepticus* (1677) is the first great example of a modern ideal of chemistry based upon a new general conception of nature and natural laws. Yet even here and in the following development of the theory of phlogiston we find only a qualitative description of chemical processes. It was not until the end of the eighteenth century, the time of Lavoisier, that chemistry learned to speak a quantitative language. From then on rapid progress is observable. When Dalton discovered his law of equivalent or multiple proportions a new way was opened to chemistry. The power of number was firmly established. Nevertheless, there still remained large fields of chemical experience which were not yet completely subjected to the rules of number. The list of the chemical elements was a mere empirical list; it did not depend on any fixed principle or show a definite systematic order. But even this last obstacle was removed by the discovery of the periodic system of the elements. Every element had found its place in a coherent system, and this place was marked by its atomic number. "The true atomic number is simply the number which gives the position of the element in the natural system when due account is taken of chemical relationships in deciding the order of each element." By arguing on the basis of the periodic system it was possible to predict unknown elements and to discover them subsequently. Thus chemistry had acquired a new mathematical and deductive structure.[14]

We can trace the same general trend of thought in the history of biology. Like all other natural sciences biology had to begin with a mere classification of facts, still guided by the class-concepts of our ordinary language. Scientific biology gave to these concepts a more definite meaning. Aristotle's zoological system and Theophrastus' botanical system show a high degree of coherence and methodological order. But in modern biology all these earlier forms of classification are eclipsed by a different ideal. Biology is slowly passing into a new stage of "deductively formulated theory." "Any science

14. For details see, for instance, Sommerfeld, *op. cit.*, chap. ii.

in its normal development," says Professor Northrop, "passes through two stages—the first which we term the natural history stage, the second the postulationally prescribed theory. To each of these stages there belongs a definite type of scientific concept. The type of concept for the natural history stage we term a concept by inspection; that for the postulationally prescribed stage a concept by postulation. A concept by inspection is one the complete meaning of which is given by something immediately apprehended. A concept by postulation is one the meaning of which is prescribed for it by the postulates of the deductive theory in which it occurs." [15] For this decisive step which leads from the merely apprehendable to the understandable we are always in need of a new instrument of thought. We must refer our observations to a system of well-ordered symbols in order to make them coherent and interpretable in terms of scientific concepts.

That mathematics is a universal symbolic language—that it is not concerned with a description of things but with general expressions of relations—is a conception which appears rather late in the history of philosophy. A theory of mathematics based upon this presupposition does not appear before the seventeenth century. Leibniz was the first great modern thinker to have a clear insight into the true character of mathematical symbolism and immediately elicit fruitful and comprehensive consequences. In this regard the history of mathematics does not differ from the history of all the other symbolic forms. Even for mathematics it proved to be extremely difficult to discover the new dimension of symbolic thought. Such thought was employed by mathematicians long before they could account for its specific logical character. Like the symbols of language and of art, mathematical symbols are from the beginning surrounded by a sort of magical atmosphere. They are looked upon with religious awe and veneration. Later on this religious and mystical faith slowly develops into a kind of metaphysical faith. In Plato's philos-

15. F. S. C. Northrop, "The method and theories of physical science in their bearing upon biological organization," *Growth* Supplement (1940), pp. 127–154.

ophy number is no longer wrapped in mystery. It is, on the contrary, regarded as the very center of the intellectual world—it has become the clue to all truth and intelligibility. When Plato in his old age gave his theory of the ideal world he tried to describe it in terms of pure number. Mathematics is to him the intermediary realm between the sensible and the supra-sensible world. He, too, is a true Pythagorean— and as a Pythagorean he is convinced that the power of number extends over the whole visible world. But the metaphysical essence of number cannot be revealed by any visible phenomenon. The phenomena partake in this essence but they cannot adequately express it—they necessarily fall short of it. It is a mistake to consider those visible numbers which we find in natural phenomena, in the movements of the celestial bodies, as the true mathematical numbers. What we see here are only "indications" (*paradeigmata*) of the pure ideal numbers. These numbers are to be apprehended by reason and intelligence but not by sight.

"The spangled heavens should be used as a pattern and with a view to that higher knowledge; their beauty is like the beauty of figures or pictures excellently wrought by the hand of Daedalus, or some other great artist, which we may chance to behold; any geometrician who saw them would appreciate the exquisiteness of their workmanship, but he would never dream of thinking that in them he could find the true equal or the true double, or the truth of any other proportion. . . . And will not a true astronomer have the same feeling when he looks at the movements of the stars? Will he not think that heaven and the things in heaven are framed by the Creator of them in the most perfect manner? But he will never imagine that the proportions of night and day, or of both to the month, or of the month to the year, or of the stars to these and to one another, and any other things that are material and visible can also be eternal and subject to no deviation— that would be absurd; and it is equally absurd to take so much pains in investigating their exact truth." [16]

Modern epistemology no longer maintains this Platonic

16. Plato, *Republic*, 529, 530 (Jowett trans.).

theory of number. It does not regard mathematics as a study of things, either visible or invisible, but as a study of relations and types of relations. If we speak of the objectivity of number, we do not think of it as a separate metaphysical or physical entity. What we wish to express is that number is an instrument for the discovery of nature and reality. The history of science gives us typical examples of this continuous intellectual process. Mathematical thought often seems to go in advance of physical investigation. Our most important mathematical theories do not spring from immediate practical or technical needs. They are conceived as general schemes of thought prior to any concrete application. When Einstein developed his general theory of relativity he went back to Riemann's geometry which had been created long before but which Riemann regarded only as a mere logical possibility. But he was convinced that we were in need of such possibilities in order to be prepared for the description of actual facts. What we need is full freedom in the construction of the various forms of our mathematical symbolism, in order to provide physical thought with all its intellectual instruments. Nature is inexhaustible—it will always pose for us new and unexpected problems. We cannot anticipate the facts, but we can make provision for the intellectual interpretation of the facts through the power of symbolic thought.

If we accept this view we can find an answer to one of the most difficult and most debated problems of modern natural science—the problem of determinism. What science needs is not a metaphysical determinism but a methodological determinism. We may repudiate that mechanical determinism which has found its expression in the famous formula of Laplace.[17] But the true scientific determinism, the determinism of number, is not liable to these objections. We no longer regard number as a mystical power or as the metaphysical essence of things. We look upon it as a specific instrument of knowledge. Obviously this conception is not called into question by any result of modern physics. The

17. For this problem, see Cassirer, *Determinismus und Indeterminismus in der modernen Physik.*

progress of quantum mechanics has shown us that our mathematical language is much richer and much more elastic and pliable than was realized in the systems of classical physics. It is adaptable to new problems and new demands. When Heisenberg put forward his theory he used a new form of algebraic symbolism, a symbolism for which some of our ordinary algebraic rules became invalid. But the general form of number is preserved in all these subsequent schemes. Gauss said that mathematics is the queen of science and arithmetic the queen of mathematics. In a historical survey of the development of mathematical thought during the nineteenth century Felix Klein declared that one of the most characteristic features of this development is the progressive "arithmetization" of mathematics.[18] Also in the history of modern physics we can follow this process of arithmetization. From Hamilton's quaternions up to the different systems of quantum mechanics we find more and more complex systems of algebraic symbolism. The scientist acts upon the principle that even in the most complicated cases he will eventually succeed in finding an adequate symbolism which will allow him to describe his observations in a universal and generally understandable language.

It is true that the scientist does not give us a logical or empirical proof of this fundamental assumption. The only proof that he gives us is his work. He accepts the principle of numerical determinism as a guiding maxim, a regulative idea that gives his work its logical coherence and its systematic unity. I find one of the best statements of this general character of the scientific process in Helmholtz' *Treatise on Physiological Optics*. If the principles of our scientific knowledge, for instance the law of causation, were nothing but empirical rules, says Helmholtz, their inductive proof would be in a very bad state. The best we could say would be that these principles were not very much more valid than rules of meteorology like the law of the rotation of the wind, etc. But these principles bear on their face the character of purely logi-

18. Felix Klein, *Vorlesungen über die Entwicklung der Mathematik im 19. Jahrhundert* (Berlin, 1926–27).

cal laws because the conclusions derived from them concern
not our actual experience and the mere facts of nature but
our interpretation of nature.

"The process of our comprehension with respect to natural
phenomena is that we try to find *general notions* and *laws of
nature*. Laws of nature are merely generic notions for the
changes in nature. . . . Hence, when we cannot trace natural
phenomena to a law . . . the very possibility of comprehending such phenomena ceases.

"However, we must try to comprehend them. There is no
other method of bringing them under the control of the intellect. And so in investigating them we must proceed on the
supposition that they are comprehensible. Accordingly, the
law of sufficient reason is really nothing more than the *urge*
of our intellect to bring all our perceptions under its own
control. It is not a law of nature. Our intellect is the faculty
of forming general conceptions. It has nothing to do with our
sense-perceptions and experiences unless it is able to form
general conceptions or laws. . . . Besides our intellect there
is no other equally systematized faculty, at any rate for comprehending the external world. Thus if we are unable to *conceive* a thing, we cannot imagine it as existing." [19]

These words describe in a very clear way the general attitude of the scientific mind. The scientist knows that there
are still very large fields of phenomena which it has not yet
been found possible to reduce to strict laws and to exact
numerical rules. Nevertheless he remains faithful to this
general Pythagorean creed: he thinks that nature, taken as a
whole and in all its special fields, is "a number and a harmony." In face of the immensity of nature many of the
greatest scientists may have had that special feeling that was
expressed in a famous saying of Newton's. They may have
thought that in their own work they were like a child who
walks along the shore of an immense ocean and amuses himself occasionally picking up a pebble whose shape or color
attracts his eyes. This modest feeling is understandable, but

19. Helmholtz, *Treatise on Physiological Optics*, trans. by James P.
C. Southall (Optical Society of America; George Banta Publishing
Co., 1925; copyright, G. E. Stechert), III, 33–35.

it gives no true and full description of the work of the scientist. The scientist cannot attain his end without strict obedience to the facts of nature. But this obedience is not passive submission. The work of all the great natural scientists —of Galileo and Newton, of Maxwell and Helmholtz, of Planck and Einstein—was not mere fact collecting; it was theoretical, and that means constructive, work. This spontaneity and productivity is the very center of all human activities. It is man's highest power and it designates at the same time the natural boundary of our human world. In language, in religion, in art, in science, man can do no more than to build up his own universe—a symbolic universe that enables him to understand and interpret, to articulate and organize, to synthesize and universalize his human experience.

12   Summary and Conclusion

If at the end of our long road we look back at our point of departure we may be uncertain whether we have attained our end. A philosophy of culture begins with the assumption that the world of human culture is not a mere aggregate of loose and detached facts. It seeks to understand these facts as a system, as an organic whole. For an empirical or historical view it would seem to be enough to collect the data of human culture. Here we are interested in the breadth of human life. We are engrossed in a study of the particular phenomena in their richness and variety; we enjoy the polychromy and the polyphony of man's nature. But a philosophical analysis sets itself a different task. Its starting point and its working hypothesis are embodied in the conviction that the varied and seemingly dispersed rays may be gathered together and brought into a common focus. The facts here are reduced to forms, and these forms themselves are supposed to possess an inner unity. But have we been able to prove this essential point? Did not all our individual analyses show us just the opposite? For we have had to stress all along the specific character and structure of the various symbolic forms—of myth, language, art, religion, history, science. Bearing in mind this aspect of our investigation we may perhaps feel inclined to favor the converse thesis, the thesis of the discontinuity and radical heterogeneity of human culture.

From a merely ontological or metaphysical point of view it would be very difficult indeed to refute this thesis. But for a critical philosophy the problem assumes another face. Here we are under no obligation to prove the substantial unity of man. Man is no longer considered as a simple substance which exists in itself and is to be known by itself. His unity is conceived as a functional unity. Such a unity does not presuppose a homogeneity of the various elements of which it consists. Not merely does it admit of, it even requires, a multiplicity and multiformity of its constituent parts. For this is a dialectic unity, a coexistence of contraries.

"Men do not understand," said Heraclitus, "how that which is torn in different directions comes into accord with itself—harmony in contrariety, as in the case of the bow and the lyre." [1] In order to demonstrate such a harmony we need not prove the identity or similarity of the different forces by which it is produced. The various forms of human culture are not held together by an identity in their nature but by a conformity in their fundamental task. If there is an equipoise in human culture it can only be described as a dynamic, not as a static equilibrium; it is the result of a struggle between opposing forces. This struggle does not exclude that "hidden harmony" which, according to Heraclitus, "is better than that which is obvious." [2]

Aristotle's definition of man as a "social animal" is not sufficiently comprehensive. It gives us a generic concept but not the specific difference. Sociability as such is not an exclusive characteristic of man, nor is it the privilege of man alone. In the so-called animal states, among bees and ants, we find a clear-cut division of labor and a surprisingly complicated social organization. But in the case of man we find

1. Heraclitus, Fragment 51, in Diels, *Die Fragmente der Vorsokratiker* (5th ed.). English trans. by Charles M. Bakewell, *Source Book in Ancient Philosophy* (New York, Charles Scribner's Sons, 1907), p. 31.
2. *Idem*, Fragment 54, in Bakewell, *op. cit.*, p. 31.

not only, as among animals, a society of action but also a society of thought and feeling. Language, myth, art, religion, science are the elements and the constitutive conditions of this higher form of society. They are the means by which the forms of social life that we find in organic nature develop into a new state, that of social consciousness. Man's social consciousness depends upon a double act, of identification and discrimination. Man cannot find himself, he cannot become aware of his individuality, save through the medium of social life. But to him this medium signifies more than an external determining force. Man, like the animals, submits to the rules of society but, in addition, he has an active share in bringing about, and an active power to change, the forms of social life. In the rudimentary stages of human society such activity is still scarcely perceptible; it appears to be at a minimum. But the farther we proceed the more explicit and significant this feature becomes. This slow development can be traced in almost all forms of human culture.

It is a well-known fact that many actions performed in animal societies are not only equal but in some respects superior to the works of man. It has often been pointed out that bees in the construction of their cells act like a perfect geometer, achieving the highest precision and accuracy. Such activity requires a very complex system of coördination and collaboration. But in all these animal performances we find no individual differentiation. They are all produced in the same way and according to the same invariable rules. No latitude remains for individual choice or ability. It is only when we arrive at the higher stages of animal life that we meet the first traces of a certain individualization. Wolfgang Koehler's observations of anthropoid apes seem to prove that there are many differences in the intelligence and skill of these animals. One of them may be able to solve a task which for another remains insoluble. And here we may even speak of individual "inventions." For the general structure of animal life, however, all this is irrelevant. This structure is determined by the general biological law according to which acquired characters are not capable of hereditary transmission. Every perfection that an organism can gain in the course of its individual life is confined to its own existence and does not influence the life of the species. Even man is no exception to this general biological rule. But man has discovered a new way to stabilize and propagate his works. He cannot live his life without expressing his life. The various modes of this expression constitute a new sphere. They have a life of their own, a sort of eternity by which they survive man's individual and ephemeral existence. In all human activities we find a fundamental polarity, which may be described in various ways. We may speak of a tension between stabilization and evolution, between a tendency that leads to fixed and stable forms of life and another tendency to break up this rigid scheme. Man is torn between these two tendencies, one of which seeks to preserve old forms whereas the other strives to produce new ones. There is a ceaseless struggle between tradition and innovation, between reproductive and creative forces. This dualism is to be found in all the domains of cultural life. What varies is the proportion of the opposing factors. Now the one factor, now the other, seems to preponderate. This preponderance to a high degree determines the character of the single forms and gives to each of them its particular physiognomy.

In myth and in primitive religion the tendency to stabilization is so strong that it entirely outweighs the opposite pole. These two cultural phenomena seem to be the most conservative powers in human life. Mythical thought is, by its origin and by its principle, traditional thought. For myth has no means of understanding, explaining, and interpreting the present form of human life other than to reduce it to a remote past. What has its roots in this mythical past, what has been ever since, what has existed from immemorial times, is firm and unquestionable. To call it into question would be a sacrilege. For the primitive mind there is no more sacred thing than the sacredness of age. It is age that gives to all things, to physical objects and to human institutions, their value, their dignity, their moral and religious worth. In order to maintain this dignity it becomes imperative to continue and to preserve the human order in the same unalterable shape. Any breach of continuity would destroy the very substance of mythical and religious life. From the point of view of primitive thought the slightest alteration in the established scheme of things is disastrous. The words of a magic formula, of a spell or incantation, the single phases of a religious act, of a sacrifice or a prayer, all this must be repeated in one and the same invariable order. Any change would annihilate the force and efficiency of the magical word or religious rite. Primitive religion can therefore leave no room for any freedom of individual thought. It prescribes its fixed, rigid, inviolable rules not only for every human action but also for every human feeling. The life of man is under a constant pressure. It is enclosed in the narrow circle of positive and negative demands, of consecrations and prohibitions, of observances and taboos. Nevertheless the history of religion shows us that this first form of religious thought by no means expresses its real meaning and its end. Here too we find a continuous advance in the opposite direction. The ban under which human life was put by primitive mythical and religious thought is gradually relaxed, and at last it seems to have lost its binding force. There arises a new dynamic form of religion that opens a fresh perspective of moral and religious life. In such a dynamic religion the individual powers have won the preponderance over the mere powers of stabilization. Religious life has reached its maturity and its freedom; it has broken the spell of a rigid traditionalism.[3]

If from the field of mythical and religious thought we pass to language we find here, in a different shape, the same fundamental process. Even language is one of the firmest conservative powers in human culture. Without this conservatism it could not fulfil its principal task, communication. Communication requires strict rules. Linguistic symbols and forms must have a stability and constancy in order to resist the dissolving and destructive influence of time. Nevertheless phonetic change and semantic change are not only accidental features in the development of language. They are inherent and necessary conditions of this development. One of the principal reasons for this continual change is the fact that language has to be transmitted from one generation to

3. For further details see above, Chap. VII, pp. 87 ff.

another. This transmission is not possible by mere reproduction of fixed and stable forms. The process of the acquisition of language always involves an active and productive attitude. Even the child's mistakes are very characteristic in this respect. Far from being mere failures that arise from an insufficient power of memory or reproduction, they are the best proofs of activity and spontaneity on the part of the child. In a comparatively early stage of its development the child seems to have gained a certain feeling of the general structure of its mother tongue without, of course, possessing any abstract consciousness of linguistic rules. It uses words or sentences that it never has heard and that are infractions of the morphologic or syntactic rules. But it is in these very attempts that the child's keen sense for analogies appears. In these he proves his ability to grasp the form of language instead of merely reproducing its matter. The transference of a language from one generation to another is, therefore, never to be compared to a simple transfer of property by which a material thing, without altering its nature, only changes possession. In his *Prinzipien der Sprachgeschichte* Hermann Paul laid special stress upon this point. He showed by concrete examples that the historical evolution of a language depends to a large degree on those slow and continual changes that take place in the transference of words and linguistic forms from parents to children. According to Paul this process is to be regarded as one of the principal reasons for the phenomena of sound shift and semantic change.[4] In all this we feel very distinctly the presence of two different tendencies —the one leading to the conservation, the other to the renovation and rejuvenation of language. We can, however, scarcely speak of an opposition between these two tendencies. They are in perfect equipoise; they are the two indispensable elements and conditions of the life of language.

A new aspect of the same problem is given us in the development of art. Here, however, the second factor—the factor of originality, individuality, creativeness—seems definitely to prevail over the first. In art we are not content with

4. H. Paul, *Prinzipien der Sprachgeschichte* (4th ed. 1909), p. 63.

the repetition or reproduction of traditional forms. We sense a new obligation; we introduce new critical standards. "Mediocribus esse poetis non di, non homines, non concessere columnae," says Horace in his *Ars Poetica* ("Mediocrity of poets is not allowed, either by the gods, or men, or the pillars which sustain the booksellers' shops"). To be sure even here tradition still plays a paramount role. As in the case of language the same forms are transmitted from one generation to another. The same fundamental motives of art recur over and over again. Nevertheless every great artist in a certain sense makes a new epoch. We become aware of this fact when comparing our ordinary forms of speech with poetical language. No poet can create an entirely new language. He has to adopt the words and he has to respect the fundamental rules of his language. To all this, however, the poet gives not only a new turn but also a new life. In poetry the words are not only significant in an abstract way; they are no mere pointers by which we wish to designate certain empirical objects. Here we meet with a sort of metamorphosis of all our common words. Every verse of Shakespeare, every stanza of Dante or Ariosto, every lyrical poem of Goethe has its peculiar sound. Lessing said that it is just as impossible to steal a verse of Shakespeare as to steal the club of Hercules. And what is even more astounding is the fact that a great poet never repeats himself. Shakespeare spoke a language that had never been heard before—and every Shakespearean character speaks his own incomparable and unmistakable language. In Lear and Macbeth, in Brutus or Hamlet, in Rosalind or Beatrice we hear this personal language which is the mirror of an individual soul. In this manner alone poetry is able to express all those innumerable nuances, those delicate shades of feeling, that are impossible in other modes of expression. If language in its development is in need of constant renovation there is no better and deeper source for this than poetry. Great poetry always makes a sharp incision, a definite caesura, in the history of language. The Italian language, the English language, the German language were not the same at the death of Dante, of Shakespeare, of Goethe as they had been at the day of their birth.

In our aesthetic theories the difference between the conservative and the productive powers on which the work of art depends was always felt and expressed. At all times there has been a tension and conflict between the theories of imitation and inspiration. The first declares that the work of art has to be judged according to fixed and constant rules or according to classical models. The second rejects all standards or canons of beauty. Beauty is unique and incomparable, it is the work of the genius. It was this conception which, after a long struggle against theories of classicism and neoclassicism, became prevalent in the eighteenth century and which paved the way for our modern aesthetic. "*Genius*," says Kant in his *Critique of Judgment*, "is the innate mental disposition (*ingenium*) *through which* Nature gives the rule to Art." It is "a *talent* for producing that for which no definite rule can be given; it is not a mere aptitude for what can be learnt by a rule. Hence *originality* must be its first property." This form of originality is the prerogative and distinction of art; it cannot be extended to other fields of human activity. "Nature by the medium of genius does not prescribe rules to Science, but to Art; and to it only in so far as it is to be beautiful Art." We may speak of Newton as a scientific genius; but in this case we speak only metaphorically. "Thus we can readily learn all that *Newton* has set forth in his immortal work on the Principles of Natural Philosophy, however great a head was required to discover it; but we cannot learn to write spirited poetry, however express may be the precepts of the art and however excellent its models." [5]

The relation between subjectivity and objectivity, individuality and universality, is indeed not the same in the work of art as it is in the work of the scientist. It is true that a great scientific discovery also bears the stamp of the individual mind of its author. In it we find not merely a new objective aspect of things but also an individual attitude of mind and even a personal style. But all this has only a psychological, not a systematic relevance. In the objective content of science

5. Kant, *Critique of Judgment*, secs. 46, 47. English trans. by J. H. Bernard (London, Macmillan, 1892), pp. 188–190.

these individual features are forgotten and effaced, for one of the principal aims of scientific thought is the elimination of all personal and anthropomorphic elements. In the words of Bacon, science strives to conceive the world "*ex analogia universi*," not "*ex analogia hominis*." [6]

Human culture taken as a whole may be described as the process of man's progressive self-liberation. Language, art, religion, science, are various phases in this process. In all of them man discovers and proves a new power—the power to build up a world of his own, an "ideal" world. Philosophy cannot give up its search for a fundamental unity in this ideal world. But it does not confound this unity with simplicity. It does not overlook the tensions and frictions, the strong contrasts and deep conflicts between the various powers of man. These cannot be reduced to a common denominator. They tend in different directions and obey different principles. But this multiplicity and disparateness do not denote discord or disharmony. All these functions complete and complement one another. Each one opens a new horizon and shows us a new aspect of humanity. The dissonant is in harmony with itself; the contraries are not mutually exclusive, but interdependent: "harmony in contrariety, as in the case of the bow and the lyre."

6. Cf. Bacon, *Novum Organum*, Liber I, Aphor. XLI.

Index

Abstraction, 61f., 174, 184f.
Accidental variations, 37
Actuality, & possibility, 79–86
Aeschylus, 119, 129, 207
Aesthetics, 176–216 (*see* Art, Beauty, Poetics); HISTORY OF: Aristotle, 177–179, 183, 198; Baumgarten, 198; Croce, 181, 193; French classicism, 179, 194, 204; Kant, 176ff., 186; Plato, 188, 191; Platonism, 207; romanticism, 195f.; Schiller, 196; Shaftesbury, 206; Swiss school, 195. THEORIES OF ART: hedonism, 202–204; metaphysical, 198, 202; naturalism, 186, 200; play, 208; theory of genius, 285.
Affections, 47, 48, 152
Agnosticism, 30. *See* Scepticism
Alchemy, 263, 271
Algebra, 69
Allegory, 177. *See* Myth
Analogies, in language, 283
Anatomy, comparative, 42, 90
Anaxagoras, 119
Ancestors, *see* Religion, Totemism
Animals: reactions, 44–45; association of ideas, 52; emotions, 48, 150; gestures, 48; imagination, 52; inner & outer world, 42f.; instincts, 77f., 90–91, 279–280; intelligence, 51f.; language, 46–53, 150f.; memory, 73; play, 210f.; reactions, 43, 45, 47–52; sense of the future, 78; signs, tokens, 45, 50; states, 279f.; symbolic processes, 46, 49. *See* Religion
Animism, 127, 136
Anthropology, Christian, 24–29; empirical, *see* Ethnology; Greek, 18–23; philosophical, 19ff., 33; primitive, 17
Anthropomorphism, 119, 129, 241
Antony, 230f.

Apes, 48, 49, 59, 60, 280
Aphasia, 48n., 62, 81
Aristophanes, 191, 192
Aristotle, 16, 36, 145, 157, 177, 179, 183, 189, 190, 198, 203, 265, 272, 279
Arithmetic, 84, 276
Art, 176–216 (*see* Aesthetics, Beauty, Poetics); categories of art, 183f., 213f. AESTHETIC EXPERIENCE: 186–194; elements of: contemplation, 187–191, 206; emotion, 187–192, 241; expression, 180–186; imagination, 194–202; imitation, 177f.; inspiration, 285f.; intuition, 184, 187; reflection, 211. PSYCHOLOGY OF ART: art & dream, 205–208; & hypnosis, 206; & intoxication, 208; pleasure, 202–205. STRUCTURE: art & life, 211–214; & language, 177, 214; & logic, 177; & morality, 177, 213; & myth, *see* Myth, Poetics; & nature, 178, 193
Arts: architecture, 197; expressive, 182, 187; music, 178, 187, 192; painting, 178, 184, 189, 197; poetry, *see* Poetics; representative, 178, 182, 187; sculpture, 184, 197, 215
Association of ideas, 52, 53, 90, 125
Astrology, 70, 71, 263–265
Astronomy, 68–71, 263, 265, 268
Atomism, 270ff.
Augustine, 25f., 76, 228
Automatism, 90; in primitive life, 119
Babylonian culture, 68–70, 265
Bacon, F., 99, 201, 286
Balzac, 200, 260
Baumgarten, A., 177
Beauty (*see* Art & Aesthetics), aesthetic & organic, 194; "easy" beauty, 192, 210; & freedom, 211ff.; & number,

ANCHOR BOOKS